TELLING OUR FAITH STORY

(Volume Two)

PERSONAL LESSONS TO OUR MINISTRY FAMILY

TELLING OUR FAITH STORY

(Volume Two)

PERSONAL LESSONS TO OUR MINISTRY FAMILY

Dr. Jim and Karon Cecy

To order this book visit *www.jaron.org* or *www.amazon.com*. A catalog of other materials is available at JARON Ministries International, 4710 N. Maple Ave., Fresno, CA 93726.

ISBN: 978-1-7357365-7-0 PAPERBACK
ISBN: 978-1-7357365-8-7 eBOOK
Library of Congress Control Number: 2024909193

Cover design by Matthew Sanchez, Awaken TV, www.awakentv.org.

Printed in the United States of America.

DEDICATION

The words of the now familiar song, *My Tribute,* written by Andrae Crouch in 1971, say it best:

How can I say thanks,
For the things You have done for me?
Things so undeserved,
Yet You gave to prove Your love for me.
The voices of a million angels,
Could not express my gratitude.
All that I am and ever hope to be,
I owe it all to Thee.

To God be the glory.
To God be the glory.
To God be the glory,
For the things He has done.

• We give God the glory for our beloved JARON Ministries International family. Without the love and support of our Board of Directors, our ministry staff, our team of pastors, ministers, missionaries, chaplains, as well as our faithful prayer warriors, and financial supporters, this ministry would falter and fail. These three and a half decades have far exceeded our initial expectations. To God be the glory.

• We give thanks for first responders who are a part of the Law Enforcement and Fire Service Community. We also express our gratitude for all of our active, retired, and veterans of the military. Most of you gave some; some gave all. All of you are worthy of honor. To God be the glory.

• We are so very grateful for our fellow pastors, ministers, and missionaries who have been such an example to us of servant-leadership. To God be the glory.

• We especially dedicate this book to all of you Skilled Helpers who serve Jesus Christ, the One who "did not come to be served, but to serve, and to give His life a ransom for many" (Mark 10:45).

To God be the glory for the things He has done.

SPECIAL DEDICATION

To Robin Dane Carter ("Rob")

> 1 Thessalonians 5:12 "But we request of you, brethren, that you appreciate those who diligently labor among you…"

• Forty-three years ago, you came into our lives as a loyal friend of our dear friends, Pastor George and Linda Posthumus. We joined them in enjoying decades of friendship with you and Vicki, without any hint of jealousy. Your love and loyalty—your lovingkindness—is a blessing to us all.

How rare is that?

• Thirty years ago, you adopted, as your own, the vision of JARON Ministries to motivate, encourage, and equip Christian leaders in the U.S. and abroad. Though you often expressed your lack of formal training, you were blessed with an amazing amount of Spirit-led capability and a willingness to do anything and go anywhere.

How praiseworthy is that?

• Soon after, you joined the missionary staff of JARON to expand the ministry globally—leading teaching, construction, and medical teams to scores of countries. No task was too great or too small. Your steadfastness and "malleability" were noticed by all.

How remarkable is that?

• Fourteen years ago, with the help of your police officer son, Joshua, you helped start CODE 3 Ministries International (as a department of JARON Ministries) to encourage and equip law enforcement officers and police chaplains. That ministry has taken you to all parts of the law enforcement community—even the families of those who have died in the line of duty. In recent days, it has been expanded to military personnel and veterans.

How important is that?

• Eleven years ago, you took on the role of JARON's Director of Ministry to oversee our expanding number of missionaries, chaplains, and pastor-teachers. Your keen and deeply personal interest in all areas of global missions is an encouragement to so many.

How incredible is that?

• In recent years, you have been recognized as being on the cutting edge of using new mass media techniques to spread the Gospel and the Word of God to countless millions.

How timely is that?

• As Jim approached his fiftieth year of ministry, you expressed a desire to spend a great deal of your time leading a team committed to sharing Jim's life work and teaching ministry with the world.

How humbling is that?

• It has been said that a life lived among the loyal is a blessed life indeed. When it comes to you, Robin, our lifelong friend and treasured co-worker, that is more than true in our lives. King David had his Mighty Men of Valor (cf. 2 Samuel 23:8). We have you!

How precious is that?

CONTENTS

PART TWO: KARON'S MINISTRY AND MISSION LESSON

PART THREE: JIM'S LESSONS FROM A MILITARY VETERAN

PART FOUR: KARON'S LESSONS FROM A COP'S DAUGHTER

CONCLUDING THOUGHTS　　335

APPENDICES　　339

INTRODUCTION TO VOLUME TWO

Telling Our Faith Story to Fellow Ministers and Skilled Helpers

When our children, who grew up in a ministry home, were deciding their careers and lifelong vocations, we did not expect them to go into the Christian ministry. We hold to the view that there are many ways to serve God by serving people. We challenged them with the timeless words of the Apostle Paul who was both a tentmaker and a minister:

> Colossians 3:23-24 "Whatever you do, do your work heartily, as for the Lord rather than for men, knowing that from the Lord you will receive the reward of the inheritance. It is the Lord Christ whom you serve."

Thus, we said to our children and will soon say to our grandchildren:

> *"We do not care what you do as a profession as long as it serves others."*

Our focus in Volume One was on our earthly family and the generations to follow. Here in Volume Two, we are concentrating on a second group of people who are equally as treasured in our hearts—a whole list of fellow ministers and people we like to call "Skilled Helpers."

Fellow ministers—pastors, missionaries, chaplains, law enforcement officers, firefighters, active military personnel, veterans, and civil servants—you, and many like you, are on our Skilled Helper list. Therefore, this book is for you as well as your precious loved ones. After all, they are too often the ones who suffer through many of our unique challenges.

Our Worlds are Not Much Different

We who spend our lives serving in some sort of ministry as Skilled Helpers share many of the same issues:

- We see what we do as a ministry and a calling.

- We are greatly disturbed by those who abuse their authority and position.

- We are often crisis-oriented and "run on adrenaline."

- We suffer higher levels of loneliness and burnout.

- We are mentally on duty 24/7 and are always "on call."

- We suffer watching our kids being treated differently.

- We sometimes wonder if our friends are really our friends.

- We struggle with trust and "sit with our back to the wall."

- We love teasing those who serve in related professions.

- We often don't tell others what we do as a profession.

- We respect and defend others in our profession.

- We feel disgust at those who bring shame to our profession.

- We are sometimes skeptical because we spend our time seeing the worst parts of humanity.

• We try not to believe everybody falls short of "telling the whole truth and nothing but the truth."

• We see rescuing, serving, and protecting as a part of our inner selves, not just what we get paid to do.

• We sometimes take home our training to "take charge" and "command authority" on the job and, consequently, our family suffers.

• We are impatient with those who expect professional favors from us.

• We admit we could use a little more respect from those we serve.

• We could use more pay and a better retirement plan.

• We love what we do—mostly. We will have difficulty retiring.

• We strive to bring credit to our profession and glory to God.

• We admit our need to improve as Skilled Helpers.

As a ministry couple with a century of combined experience, we are here to help with all of these—although we can't guarantee more income and better retirement benefits! We remind you of the words we heard when we began to minister fifty years ago:

"Serving the Lord doesn't pay much, but the retirement plan is out of this world."

Our Motivation is to Honor Leaders

> 1 Thessalonians 5:12-13 "But we request of you, brethren, that you appreciate those who diligently labor among you, and have charge over you in the Lord and give you instruction, and that you esteem them very highly in love because of their work. Live in peace with one another."

In her life journey from a high-profile cop's daughter to a pastor's wife, minister, counselor, mentor, and missionary, Karon has a unique perspective. As a seasoned Pastor-Teacher, minister, and missionary, Jim has certainly "bled the blood."

This biblically-sound, story-based devotional is presented as a celebration of God's faithfulness. It presents a wide variety of stories and practical lessons from our enjoined lives, representing a century of combined years of ministry experience.

Over each of our five decades of ministry, we have come to deeply love and esteem leaders—all kinds of leaders. We appreciate those who work on the front lines as first and second responders, as well as those who serve behind the scenes in many support roles.

We have written this book—Volume Two of our *Telling Our Faith Story"* series—especially to encourage our fellow ministers and other Skilled Helpers. All of us have been called, in some way, to feed, love, minister—i.e., to protect and serve. Many of us have families who often pay the price for our sacrifice for others. We trust these devotional stories will stimulate us even further to do our work heartily to the Lord:

> Colossians 1:29 "For this purpose also I labor, striving according to His power, which mightily works within me."

Our Mandate is to Never Give Up

All of us who have been called to serve people have also been called to never give up. Sadly, too many of my fellow ministers quit a long time ago—they just haven't told anyone—and barely admit it themselves. May these devotionals encourage your hearts and help you to "keep on keeping on." May we hold on to:

> Galatians 6:9 "Let us not lose heart in doing good, for in due time we will reap if we do not grow weary."

> 2 Thessalonians 3:13 "But as for you, brethren, do not grow weary of doing good."

Our Method is to Encourage Fellow Ministers

Normally, devotionals are balanced, somewhat formulaic, and organized; stories are not. Some of our faith stories are short and lack detail while others are much more "beefy." Some are more anecdotal while others are more Bible studies with personal applications. In some cases, you will find similar stories with different spiritual applications. This is as it should be.

There is no forced reading plan. Skip around as you desire. These faith story devotionals are laid out in four parts, in hopes of encouraging your hearts "where you live":

> Part One: Jim's Ministry and Mission Lessons

> Part Two: Karon's Ministry and Mission Lessons

> Part Three: Jim's Lessons from a Military Veteran

> Part Four: Karon's Lessons from a Cop's Daughter

Included in each of the devotions is a section, *"For Personal Reflection,"* to challenge you to further thought and subsequent action. There is also an extensive Scripture and Foreign Word Index. Helpful tools are also included in the Appendix to help equip you to minister.

Soli Deo Gloria.
To God Alone be the Glory!

Dr. Jim and Karon Cecy
Fresno, California

PART ONE

JIM'S
MINISTRY AND MISSION
LESSONS

Jim's Ministry Devotional #1

My Plans or God's?

> Proverbs 16:1-3 "The plans of the heart belong to man, but the answer of the tongue is from the LORD. All the ways of a man are clean in his own sight, but the LORD weighs the motives. Commit your works to the LORD and your plans will be established."

Growing up, I wanted to be a singer. The only problem: I didn't sing well! In my last years of high school I considered pursuing a career in law—perhaps so I could say such cool things as *res ipsa loquitur* –"The thing speaks for itself." Or does it?

In my first year of college, I believed I was headed to be an elementary teacher. At the end of my second year, I joined the U.S. Navy as a damage-controlman. During battle, I was assigned to a shipboard fire control station. My daily job was working in personnel administration and legal affairs. Little did I know God was nonetheless working His plan.

I accepted Christ at twenty-one, on the very day I finished my active naval service. I remember telling God, *"I will do anything for You, except go into the ministry."* I think God laughed and said, *"We'll talk about that later, young man!"*

I got married to a cop's daughter and seriously considered becoming a deputy sheriff. God had a much different plan for me than law enforcement. In the meantime, I manufactured ice cream and trained to manage a store. At least, that's what I thought.

Later, as I expressed a willingness to become involved in ministry, my initial plan was to train as a missionary in Asia. I graduated college with a degree in speech-communications and eventually decided to go to seminary where I told my advisors I would prepare to be a Christian missionary, educator, professor, and counselor, but definitely not a pastor of a local church. I was especially intimidated by the necessary studies in Greek and Hebrew. They would eventually become some of my best subjects.

Obviously, many of my plans did not come to pass. I am not a singer, lawyer, elementary teacher, cop, store manager, nor a full-time missionary.

For fifty years, I have been what I never planned to be—a local church pastor-teacher. Like the Apostle Paul I was "appointed" a preacher (cf. 2 Timothy 1:11). Along the way, that role has taken me to doctoral studies in pastoral counseling, starting an international ministry, traveling to hundreds of cities in over thirty-five countries (many in Asia), writing books and study materials, counseling, and providing pastoral care for countless people. And, to my surprise, in recent years, we started a ministry department to train police chaplains internationally. And yes, I even get to sing publicly, though I still sound best when drowned out by other singers. I also, according to my fifteen grandchildren, make the best milkshake this side of heaven! Apparently, that skill never left me.

By the way, my wife and I experienced four miscarriages and were unable to have children of our own. However, we adopted three daughters and became foster parents to twenty-three children, some who stayed with us for decades—thus the fifteen precious, milkshake-loving grandchildren. Being a husband of fifty years, a father for decades, and a grandfather is, without a doubt, my ultimate accomplishment.

I am so grateful God interrupted my many plans with His. Expect Him to do the same for you. If you trust your life to Him with all your heart and do not insist on your own plans, He will make your paths straight (cf. Proverbs 3:5-6), and "your plans (i.e., His plan for you) will be established" (cf. Proverbs 16:1-3). Along the way, He might even let you do many of the things you had planned and even more that are beyond your lifelong dreams—so much so, that you can proclaim with the Apostle Paul, who was equally surprised at God's perfect will for his life:

Ephesians 3:20-21 "Now to Him who is able to do far more abundantly beyond all that we ask or think, according to the power that works within us, to Him be the glory in the church and in Christ Jesus to all generations forever and ever. Amen."

To this day, my congregation often hears me recite the old Jewish saying: *"The plans are man's; the odds are God's."* And so it is!

For Personal Reflection:

1. In what ways has God's plan for your life changed your plans for the better?

2. You may be content, but are you fulfilled in what you are doing?

3. Read Proverbs 16:1-3 and Proverbs 3:5-6. In what ways do these passages apply to you today?

4. We refer you to the worksheets related to Planning in *"The Accountable Life: Protecting Myself and Others"* by Dr. James M. Cecy. Available at www.amazon.com or www.jaron.org.

© Dr. James M. and Karon M. Cecy.

Jim's Ministry Devotional #2

The Purpose of God in My Life

> Acts 13:36 "For David, after he had served the purpose of God in his own generation, fell asleep…"

I recently became aware of what many say is a familiar quote from Mark Twain:

> "The two most important days in your life are the day you are born and the day you find out why."

Even as a child, I struggled with the question, *"Why am I here?"* I remember one "dark night of the soul" at the age of nine when I was afraid I was going to die. I wept before God: *"Lord, what do You want with my life?"* I went to sleep with a great sense of peace that God had His hand on me. I prayed the familiar childlike prayer:

> *Now I lay me down to sleep.*
> *I pray the Lord my soul to keep.*
> *If I should die before I wake,*
> *I pray the Lord my soul to take.*

As a young adult, during a very heavy season of discouragement, I cried out often, *"God, if You are real, show me."* He answered that cry of my heart in 1971 when I gave my life to Jesus Christ. Even after I became a disciple of Jesus, I often asked, *"What is Your purpose for my life?"* I knew the popular theological answer was to glorify God and enjoy Him forever. But I craved more specifics.

While reading Proverbs 16:4, I was reminded the Lord has made "everything" for its own purpose. I asked myself, *"Might that also include me?"* I needed to begin the practice of rehearsing a few of God's purposes for keeping me alive. Perhaps you need to do the same:

> • *"I am a Beloved Child of God. Today, I will not lose focus on who I am and what I am called to do."*

> • *"I am a Soldier of the Cross. Today, I will not let myself get distracted from my duty to my Supreme Commander."*

> • *"I am a Servant of God. Today, I will obey my Master at all costs."*

> • *"I am an Ambassador of Jesus Christ. Today, I will represent my King in everything I say and do."*

> • *"I am a Messenger of the Gospel. Today, I will join with others in praying and participating in sharing the good news with the world."*

Based on these promises and others, I rewrote that old childhood prayer:

> *Now I lay me down to sleep.*
> *I pray the Lord my soul to keep.*
> *Give me the peace to make me still,*
> *That I may wake to do Your will.*

In summary, these declarations reflect God's purposes for helping us live *unum diem ad tempus*—one day at a time.

For Personal Reflection:

1. Carefully read the above "I am…" statements.

2. Memorize Acts 13:36 "For David, after he had served the purpose of God in his own generation, fell asleep."

3. Reflect on why you think God has given you another day to live.

4. Share your thoughts with a loved one or a faithful friend.

© Dr. James M. and Karon M. Cecy.

Jim's Ministry Devotional #3

Pastoral Callings

> 2 Chronicles 20:15, 17 "…the battle is not yours but God's….You need not fight in this battle; station yourselves, stand and see the salvation of the LORD on your behalf….Do not fear or be dismayed; tomorrow go out to face them, for the LORD is with you."

Facing My Inner Battles

Permit me time to reflect on my life journey from self-centeredness to submission to Christ's lordship as an object of His mercy and grace.

Inner Battle #1: *"God would never save someone like me."*

God's Faithful Answer:

1 Timothy 1:15 "It is a trustworthy statement, deserving full acceptance, that Christ Jesus came into the world to save sinners, among whom I am foremost of all."

Romans 10:9-10 "…if you confess with your mouth Jesus as Lord (i.e., the Master/The One in Charge), and believe in your heart that God raised Him from the dead, you will be saved; for with the heart a person believes, resulting in righteousness, and with the mouth he confesses, resulting in salvation" (My addition).

Titus 3:5-7 "He saved us, not on the basis of deeds which we have done in righteousness, but according to His mercy, by the washing of regeneration and renewing by the Holy Spirit, whom He poured out upon us richly through Jesus Christ our Savior, so that being justified by His grace we would be made heirs according to the hope of eternal life."

My Present Reality:

In 1971, God reached into the flock of sinful humanity and chose me to be His own. I am an object of His love and mercy.

Inner Battle #2: *"I am not good enough, experienced enough, or smart enough to do ministry."*

God's Faithful Answer:

2 Corinthians 3:4-6 "Such confidence we have through Christ toward God. Not that we are adequate in ourselves to consider anything as coming from ourselves, but our adequacy is from God, who also made us adequate as servants of a new covenant..."

2 Corinthians 4:7 "But we have this treasure in earthen vessels, so that the surpassing greatness of the power will be of God and not from ourselves..."

My Present Reality:

By God's grace, I have been ministering for five decades. He is able!

Inner Battle #3: *"Given my history, I'll never have a normal family life."*

God's Faithful Answer:

Proverbs 18:22 "He who finds a wife finds a good thing and obtains favor from the LORD."

Psalm 113:9 "He makes the barren [i.e., childless] woman abide in the house as a joyful mother of children. Praise the LORD!" (My addition).

Psalm 71:17-18 "O God, You have taught me from my youth, and I still declare Your wondrous deeds. And even when I am old and gray, O God, do not forsake me, until I declare Your strength to this generation, Your power to all who are to come."

My Present Reality:

I've been married to my best friend and fellow ministry partner for over fifty years. We are blessed with three adopted daughters and have enjoyed caring for twenty-three foster children—two who are a permanent part of our family. We now have a boatload of fifteen grandchildren and we hope to live long enough to become great-grandparents to many.

Psalm 128:6 "Indeed, may you see your children's children."

Inner Battle #4: *"I will never know the Bible enough to be a good teacher."*

God's Faithful Answer:

1 Peter 2:2 "…like newborn babies, long for the pure milk of the word, so that by it you may grow in respect to salvation…"

2 Timothy 2:15 "Be diligent to present yourself approved to God as a workman who does not need to be ashamed, accurately handling the word of truth."

My Present Reality:

God gave this biblically ignorant young man a lifelong thirst to study the Word of God.

Inner Battle #5: *"I could never be an effective preacher."*

God's Faithful Answer:

1 Corinthians 9:16 "…if I preach the gospel, I have nothing to boast of, for I am under compulsion; for woe is me if I do not preach the gospel."

2 Timothy 1:11 "…I was appointed a preacher and an apostle and a teacher."

My Present Reality:

As a young man, I was terrified to stand before people and speak. Now, without exaggeration, I have spoken to hundreds of thousands of people throughout the world. No one is more surprised than I am.

Inner Battle #6: *"I could never be a part of a global ministry."*

God's Faithful Answer:

Daniel 11:32 "….the people who know their God will display strength and take action."

My Present Reality:

In 1990, I founded JARON Ministries International (incorporated in 1992). Through its many missionaries and projects, our teams minister throughout the world. (See the Appendix for an overview.)

Inner Battle #7: *"I'm getting too old to be effective."*

God's Faithful Answer:

Psalm 71:9 "Do not cast me off in the time of old age; do not forsake me when my strength fails."

Acts 13:36 "…[he] served the purpose of God in his own generation, fell asleep, and was laid among his fathers…" (My addition).

My Present Reality:

At seventy-four years old, I am still kicking and highly motivated.

Inner Battle #8: *"I'll never be able to finish this book. And besides, who would want to read it?"*

My Present Reality:

Here you are. And Volume Three is coming soon.

Gloria in Excelsis Deo.
Glory to God in the Highest!

For Personal Reflection:

1. What are your inner battles and excuses that prevent you from experiencing all God wants for you?

2. Reflect on God's Faithful Answer:

2 Chronicles 20:15, 17 "...the battle is not yours but God's....You need not fight in this battle; station yourselves, stand and see the salvation (i.e., the deliverance) of the LORD on your behalf....Do not fear or be dismayed (i.e., by those outer and inner battles); tomorrow go out to face them, for the LORD is with you" (My additions).

3. Now it's time to celebrate your present realities. Write them out and share them with someone who can use the encouragement from your faith story.

© Dr. James M. and Karon M. Cecy.

Jim's Ministry Devotional #4

Magnum Opus

> Matthew 25:23 "His master said to him, 'Well done, good and faithful slave. You were faithful with a few things, I will put you in charge of many things; enter into the joy of your master.'"

Magnum opus is Latin for what is considered the most important work of a person. It is the opposite of what some might see as a failure, a clunker, a debacle…even a bomb! After seventy-four years of life, I have quite a list of failures:

• I bombed at being a singer. My junior high dream.

• I failed at breaking the two-minute half-mile. My high school aspiration.

• I have yet to finish writing an extensive commentary on the Book of Proverbs. My goal before I die.

So, what then is my *magnum opus*—my most important work? The simple answer: I am not quite sure.

• Is it over fifty years of marriage?

• Is it forty-four years of children, foster children, and now fifteen grandchildren?

• Is it five decades of pastoral ministry and overseas ministry in thirty-five countries?

• Is it these "later years" when I get to disciple so many ministers, missionaries, and Skilled Helpers?

I think my best accomplishment has yet to be revealed. I pray it will be at my death when I hope I will hear from My Savior:

Well done, Jim, My good and faithful servant. You were faithful with the few things I gave you to do. In the future, I will put you in charge of many things. Enter into the joy of your Master (cf. Matthew 25:23).

Dei Gratia.
By the Grace of God!

For Personal Reflection:

1. What are the things you never accomplished?

2. What accomplishments bring you the most joy?

3. What is your *magnum opus*—your next and most important work yet to be done?

4. What is keeping that from happening?

© Dr. James M. and Karon M. Cecy.

Jim's Ministry Devotional #5

My Life is an Embassy

> 2 Corinthians 5:20 "Therefore, we are ambassadors for Christ, as though God were making an appeal through us..."

When I was thirty years old, I took my first overseas ministry trip to India. I will never forget the sights and sounds (and even the smells) of what was for me an incredibly foreign country. Towards the end of our month-long trip, we walked into the American Embassy in New Delhi, the Indian capital. There, my senses were filled with reminders of home: an American flag, American Marines, American music, and American art. Although it may have been my famished imagination, I could even smell American hamburgers and fries! All thirty fellow pastors sang, *"God Bless America"* in the echoing rotunda of the beautiful, American-style building. What a memorable experience! I often reflect on that welcome taste of home in a foreign land.

As one who has trusted in Jesus Christ alone for his salvation, I do not consider this world my home. As born-again Christians, we are aliens and strangers in this foreign land. Our true citizenship is in heaven (cf. Ephesians 2:19; Philippians 3:20-21). Therefore, our primary allegiance is to the King of kings under whom we serve as emissaries. The Apostle Paul reminds us of our unique calling: "Therefore, we are ambassadors for Christ, as though God were making an appeal through us..." (2 Corinthians 5:20).

Our job description as ambassadors of Jesus Christ is to live in this foreign land, Earth, as representatives of our home country, Heaven. Though our heavenly citizenship comes with tremendous privileges, it also comes with substantial responsibility to live in such a way that reflects the values of the Sovereign King we represent.

Furthermore, each Christian family and local church is to be an

Embassy of Heaven where those godly virtues exist and are readily seen by all people, so they will glorify our Father in Heaven (cf. Matthew 5:16). Put simply, my life is to be an embassy, a taste of Heaven on Earth.

I hasten to admit being an ambassador and representing eternal values are certainly not easy. In his letter to the Ephesians, the Apostle Paul spoke about being an "ambassador in chains" (Ephesians 6:20). He was, in my opinion, talking about the physical chains that bound him during his imprisonment in Rome. There are, however, many Christians who are ambassadors living in chains brought about by their own sinful choices. They are still ambassadors of Christ but, nonetheless, ambassadors in chains.

I am committed to enable and equip even more fellow ambassadors to be freed from the shackles of sin. It is also a call for every Ambassador of Jesus Christ to become an Ambassador of Purity, a diplomat representing God's holiness in an ungodly world. To change the metaphor, this also means serving as a Soldier of the Cross (cf. 2 Timothy 2:3-4), fighting trench warfare against this never-ending battle with ungodliness.

The training isn't easy. Ask anyone who has served in the Foreign Service or the military. Beyond the initial education needed, it takes years of on-the-job training to properly represent a country and battle an enemy. Our instructions on how to be effective Ambassadors and Soldiers of the Cross are as close as our Bible. Most of our training, however, will be in the trenches as we live out these biblical principles as resident aliens on foreign soil. Our orders are clear:

> 1 Peter 2:11 "Beloved, I urge you as aliens and strangers to abstain from fleshly lusts which wage war against the soul."

For Personal Reflection:

1. Take some time to consider your life as an ambassador as well as your family and church as an embassy.

2. In what specific ways do you represent Christ at home, work, school, and in the community?

3. What are the heavenly values you hope will exist in your earthly life and family?

(Adapted from *"The Purity War: A Biblical Guide to Living in an Immoral World"* by Dr. James M. Cecy. Available at www.amazon.com and www.jaron.org.)

Jim's Ministry Devotional #6

Real People, Real Needs

> Matthew 9:36-38 "Seeing the people, He felt compassion for them, because they were distressed and dispirited like sheep without a shepherd. Then He said to His disciples, 'The harvest is plentiful, but the workers are few. Therefore beseech the Lord of the harvest to send out workers into His harvest.'"

We live in a world of fifty-eight million square miles of land with a recent count of about eight billion people. My personal piece of planetary real estate, here in Fresno, California, is so very small. (Sometimes I tease that Fresno is not the end of the world, but I can see it from here!)

Every morning, I pray for a different country or region of the world. I am often prompted by a small globe I have next to my chair or a coffee cup with a map or the name of a country. I also have a wooden rack with a number of souvenir spoons from around the world. Close by I keep the latest edition of the book, *Operation World: The Definitive Prayer Guide to Every Nation* by Jason Mandryk. It lays out the spiritual condition of every country. I am certainly well-equipped to pray more specifically.

To date, I have been privileged to minister in some thirty-five foreign countries plus half of the states in the U.S. I have traveled to some of these places as many as thirty times. My dear friend and renowned missiologist, Dr. Monnie Brewer, has traveled to five times as many countries, some of them scores of times.

Take the time to slowly read through the following list of countries where I have ministered and served. I remind us these are more than geo-political entities. These are places where real people with real needs inhabit and where we pray God is raising up His workers to share with them the good news about the life and love of the Lord Jesus Christ:

> • Albania • Australia • Belarus • Bosnia • Bulgaria • Canada • Czech Republic • Democratic Republic of the Congo • England (U.K.) • Ethiopia • France • Germany • Hong Kong (China) • Hungary • India • Northern Ireland (U.K.) • Israel • Italy • Mexico • Moldova • Montenegro • Norway • Philippines • Poland • Republic of Ireland • Romania • Scotland (U.K.) • Serbia • Singapore • South Africa • Sri Lanka • Taiwan • Turkey • Ukraine • United States

Now, I encourage you to move on to praying for the rest of the world's eight billion people, one continent, one country, or one region at a time. Here's a sobering thought: Millions of people on Earth right now will still be here on New Year's Eve in the year 2099. A child born in 2025 will be in his or her seventies. Then the population is expected to be over ten billion. So many needy souls!

The story is told of the passionate Christian leader, A. B. Simpson, the founder of the Christian and Missionary Alliance, who was found in his office hugging a globe and weeping before the Lord for a lost world. I feel like that and hope you do, as well.

Our daily prayer needs to be similar to the famous prayer of Bob Pierce, who, after a visit to suffering children on an island in Korea, wrote in his Bible:

> "Let my heart be broken by the things that break the heart of God."

For Personal Reflection:

1. Make a list of the countries and U.S. states you have visited or where you have family and friends.

2. Spin a globe or randomly point to a country on a map. Do some research regarding the spiritual needs of that region. For further reference go to *www.operationworld.org.*

3. Pray to the Lord of the Harvest to send His workers there who will share the good news of the Gospel. Encourage others to join you in praying.

© Dr. James M. and Karon M. Cecy.

Jim's Ministry Devotional #7

Facing Disaster

> Psalm 46:1-3, 10 "God is our refuge and strength, a very present help in trouble. Therefore we will not fear, though the earth should change and though the mountains slip into the heart of the sea; though its waters roar and foam, though the mountains quake at its swelling pride. Selah....Cease striving and know that I am God; I will be exalted among the nations, I will be exalted in the earth."

Almost forty-five years ago, as a thirty-one-year-old pastor, God called me to lead my local church through a time of disaster—a 1982 superstorm that ultimately killed twenty-two people in our San Lorenzo Valley.

The sheets of rain had been coming down for days and days. The rivers overflowed and we had severe county-wide flooding. People were cut off. Many were evacuated. A dozen people were killed in the first days of the storm.

We were without power for many days. Sadly, the whole side of a mountain slid down, burying scores of homes, and killing another ten people. It was our county's deadliest disaster.

In response, our local church became a Disaster Relief Center. In the midst of the crisis, the Body of Christ was united as we had never seen in our Valley.

After a recent injury, I was in a full-leg cast and unable to walk. However, I needed to do something more. A California Highway Patrol officer who attended my church offered to carry me on his back through the mud, up on a rooftop of a buried house, as I wept and prayed for the family who had perished below. It was one of the saddest moments of my ministry.

On that still rainy Sunday morning, I came before the church and held up my Bible. I was numb, scared, feeling helpless, and begging God for the wisdom to lead. I asked people to share their needs, their tears, and even their frustrations with the government and the church. In their minds, we just weren't doing enough.

I felt so inadequate as I heard the stories. I couldn't preach that day. I had no words! I held my Bible in my hands and wept as I slowly read each line to the congregation:

Psalm 46:1-3 "God is our refuge and strength, a very present help in trouble. Therefore we will not fear, though the earth should change and though the mountains slip into the heart of the sea; though its waters roar and foam, though the mountains quake at its swelling pride. Selah."

The word *selah* is an ancient musical notation used in the Psalms that calls us to pause—to stop and think deeply about what we just read. I gave time for the congregation to reflect on these comforting words. I could hear the soft cries of many. I went on to read quietly:

Psalm 46:10 "Cease striving and know that I am God; I will be exalted among the nations, I will be exalted in the earth."

Twenty years later, on the Sunday after the 911 attack, I quietly read the same passages to an equally distraught congregation here in Fresno. We were once again consoled by the knowledge that God was still on His throne.

Here I am, decades later, and there are times when I feel as inadequate as when I was thirty-one. However, I also have the same hope. Therefore, no matter what the disaster, we will not succumb to panic or fear. We will call for a moratorium on grumbling,

43

criticizing, and whining. We will bombard the many voices and opinions with prayer and praise. We will be the Church—the Praying Church and the Hope-Filled church.

God is our refuge and our strength. He is a very present help. God is in our midst. We will cease striving. We will exalt Him in the midst of any disaster. *Selah*. Stop and think about that!

For Personal Reflection:

1. Read Psalm 46:1-3, 10 once again.

2. Reflect on a time when you experienced panic or disaster. How well did you live out the reminders and the promises of this psalm?

© Dr. James M. and Karon M. Cecy.

Jim's Ministry Devotional #8

Qualities of a Servant-Leader

2 Timothy 1:1-7 "Paul, an apostle of Christ Jesus by the will of God, according to the promise of life in Christ Jesus, to Timothy, my beloved son: Grace, mercy and peace from God the Father and Christ Jesus our Lord. I thank God, whom I serve with a clear conscience the way my forefathers did, as I constantly remember you in my prayers night and day, longing to see you, even as I recall your tears, so that I may be filled with joy. For I am mindful of the sincere faith within you, which first dwelt in your grandmother Lois, and your mother Eunice, and I am sure that it is in you as well. And for this reason I remind you to kindle afresh the gift of God which is in you through the laying on of my hands. For God has not given us a spirit of timidity, but of power and love and discipline."

The world says a true leader:

- Stands above a crowd.
- Speaks with eloquence and confidence.
- Shows he or she is powerful and popular.

The Bible, however, says a true leader is a humble servant:

Luke 22:26-27 "But it is not this way with you, but the one who is the greatest among you must become like the youngest, and the leader like the servant. For who is greater, the one who reclines at the table or the one who serves? Is it not the one who reclines at the table? But I am among you as the one who serves."

The Apostle Paul's Last Will and Testament

The date is around A.D. 65-67. The Apostle Paul is in prison once again in the city of Rome. He is writing to Timothy, his beloved younger disciple who is now serving in the Church of Ephesus. The letter arrives after Paul is beheaded under orders from the Emperor Nero.

You might say this is *The Apostle Paul's Last Will and Testament.* You might also say this is his *Treatise on the Qualities of an Effective Servant-Leader.* The only difference is he doesn't come out and list them—he just exudes them. They flow from his life, not just his head. Take to heart his example. Not much more needs to be said:

- **The effective servant-leader thanks God for fellow Christian workers.**

    2 Timothy 1:3 "I thank God..."

- **The effective servant-leader serves God in the purity of a God-centered life.**

    2 Timothy 1:3 "...whom I serve with a clear conscience the way my forefathers did..."

- **The effective servant-leader communicates with God continually.**

    2 Timothy 1:3 "...as I constantly remember you in my prayers night and day..."

- **The effective servant-leader longs to fellowship with God's people.**

2 Timothy 1:4 "…longing to see you even as I recall your tears…"

• **The effective servant-leader acknowledges his need for other Christians.**

2 Timothy 1:4 "…so that I may be filled with joy."

• **The effective servant-leader expresses confidence in the faith of other believers.**

2 Timothy 1:5 "For I am mindful of the sincere faith within you, which first dwelt in your grandmother Lois and your mother Eunice, and I am sure that it is in you as well."

• **The effective servant-leader exhorts and encourages fellow Christians.**

2 Timothy 1:6 "For this reason I remind you to kindle afresh the gift of God which is in you through the laying on of my hands."

• **The effective servant-leader relies on God for boldness in ministry.**

2 Timothy 1:7 "For God has not given us a spirit of timidity, but of power…"

• **The effective servant-leader relies on God for an ability to love those he ministers to.**

2 Timothy 1:7 "For God has not given us a spirit of timidity, but of power <u>and love</u>…" (My emphasis).

- **The effective servant-leader relies on God for self-control.**

  2 Timothy 1:7 "For God has not given us a spirit of timidity, but of power and love <u>and discipline</u>" (My emphasis).

For Personal Reflection:

1. Look over these qualities of an effective servant-leader demonstrated by the Apostle Paul.

2. Circle the ones you feel you are exemplifying the best.

3. Put an X next to the ones concerning which you need the most work.

(Adapted from *"Men in Action: Equipping Men to Lead in the Home, the Church, and the Community"* by Dr. James M. Cecy. Available at www.amazon.com and www.jaron.org.)

© Dr. James M. and Karon M. Cecy.

Jim's Ministry Devotional #9

"Well, Stop It!"

> 1 Corinthians 15:34 "Become sober-minded as you ought, and stop sinning…"

I wish I could say it was easy for this lifelong city boy to move to the agriculturally blessed San Joaquin Valley. I have since learned to deeply love its people and this city. I am especially grateful to God for the unity of the churches in this community. It truly is a great place to live, raise a family, and minister.

My dramatic change of heart began one morning at the local Salvation Army Thrift Store. I was standing at the door, waiting for my wife and daughters to finish looking through endless rows of used clothing. They were having a great time; I was not. My face must have revealed my misery.

A little girl, who looked about seven years old, approached me at the door. She gazed up at me with her beautiful brown eyes and without any shyness proclaimed, "Jesus died for your sins!" Frankly, I was not in the mood to have this little girl witness to me. I gave a dismissive mumble, "I know." Undaunted, she continued, "Well, you're a sinner!" My sour face turned into a smile and I responded, "I know that, too!" Then to my amazement, she put her hands on her hips and raised her voice, "Well, stop it!" She turned on her heels and sauntered away.

I decided that day I wanted to live in a city where a seven-year-old is used by God to confront a Pastor-Sinner like me. In that spirit, I remind us of some of the clear and pithy mandates of Scripture regarding the sins we need to stop immediately and the lives we need to pursue now:

> 1 Corinthians 6:18 "Flee immorality."

1 Corinthians 10:14 "Therefore, my beloved, flee from idolatry."

1 Timothy 6:11 "But flee from these things, you man of God, and pursue righteousness, godliness, faith, love, perseverance and gentleness."

2 Timothy 2:22 "Now flee from youthful lusts and pursue righteousness, faith, love and peace, with those who call on the Lord from a pure heart."

That young girl in the thrift shop sounded very much like the old Apostle Paul:

1 Corinthians 15:34 "Become sober-minded as you ought, and stop sinning…"

Just stop it!

For Personal Reflection:

1. What do you need to stop now?

2. Well…just stop it!

(Adapted from *"The Purity War: A Biblical Guide for Living in an Immoral World"* by Dr. James M. Cecy. Available at www.amazon.com or www.jaron.org.)

© Dr. James M. and Karon M. Cecy

Jim's Ministry Devotional #10

My Firsts

> Philippians 3:12-14 "Not that I have already obtained it or have already become perfect, but I press on so that I may lay hold of that for which also I was laid hold of by Christ Jesus. Brethren, I do not regard myself as having laid hold of it yet; but one thing I do: forgetting what lies behind and reaching forward to what lies ahead, I press on toward the goal for the prize of the upward call of God in Christ Jesus."

Ministry life is full of firsts. Some of them are great experiences; others open the doors for painful but much-needed lessons. Nelson Mandela is known to have said, "I never lose. I either win or I learn." He went on to say, "Do not judge me by my success, judge me by how many times I fell down and got back up again."

My First Worst Sermon

I was invited to speak at a chapel service for a Christian junior high school. I worked hard to prepare a message I had hoped would encourage these teenagers. Things went well, at first. But on Point #17, I was well aware I was losing my audience. Actually, I lost them on Point #4! I have since learned the three vital points of a sermon: 1. Be sincere. 2. Be brief. 3. Be seated. This was my first worst sermon; there were plenty more to follow.

My First Church Board Proposal

I was asked to make a proposal for a remote-controlled projector screen that would unfold over the front of our baptistry. I did my

TELLING OUR FAITH STORY (VOLUME TWO)

homework and presented to the Board of Elders a ten-minute, extensive list of reasons why we needed the screen. One of the older elders simply said, "Why are you wasting our time with all this? Just buy it!" Oh, the uselessness of overkill! Lesson learned.

My First Greek Test

I was absolutely intimidated by my first semester New Testament Greek class—a requirement for graduation in my seminary. On the day of the final exam, we got word one of our seminary professors had died suddenly. As a new seminarian, I did not know him well but I was grieved for his family and his fellow professors. Whereas my normal practice would have been to study right up to the time of the final test, I could not. I looked at a fellow seminarian and said, "Do you want to go pray?" Surprisingly, he agreed to leave the class with me about a half hour before the test. We prayed for as long as we could and then re-entered the classroom where our fellow students were cramming for the exam. We took the test, thinking we had blown our chances by forsaking our last-minute opportunity for review. In a few days, the test results came in. He and I got the highest grades, not only in that class, but in all the first-semester Greek classes in the seminary! I believe God honored our putting Him and the needs of the professor's family first. I have never forgotten that lesson. Seek Him first! (cf. Matthew 6:33-34; Colossians 3:1-2).

My First Death of a Parishioner

As a new pastor, I had never been with a person on their deathbed. The doctors informed the family there was no evidence of brain activity and their beloved mother and grandmother had "most likely" expired. All that was left was to "pull the plug." None of the family could agree and one of them said to me, "Pastor, please make this decision for us. We will trust you." They all nodded.

I was in my twenties and ill-equipped to know what to do next. The doctor, seeing my consternation, guided me into a side room. He spoke gently, "Pastor, these are tough decisions to make, but based on my best medical experience, I believe she is just being kept alive by the machines." I went to her bedside, held her hands, and prayed. I drew close and whispered in her ear, *"When you get to heaven, tell Jesus I love Him and I am sorry if I made a mistake."* I then signaled the nurse to stop life support. I waited for what felt like an eternity as I watched for the steady beat on the heart monitor to become a flat line. Sadly, that was my first but, after fifty years of ministry, certainly not my last experience with death.

My First Real Look at Grief

I stood at the casket just inches long. A sweet baby girl had died of crib death. I stood with the young mother as she gently stroked the arms of her precious child. This grieving mother then folded her own arms and moaned deeply, *"O God! O God!"*

A woman was in my church office as she heard the confession of her husband who had committed adultery—again. Like the young mother responding to the death of her infant daughter, this betrayed wife cradled her arms and moaned the exact same words, *"O God! O God!"* I will never forget the looks of grief on both of these precious ladies' faces. Grief comes in many forms.

My First Wedding at a Bar

No kidding! I performed the wedding for the parents of our foster sons who were being reunited with their family. I had the joy of counseling them and officiating their wedding. The look on our children's faces was priceless as the bartender shouted to the patrons, "Hey you all, keep it quiet and no more ordering drinks. We're about to do a wedding." The place got strangely quiet as some of the patrons moved the furniture so we could proceed under the lighted beer sign over the pool table. "Do you take this woman....?" "Do you take this man....?" Watching those "good old boys" quiet down and respectfully stop drinking for a few minutes was, frankly, rather "church-ish." However, it was short-lived as the bartender shouted, "The bar is now open!"

My First Seminary Class as an Adjunct Professor

I was teaching as an adjunct professor at a seminary. One of my students shuffled his way to the front. He was obviously quite agitated. "Dr. Cecy, I just don't know what I am called to be. A pastor? A missionary? A Bible scholar?" I smiled a bit knowing his grades reflected that most likely he would not be a Bible scholar. I looked at this sincere brother and responded, "It doesn't matter what you are called to be as long as you keep in mind 1 Thessalonians 4:7 'God has not called us for the purpose of impurity, but in sanctification.' In other words, whatever He calls you to do, you are called to be pure—whether a pure pastor, a pure missionary, or a pure Bible scholar. You can even be a pure lawyer!" We both smiled as he went back to his seat.

Fellow ministers, press on past your firsts!

For Personal Reflection:

Write down some of your "firsts" and reflect on how you felt and what you learned. Share these with your loved ones and friends.

© Dr. James M. and Karon M. Cecy

Jim's Ministry Devotional #11

Pastor-Bloopers

Psalm 103:14 "For He Himself knows our frame; He is mindful that we are but dust."

I first heard these stories in seminary. They were told as if true:

• A new pastor, officiating his first funeral, stood in front of the open casket and said, "This body is just a shell; the nut is in heaven!"

• The keynote speaker, addressing a large audience at a popular Christian conference center, was not prepared for his series of bloopers. He initially spoke with confidence, "Satan, like a giant octopus, will grab you by his testicles." Of course, he meant to say, tentacles but the damage was done—he thought. He continued in the same sermon, speaking about the "fiery darts" of Satan. The only problem? He reversed the letters!

For some examples of my own pastor-bloopers, read on:

• While performing my first wedding, I nervously stood before the crowd and said: "For those of you who are single, this is a time for you to thank God...(At that point I ran out of air and gulped as I finished my sentence)...for His perfect timing and will in your life." I could hear the wave of laughter drifting from the back row to the front.

• While I was preaching one of my first sermons, I spilled a glass of ice water on the front of my light grey pants. It was impossible to hide what truly looked like a "real" accident. I decided to step from behind the pulpit and just face what was next. The laughter did not stop for what felt like an eternity of minutes.

• As a new pastor, I asked a woman in my church when her baby was due. She wasn't pregnant. I never made that mistake again!

• Not too long after, I saw a woman cradling her baby in a blanket. In order to comment on how cute the baby was, I pulled the blanket away from the baby's face. She was nursing.

• I did not have the strength to lift a professional football player out of our church baptismal. He was solid muscle; I was not. I will never forget his eyes as he most likely thought, "I am going to die." He survived; I'm the one who died…of embarrassment.

• While ministering in Manila, I pointed to a young Filipino girl and said in broken Tagalog (Filipino), *Halika dito* instead of *Halikan dito*. *Halika dito* means "Come here." *Halikan dito* means "Kiss me." What a difference one letter makes.

• My executive pastor and I had arranged for our church's Staff Christmas Party to be held at an expensive Brazilian barbecue restaurant. All was well until the door of our private banquet room opened, and two scantily clad belly dancers began prancing from table to table. That Christmas, my secretary gave me a pink bolo and a black mask.

• After being announced as Dr. Cecy at the Mayor's reception for our medical team in Manila, a missionary woman pulled me aside and began to ask some very personal gynecological questions. I quickly interrupted, "Oh…no…no…I am a…(I couldn't think of the right words)…I am a Bible Doctor!" She just laughed as I slid behind my fellow missionaries.

• I was preaching on "stimulating one another to love and good deeds" (Hebrews 10:24). After a bit of study, I learned the Greek phrase referred to the use of a cattle prod. Being a city boy, I asked my secretary to bring one to my office. I placed my finger on the end of the probes and pulled the trigger. I screamed like a six-year-old child, loud enough for my office staff to hear. I was certainly "stimulated." Lesson well-learned.

• I was trying to use an illustration in my sermon and I just could not think of the right word. After a few seconds of stuttering, I finally described it as "a steel rod with a long hole down the center." Someone from the back shouted out, "Do you mean a pipe?" I shouted, "Right!" It was a senior moment before I was a senior.

• While speaking at a Mennonite school, which was historically pacifistic, I used a target pistol illustration, "I am sure you all know when shooting at a target with a gun, you must not shoot first and draw the circle later." I didn't expect the blank stares and the sounds of muffled laughter. They forgave me. Years later I was invited as their graduation commencement speaker. Of course, I refrained from any "ballistic" comments.

• It had been a very long day of travel home from the Philippines. I arrived at Los Angeles Airport, exhausted and barely able to walk to the gate connecting to my flight to Fresno. I decided to freshen up and change my clothes in a nearby restroom. As I left the private stall, I went to the sink to wash my face and hands. To my surprise, I could see in the mirror a woman opening the door of the stall next to the one I had just occupied. Yes, I was in the women's restroom! I decided to play dumb. I dried my hands and left the restroom; embarrassed and afraid this shocked woman was flying on the same plane to Fresno. I must admit, I was tempted to greet her in Italian in hopes she would think I was a misguided foreigner. Instead, I boarded the plane, covered my face with a mask, and fell asleep. I was thankful she was not on that small plane. I cannot imagine sitting next to her and facing the temptation to use my very limited Italian vocabulary. *"Mi scusi Signora."* "Excuse me Madam." I would expect her response to be, *"Stupido!"* (No translation needed.) Given the way my day was going, I would not have been surprised if she spoke more fluent Italian and to hear her say, *"Niente scuse."*—"No excuses."—in other words, It's time to 'fess up!' You're an idiot!"

My Most Embarrassing Ministry Moment

It is common for pastors to share their most embarrassing ministry moments at ministry retreats and conferences. This next blooper often gets first prize from my fellow ministers.

While reading a letter of confession before the whole congregation at the request of a young single woman who was pregnant, I read the wrong name. Instead, I stated it was a letter from another young single woman in our church with a similar name. She and her parents were in the room. I will never forget the gasps!

These are only a few of my many pastoral bloopers. I expect there will be more as the years unfold. To err is very human. To forgive oneself is not easy. To expect there will be many more mistakes is…well…terrifying!

For Personal Reflection:

1. Reflect on some of your most embarrassing moments.

2. What lessons did you learn from this experience?

© Dr. James M. and Karon M. Cecy

Jim's Ministry Devotional #12

God's Love Language

> Ephesians 2:10 "For we are His workmanship, created in Christ Jesus for good works, which God prepared beforehand so that we would walk in them."

Counselors often speak of "love languages"—the actions people experience when they are feeling most loved. Many of us are familiar with the most popular list:

#1. Words of Affirmation

#2. Acts of Service

#3. Gifts

#4. Quality Time

#5. Physical Touch

Of these five ways most express love, my preference is "acts of service." My wife knows it. Some of the greatest expressions of her love is when I come home from a ministry trip and see projects done that are on my impossible-to-accomplish "To Do" list. Sometimes they are complete surprises.

Some of our greatest expressions of our love for the Lord are also expressed in our acts of service. When I first became a follower of Christ, I wanted to simplify what I had come to believe about my personal relationship with Him. Beyond trusting Him alone to forgive my sins and give me eternal life, I wanted to experience the abundant life He promised this side of Heaven (cf. John 10:10). Over fifty years ago, I laid it out this way:

To know Him is to love Him.
To love Him is to obey Him.
To obey Him is to serve Him.

Service is also one of God's love languages. Yes, some people express their love for God in other ways but after fifty years of serving the Lord, I echo the prayers of the Apostle Paul:

1 Timothy 1:12 "I thank Christ Jesus our Lord, who has strengthened me, because He considered me faithful, putting me into service..."

1 Corinthians 16:9 "...a wide door for effective service has opened to me..."

Over the timeline of my Christian life, such a wide door has been opened to me. I hesitate to list these out for fear it can seem arrogant. However, as I wrote this list, my heart was filled with sincere praise God would use a "wretch like me." I have been honored to serve the Lord:

• As a local church member, giving of my time, talent, and treasures.

• As a Sunday School teacher.

• As a Youth Director, eventually licensed as a Pastor.

• As a seminary student, serving in a local church as a ministry intern.

• As an associate pastor.

• As a Christian education director.

• As an interim senior pastor.

• As a senior pastor.

• As a biblical counselor.

• As an elder.

• As a board member.

• As a missionary.

• As a conference speaker.

• As a Bible institute professor.

• As an adjunct seminary professor.

• As a trainer of fellow ministers, pastors, chaplains, and missionaries.

• As the founder and president of a mission organization.

• As a consultant, advisor, and mentor.

• As a curriculum developer and an author.

And let's not forget my calling as a member of my earthly family:

• As a sibling, brother-in-law, and cousin.

• As an uncle, great uncle, and great-great uncle.

• As a husband.

• As a father, grandfather, and hopefully someday, great-grandfather.

The Apostle Paul gave the requirements for such service:

Romans 12:11 "...not lagging behind in diligence, fervent (Greek: *zeo*, "boiling" and "zealous") in spirit, serving the Lord..."

The word *fervent* is used only in one other place in the New Testament to describe Apollos, a man who was "mighty in the Scriptures" and "fervent in spirit" (cf. Acts 18:24-25).

Not lagging behind in diligence. Boiling in fervency and zeal. Serving the Lord as a form of worship. Talk about a love language that blesses the heart of God!

For Personal Reflection:

1. What is your love language?

2. In what way does God most communicate His love for you?

3. In what way do you most communicate your love for God?

Jim's Ministry Devotional #13

Exception Clauses. Famous Excuses

Luke 14:18 "…they all alike began to make excuses."

On November 17, 1971, I prayed to receive Christ as my Lord and Savior. My whispered prayer was simple and heartfelt:

"Lord Jesus…come into my heart and be my Lord and Savior."

Sadly, my prayer also had some conditions that reflected my ignorance of His sovereignty:

"I will do anything for You, Lord…except go into the ministry."

My reasons were simple: I felt unworthy, unqualified, and ill-equipped. I had no idea God would use someone like me.

In those days, when people suggested God may be calling me to full-time vocational ministry, I often teased, *"I don't want to be paid to be good; I want to remain, 'good for nothing.'"* Oh, how my life was filled with excuses. However, it didn't take long to learn from the Bible that I was in good company with some pretty famous excuse-makers, who had their own exception clauses. Let me paraphrase a few:

• Moses: "I will do anything for You, Lord, except I don't speak very well. Send someone else" (cf. Exodus 4:10, 13).

• Gideon: "I would do what you ask, Lord, except I am not qualified" (cf. Judges 6:15).

• Jeremiah: "I would preach to your rebellious people, Lord, except I am too young and inexperienced" (cf. Jeremiah 1:6).

• Jonah: "I would offer your forgiveness to these unbelievers, Lord, except..." Then he just fled from the Lord! (Jonah 1:3). Later he cries out: "Lord, I'd rather die than do what You are asking me to do" (cf. Jonah 4:3, 8).

God's answer to most of these excuses was the same:

"I am with you." (cf. Exodus 4:11-12; Judges 6:16; Jeremiah 1:7-8). God also heard Jonah's cry for help (cf. Jonah 2:1-2).

God's answer to all our excuses is even more amazing:

Matthew 28:20 "I am with you always, even to the end of the age" (My emphasis).

Having served in vocational ministry for five decades, I am thanking God for His sovereign will that overruled many of my foolish excuses and exception clauses. I am especially grateful for the timeless words of the Apostle Paul:

Ephesians 2:10 "For we are His workmanship, created in Christ Jesus for good works, which God prepared beforehand so that we would walk in them."

So, what are your "exception clauses"?

"I will do anything for You, Lord, EXCEPT_____!"

For Personal Reflection:

What are your excuses for not doing what God is asking you to do?

God wants me to: My excuse: God's answer:

_____   _____   _____

Comment:

God wants me to: My excuse: God's answer:

_____   _____   _____

Comment:

"Thank you, Lord, for using us in spite of ourselves. I hear You speaking to my excuse-making heart, 'I am with you always!'"

© Dr. James M. and Karon M. Cecy.

Jim's Ministry Devotional #14

The Many Facets of Leadership

> Matthew 20:25-28 "But Jesus called them to Himself and said, 'You know that the rulers of the Gentiles lord it over them, and their great men exercise authority over them. It is not this way among you, but whoever wishes to become great among you shall be your servant, and whoever wishes to be first among you shall be your slave; just as the Son of Man did not come to be served, but to serve, and to give His life a ransom for many'" (cf. Luke 22:24-27).

Some of the characteristics of a true leader, biblically speaking, were as foreign in ancient cultures as they are today. Like the facets of a brilliant diamond, we are presented in the Greek New Testament with the many facets of godly leadership as prescribed by God.

1. The Up-Front Leader (Greek: *prohistemi*)

This is the one who "stands before" a crowd, the one who presides over, rules, governs, and gives direction. This is the person who sticks his head above a crowd, knowing someone may throw a brick at it. This is also the person who turns around and sees people are following.

2. The Intentional Leader (Greek: *hegoumenos*)

This is the person who is careful, thoughtful, and intentional. He or she doesn't shoot first and draw the target later.

3. The Mature Leader (Greek: *presbuteros*)

This is the leader with the emotional, and spiritual maturity who comes with wisdom and experience, regardless of age.

4. The Overseeing Leader (Greek: *episcopos*)

The basic meaning of the word speaks of one who "sees from above." This is the leader who can view the whole situation, rather than just the parts.

5. The Shepherd Leader (Greek: *poimen*)

The words speak of one who cares, feeds, protects, and warns. This is a person who cares enough to be well-prepared for any situation.

6. The Chief Leader (Greek: *kephale*)

This is the leader who obediently accepts an assigned position of headship and responsibility, regardless of the challenges.

7. The Teaching Leader (Greek: *didaskalos*)

This is the one who teaches by both precept and example and is a person of content, not just opinions.

8. The Managing Leader (Greek: *oikonomos*)

This is one who is able to steward and manage. (The word *oikonomos* refers to one who knows the rules of the house.) This is the person who can be trusted to manage life in all its facets (personal, financial, relational, physical, etc.).

9. The Hands-On Leader (Greek: *diakonos*)

The word, sometimes translated as deacon, speaks of one who ministers hands-on and whose life of service leads others to do the same.

10. The Servant-Leader (Greek: *doulos*)

The word refers to one who leads as a servant (i.e., a bondslave). It is related to the word *huperetes* which speaks of the under-rower slave, chained to the lowest and most dangerous level of a Roman ship (cf. Acts 26:16, where Jesus appoints us to that kind of ministry). These are the leaders who are "chained" to their responsibilities.

11. The Humble Leader (Greek: *tapeinophrosune*)

From the words of Jesus Himself comes an aspect of leadership that is especially foreign to us humans. It was one of His deepest concerns:

> John 13:14-16 "If I then, the Lord and the Teacher, washed your feet, you also ought to wash one another's feet. For I gave you an example that you also should do as I did to you. Truly, truly, I say to you, a slave is not greater than his master, nor is one who is sent greater than the one who sent him."

> Luke 9:48 "...for the one who is least among all of you, this is the one who is great."

The Apostle Paul would agree:

Philippians 2:3 "Do nothing from selfishness or empty conceit, but with humility of mind regard one another as more important than yourselves…"

We would do well to look at many more passages that present the attributes of a leader. One of my favorites is:

Colossians 3:12-15 "So, as those who have been chosen of God, holy and beloved, put on a heart of compassion, kindness, humility, gentleness and patience; bearing with one another, and forgiving each other, whoever has a complaint against anyone; just as the Lord forgave you, so also should you. Beyond all these things put on love, which is the perfect bond of unity. Let the peace of Christ rule in your hearts, to which indeed you were called in one body; and be thankful."

Imagine meeting a leader who is:

- Chosen of God.

- Holy and beloved.

- Compassionate.

- Kind.

- Humble.

- Gentle.

- Patient.

- Forbearing.

- Forgiving.

- Loving.

- Committed to unity.

- Ruled by the peace of Christ.

- Grateful.

How unlike the world's view of leadership. How like Jesus!

For Personal Reflection:

1. Which of the above facets of godly leadership most describes you?

2. Which of the above characteristics of a leader are most in need of improvement in your life?

3. Write a summary of the strengths and weaknesses of your leadership style.

(Adapted from *"Men in Action: Equipping Men to Lead in the Home, the Church, and the Community"* by Dr. James M. Cecy. Available at www.amazon.com and www.jaron.org.)

© Dr. James M. and Karon M. Cecy.

Jim's Ministry Devotional #15

Preparing My Heart for Effective Ministry

> 1 Thessalonians 2:4 "...we speak, not as pleasing men but God, who examines our hearts."

I have been blessed to travel to many places and minister to a myriad of people in hundreds of locations. I have come to learn effective and lasting ministry demands our souls be as prepared as our minds and bodies.

Reflecting on the Apostle Paul's own personal testimony regarding his challenging ministry in ancient Thessalonica, I invite you to briefly consider twenty-four heart-felt "ministry covenants" that need to be made before embarking on our own discipleship meetings, teaching opportunities, and ministry adventures. This checklist is based on what the Apostle Paul wrote in 1 Thessalonians 2:1-20 as he presented the defense of his brief ministry in Thessalonica (cf. 1 Thessalonians 1-2; Acts 17:1-9). May the example of his ministry success be our own:

Ministry Covenant #1. "I will not waste the gifts and resources God has entrusted to me."

> 1 Thessalonians 2:1 "For you yourselves know, brethren, that our coming to you was not in vain..."

Ministry Covenant #2. "I will boldly speak the truth, even in the midst of opposition."

> 1 Thessalonians 2:2 "...but after we had already suffered and been mistreated in Philippi, as you know, we had the

boldness in our God to speak to you the gospel of God amid much opposition."

Ministry Covenant #3. "I will strive to make sure my ministry is accurate."

1 Thessalonians 2:3 "For our exhortation does not come from error…"

Ministry Covenant #4. "I will strive to make sure my ministry is pure."

1 Thessalonians 2:3 "For our exhortation does not come from error or impurity..." (My emphasis).

Ministry Covenant #5. "I will strive to make sure that my ministry has integrity."

1 Thessalonians 2:3 "For our exhortation does not come from error or impurity or by way of deceit..." (My emphasis).

Ministry Covenant #6. "I will minister from the depth of God's approval and calling in my life."

1 Thessalonians 2:4 "...but just as we have been approved by God to be entrusted with the gospel, so we speak..."

Ministry Covenant #7. "I will strive to please God, even if it means not pleasing men."

1 Thessalonians 2:4 "...so we speak, not as pleasing men but God, who examines our hearts."

Ministry Covenant #8. "I will not engage in flattery."

1 Thessalonians 2:5 "For we never came with flattering speech, as you know..."

Ministry Covenant #9. "I will not allow greed to motivate my ministry."

1 Thessalonians 2:5 "For we never came with flattering speech, as you know, <u>nor with a pretext for greed</u>—God is witness..." (My emphasis).

Ministry Covenant #10. "I will not seek the praise and glory of men."

1 Thessalonians 2:6 "...nor did we seek glory from men, either from you or from others..."

Ministry Covenant #11. "I will not assert or abuse my position."

1 Thessalonians 2:6 "...even though as apostles of Christ we might have asserted our authority."

Ministry Covenant #12. "I will be as gentle as a mother tenderly caring for her children."

1 Thessalonians 2:7 "But we proved to be gentle among you, as a nursing mother tenderly cares for her own children."

Ministry Covenant #13. "I will strive to have a fond affection for the people I am serving."

1 Thessalonians 2:8 "Having so fond an affection for you..."

Ministry Covenant #14. "I will impart not only my message and ministry but also my life."

> 1 Thessalonians 2:8 "...we were well-pleased to impart to you not only the gospel of God but also our own lives, because you had become very dear to us."

Ministry Covenant #15. "I will labor diligently so as not to pose a financial burden on God's people."

> 1 Thessalonians 2:9 "For you recall, brethren, our labor and hardship, how working night and day so as not to be a burden to any of you, we proclaimed to you the gospel of God."

Ministry Covenant #16. "I will behave in a godly manner."

> 1 Thessalonians 2:10 "You are witnesses, and so is God, how devoutly and uprightly and blamelessly we behaved toward you believers..."

Ministry Covenant #17. "I will be as forthright as a father lovingly correcting his children."

> 1 Thessalonians 2:11 "...just as you know how we were exhorting and encouraging and imploring each one of you as a father would his own children..."

Ministry Covenant #18. "I will equip people to walk in a manner that is worthy of the God who called them."

> 1 Thessalonians 2:12 "...so that you would walk in a manner worthy of the God who calls you into His own kingdom and glory."

Ministry Covenant #19. "I will strive to teach that which is truly based on the Word of God and not the word of men."

> 1 Thessalonians 2:13 "For this reason we also constantly thank God that when you received the word of God which you heard from us, you accepted it not as the word of men, but for what it really is, the word of God…"

Ministry Covenant #20. "I will confidently expect God's Word will mightily work in the people I am serving."

> 1 Thessalonians 2:13 "…you accepted it not as the word of men, but for what it really is, the word of God, which also performs its work in you who believe" (My emphasis).

Ministry Covenant #21. "I will encourage Bible-believing disciples to be prepared to endure persecution for the cause of Christ."

> 1 Thessalonians 2:14-16 "For you, brethren, became imitators of the churches of God in Christ Jesus that are in Judea, for you also endured the same sufferings at the hands of your own countrymen, even as they did from the Jews, who both killed the Lord Jesus and the prophets, and drove us out. They are not pleasing to God, but hostile to all men, hindering us from speaking to the Gentiles so that they may be saved; with the result that they always fill up the measure of their sins. But wrath has come upon them to the utmost."

Ministry Covenant #22. "I will strive for such a relationship with the people I am serving that, once I leave, I will be eager to see them again."

1 Thessalonians 2:17 "But we, brethren, having been taken away from you for a short while—in person, not in spirit—were all the more eager with great desire to see your face."

Ministry Covenant #23. "I will pray God will remove the hindrances and clear the way for more effective ministry."

1 Thessalonians 2:18 "For we wanted to come to you—I, Paul, more than once and yet Satan hindered us."

Ministry Covenant #24. "I will pray the people I am serving will be a source of blessing when Jesus returns."

1 Thessalonians 2:19-20 "For who is our hope or joy or crown of exultation? Is it not even you, in the presence of our Lord Jesus at His coming? For you are our glory and joy."

For Personal Reflection:

Read and pray through these Ministry Covenants before your ministry events.

© Dr. James M. and Karon M. Cecy.

Jim's Ministry Devotional #16

The Minister's Hands

Psalm 24:3-4 "Who may ascend into the hill of the LORD? And who may stand in His holy place? He who has clean hands and a pure heart, who has not lifted up his soul to falsehood and has not sworn deceitfully."

Psalm 63:4 "So I will bless You as long as I live; I will lift up my hands in Your name."

Proverbs 12:14 "A man will be satisfied with good by the fruit of his words, and the deeds of a man's hands will return to him."

1 Timothy 2:8 "Therefore I want the men in every place to pray, lifting up holy hands, without wrath and dissension."

Of all the physical attributes of my first pastor, I remember his hands. He would stand at the door of the church and shake my hand, look in my eyes, and convince me I was the most important person in his life, at least for that moment.

While I was in seminary, Josh McDowell came to our chapel service. Although he was well known to us all, he grabbed my hand and said, "Hi, I'm Josh McDowell. What's your name?"

Why would a famous guy like McDowell introduce himself as if I didn't know his name? I was struck by his sincerity and humility. That was in 1975, and I have never forgotten the feel of his hand and the look in his eye. I, a lowly seminary student and new Christian, was the most important person in the crowd. In that memorable moment, I learned a life-long ministry lesson.

There is something about our hands that convey strong messages. A clenched fist displays anger and the desire to use force. An open-handed salute is more than a sign of respect; it signals to a superior there is no weapon or threat. A pat on the back communicates affirmation of a person. Applause is simply an affirming pat on the back from a distance. Open hands can also be a sign of peace (1 Timothy 2:8). We endeavor daily to lift up "holy hands" to the Lord (cf. 1 Timothy 2:8) as a symbol of His peace prevailing over our "anger, wrath, malice, slander, and abusive speech" (cf. Colossians 3:8). We also "lay hands on" and pray for those who are heading out on a new challenge in which they need our support and encouragement.

In addition to a symbol of the healing power of God, the Bible speaks of "laying hands" on someone as a means of endorsing and identifying with a person being sent to use their God-given gifts and talents in a ministry (cf. Acts 13:3; 1 Timothy 4:14; 5:22; 2 Timothy 1:6; etc.).

As those who minister to others, let's reflect on our hands:

• **We lift our hands to the Lord with a desire for His peace to prevail in our lives.**

> 1 Timothy 2:8 "Therefore I want the men in every place to pray, lifting up holy hands, without wrath and dissension."

• **We open our hands to reveal we have no anger or malice toward others.**

> 1 Samuel 24:11, 13) "...there is no evil or rebellion in my hands, and I have not sinned against you, though you are lying in wait for my life to take it...my hand shall not be against you."

• We <u>pat</u> others on the back in recognition we believe in what God is doing in our midst.

> Philippians 1:6 "For I am confident of this very thing, that He who began a good work in you will perfect it until the day of Christ Jesus."

• We <u>applaud</u> others when they make the right choices.

> 1 Corinthians 12:26 "…if one member is honored, all the members rejoice with it."

• We <u>lay our hands</u> on others in recognition they are commissioned for a holy purpose.

> 1 Timothy 4:14 "Do not neglect the spiritual gift within you, which was bestowed on you through prophetic utterance with the laying on of hands..."

• We <u>join hands with</u> others as Soldiers of the Cross, <u>saluting</u> our divine Commander in Chief.

> 2 Timothy 2:1-4 "You therefore, my son, be strong in the grace that is in Christ Jesus. The things which you have heard from me in the presence of many witnesses, entrust these to faithful men who will be able to teach others also. Suffer hardship with me, as a good soldier of Christ Jesus. No soldier in active service entangles himself in the affairs of everyday life, so that he may please the one who enlisted him as a soldier."

• We <u>shake hands</u> with as many people as possible.

While looking into their eyes, we give them our full attention because they are important—especially to God.

It is not surprising I often say to my pastoral staff, "All hands on deck." It is not just reminiscent of my Navy days. Hopefully, it reminds us to:

• Lift our hands to the Lord in prayer.

• Open our hands in peace toward others.

• Pat others on the back to encourage them.

• Applaud others when they do well.

• Lay hands on others to affirm them.

• Salute and worship our King of kings and Lord of lords.

• Shake hands with as many people as possible—because we love them with the love of the Lord.

That's what I call "hands on" ministry!

For Personal Reflection:

1. Reflect on the impact of your hands to worship, encourage, and affirm.

2. What are some of the improper uses of your hands (e.g., striking out in anger, etc.)?

3. Which of the positive actions of your hands is most needed?

(Adapted from *"Men in Action: Equipping Men to Lead in the Home, the Church, and the Community"* by Dr. James M. Cecy. Available at www.amazon.com and www.jaron.org.)

Jim's Ministry Devotional #17

The Accountable Life

I was at the Los Angeles airport talking to the agent at the check-in counter. A tall gentleman behind me interrupted, "Are you Dr. Cecy?" I turned and responded, "Well, yes, I am." He continued, "I recognize your voice because I listen to your radio program all the time."

I was initially flattered until he blurted out, "I would have thought you were better looking, but..." He paused only for a second and then finished his abrupt comment, "...you are rather short and... f...f...featured." I think he meant to say, "fat" but at least he had enough sense to hold back a bit. Usually not at a loss for words, I didn't know what to say, so I just turned and attended to my business.

My fellow missionaries could not stop laughing. On our very long trip to Manila, they kept asking me, "Are you Dr. Cecy—the short and...f... f...featured guy?" Those words have often served to keep me moving and watching those wasted calories. I am still short. Not much I can do about that. But I can do something about being a little less "featured." So it is with every arena of my life—and yours, as well.

Call it the examined life, the disclosed life, the transparent life, the vulnerable life, the defendable life, the reporting life, the responsible life, or the honest life. It is one of the keys to what Jesus came to offer—the abundant life (cf. John 10:10).

The accountable life is one that lives in the knowledge of an omniscient and loving God who not only knows us intimately but cares about everything we think, say, and do. It is also the life that takes seriously the responsibility to enlist the help of others on this path to living the way God desires for us. A few reminders from the Word of God:

Ephesians 4:1 "Therefore I, the prisoner of the Lord, implore you to <u>walk in a manner worthy</u> of the calling with which you have been called..." (My emphasis).

Colossians 1:9-10 "For this reason also, since the day we heard of it, we have not ceased to pray for you and to ask that you may be filled with the knowledge of His will in all spiritual wisdom and understanding, so that you will <u>walk in a manner worthy</u> of the Lord, to please Him in all respects, bearing fruit in every good work and increasing in the knowledge of God..." (My emphasis; cf. 1 John 2:6; 3 John 1:6).

1 Thessalonians 2:11-12 "...we were exhorting and encouraging and imploring each one of you as a father would his own children, so that you would <u>walk in a manner worthy</u> of the God who calls you into His own kingdom and glory" (My emphasis).

For Personal Reflection:

1. Reflect on your level of accountability to God, yourself, and others.

2. In what area of accountability do you struggle the most?

(Adapted from *"The Accountable Life: Protecting Myself and Others"* by Dr. James M. Cecy. Available at www.amazon.com and www.jaron.org.)

© Dr. James M. and Karon M. Cecy.

Jim's Ministry Devotional #18

"Get Out of Bed!"

> Colossians 1:28-29 "We proclaim Him, admonishing every man and teaching every man with all wisdom, so that we may present every man complete in Christ. For this purpose also I labor, striving according to His power, which mightily works within me."

I am one of those people who, on most days, wakes up early without an alarm clock. But, then again, there are those days when I grumble, "Good Lord, it's morning," rather than "Good morning, Lord."

I love the old story of the mother who called her son on Sunday morning to make sure he got out of bed and was ready for church.

"I'm not going," he replied.

"Yes, you are going, so get out of that bed!" his mother demanded.

"Give me one good reason why I should go," said her son.

"I'll give you three good reasons. One, I'm your mother and I say you're going. Two, you're forty years old, so you're old enough to know better. And three, you're the pastor, so you need to be there!"

I have been doing some kind of ministry for fifty years—as a teacher, ministry leader, pastor, counselor, professor, and missionary. I wish I could tell you every day has been a joy, but I would be lying. Over the years I have observed there are three kinds of people:

- VNP – Very Needy People – which can be rightly said of all of us who need to be equipped.

- VHP – Very Helpful People – who use their gifts and talents to help care for very needy people.

- VDP – Very Draining People – who do more taking than giving and are most demanding.

In order to faithfully serve people from each of these groups, I have needed to constantly remind myself of the words of the Apostle Paul in Colossians 1:28-29. They're worth repeating:

Colossians 1:28-29 "We proclaim Him, admonishing every man and teaching every man with all wisdom, so that we may present every man complete in Christ. For this purpose also I labor, striving according to His power, which mightily works within me."

Many of my fellow ministers have declared these verses as best describing their philosophy of ministry. I agree with them. This passage often stimulates my heart to rehearse the following declarations:

Declaration #1: "Today, I will keep proclaiming Christ as my central focus."

Declaration #2: "Today, I will be willing to admonish (i.e., warn and confront) people."

Declaration #3: "Today, I will work hard to teach the Word of God with wisdom."

Declaration #4: "Today, I will strive to present people complete (i.e., mature) in Christ as a special offering to Him."

Declaration #5: "Today, I will labor to lovingly serve all kinds of people, according to Christ's power mightily working in me."

Yes, it's hard work but well worth it. It's what gets me out of bed even without my mother as my alarm clock!

For Personal Reflection:

1. What are the things that keep you from "getting out of bed"?

2. Read Colossians 1:28-29 forty times as you make it your philosophy of ministry.

3. Make a copy and rehearse the five declarations stated in this devotional.

© Dr. James M. and Karon M. Cecy.

Jim's Ministry Devotional #19

My Office

> John 13:14-15 "If I then, the Lord and the Teacher, washed your feet, you also ought to wash one another's feet. For I gave you an example that you also should do as I did to you."

As you walk into my church office, you are immediately faced with what is obviously a former sailor's décor. A ship's bell hangs by the door. Models of masted ships sit on shelves around the room. Pictures and models of my Navy ship, the *U.S.S. Kitty Hawk*, are everywhere. On the cabinet shelves are artifacts, military hats, and police patches, many given to me over the years. Most of them have a story. Let me share a couple:

The Ukrainian Officer's Hat

On one of my many trips to Ukraine, I met an associate pastor who was once a MIG fighter pilot for the U.S.S.R. He shared that, at one time, he was involved with the missiles pointed at America and her allies at the same time I was serving on a well-equipped warship prepared to defend against such attacks. We spoke of the times the bombers from the U.S.S.R. would fly over our ship and our planes would tail them in a dangerous game of "cat and mouse." The fact is, we were once enemies!

Now, here we were, serving the Lord as pastors. We became close friends very quickly. One day, he took me to a museum celebrating the former glory of the Soviet military. I even got to stand next to the cockpit of the type of MIG fighter jet he flew.

Two Cold War army tanks were stationed in front of the museum—one Soviet and one American. They were facing each other in obvious combat position. However, someone had attached a long cord between both barrels. It was a touching sight. There, in front of those two deadly weapons of destruction, we stood and prayed for peace.

Back at the church, we stood before some 1,600 people at a Sunday service. He presented me with his Ukrainian Air Force Hat. We hugged as former enemies and now brothers in Christ. The place exploded with applause. His hat now sits in a prominent place in my office. It reminds me to pray for him and especially for peace in that turbulent part of the world.

The Ukrainian Man's Shoeshine Kit

On the same trip an old man came to me at the end of the church service. He could not speak English. Through a translator he said, "May I honor you? I would like to shine your shoes right now." I didn't know what to say.

As we talked further, I found out this old man's only income came from polishing shoes. In his hand he held a small tin can that contained polish and a very small rag. He handed me his shoeshine kit and his scarf. "May I honor you by giving you these?" I began to cry as did he. We embraced. I tried to give him his belongings back, but he insisted. The pastor with me expressed it would be an insult to not take them.

Now, those precious items have a prominent place in my office. What a reminder to pray for the everyday folks of Ukraine who are eking out a living in the midst of the great challenges their nation is facing.

There are many more items in my office, most with a touching story. Many prompt me to pray. All of them stir my memories of precious times of ministry around the world, especially watching the people of God follow Jesus's example of humility and self-sacrifice. Their lives are such an example to me.

For Personal Reflection:

1. Show your family and friends some of the relics in your "museum of memories" that hold special value to you.

2. Share the reasons they are important to you.

© Dr. James M. and Karon M. Cecy.

Jim's Ministry Devotional #20

His Door is Always Open

James 4:8 "Draw near to God and He will draw near to you."

My family has always known they have immediate access to me no matter how busy I am. When they were young, my secretaries were told to inform me whenever my children stepped into the church office. Regardless of what I was doing, I came out to give them a big hug and a piece of candy. My ministry staff also knows I will answer their calls as soon as possible. Unless I am counseling someone, my door is always open. They also know they can have fifteen minutes of uninterrupted time no matter what I am doing.

I am reminded today of the many wonderful passages in the Bible showing how accessible our great God is:

• Psalm 46:1 "God is our refuge and strength, a very present help in trouble."

• Psalm 73:28 "…the nearness of God is my good…"

• Hebrews 4:16 "…let us draw near with confidence to the throne of grace, so that we may receive mercy and find grace to help in time of need."

• Hebrews 10:22 "…let us draw near with a sincere heart in full assurance."

I am also blessed by the timeless words of the old hymn, *Day by Day*, written in 1865 by Swedish poet, Lina Sandell, several years after she witnessed the tragic drowning of her father. The song begins:

Day by day, and with each passing moment,
Strength I find to meet my trials here.

I am especially prompted in my daily activities to consider the words from the second stanza:

Every day the Lord Himself is near me,
With a special mercy for each hour.
All my cares He fain would bear and cheer me,
He whose name is Counselor and Power.

Precious brothers and sisters in Christ, God is with us today. What an incredible thought! But there's another side of this great truth to consider. I am intrigued by King David's prayer in Psalm 139. After elaborating on the wonder of <u>God's</u> presence with him, David ends with a declaration of <u>his</u> presence with God:

Psalm 139:17-18 "How precious also are Your thoughts to me, O God! How vast is the sum of them. <u>When I awake, I am still with You</u>" (My emphasis).

Simply stated: God is with us. It's time to ask: Are we with Him? Draw near to Him today! His door is always open! In the words of the old saying:

"If you don't feel close to God, guess who moved!"

For Personal Reflection:

Reflect on how accessible God is to you. How does that affect your attitude and actions today?

© Dr. James M. and Karon M. Cecy.

Jim's Ministry Devotional #21

Jim's Acrostics and Acronyms

> Luke 16:17 "But it is easier for heaven and earth to pass away than for one stroke of a letter of the Law to fail."

Mnemonic devices are memory techniques. Some people use lists; others make up songs: *"This is the way I wash my car, wash my car, wash my car...so early in the morning."*

An acrostic is a set of initials that, if taken in order, form a word or phrase. For example, F.B.I., or FBI, refers to the Federal Bureau of Investigation. In my family, FBI means Full-Blooded Italian. To be honest, too many of my FBI family have spent time talking to the FBI agency.

On the other hand, an acronym is an abbreviation composed of the initial letters of a set of words but these letters form a word that is pronounceable. Most of us refer to the National Aeronautics and Space Administration with the acronym NASA. Of course, there is a joke that when you put the word "The" and "IRS" together, it spells "Theirs." That is both pronounceable and painful!

Then we have to mention an abbreviation, like U.S.A. Apparently, this is neither an acrostic nor an acronym. Why? I don't know. Are you confused yet? I certainly am! Today, due to text messaging, there is even more banter over initialisms—I suspect designed to keep parents and grandparents permanently baffled.

Psalm 119 is actually an acrostic poem in Hebrew. If you read it in any other language, you miss it. The Psalm, written by King David, is composed of 176 verses divided into twenty-two stanzas. Each stanza begins with a word that corresponds to a letter in the Hebrew alphabet—from *aleph*, the first letter of the alphabet to *tav*, the last letter. Then, each of the eight verses of each stanza begins with the same Hebrew letter. Why did King David do this?

How else would his readers be able to memorize 176 verses? He knew most every Hebrew-speaker knew the alphabet. Are you confused yet? Thankfully, having studied basic Hebrew, I am not.

However, I have used these mnemonic devices as memory techniques all my life. Let's look at a few of my acrostics, acronyms, abbreviations and initialisms. You decide which they are:

5 – 12 – 5 – 5 – 12

This is how I remember the Old Testament books.

    5 – Books of the Pentateuch (Torah)

    12 – Historical Books

    5 – Wisdom Books

    5 – Major Prophets

    12 – Minor Prophets

A.C.T.S.

The process by which I deal with my sin:

    A – <u>Admit</u> my sin

    C – <u>Confess</u> my sin

    T – <u>Turn</u> from my sin

    S – <u>Serve</u> others from my repentant life

B.A.A.A.A.

This is the way I share the Gospel, reminding people they, by trusting in Christ alone, become a part of His precious flock of sheep (cf. John 10:27-28). Thus, the word: *"Baaaa"*:

B – You must <u>believe</u> Jesus Christ died on the cross and bodily rose from the grave.

A – You must <u>admit</u> you are a sinner.

A – You must <u>agree</u> to turn from sin to God.

A – You must <u>acknowledge</u> Jesus Christ is the Risen Lord.

A – You must <u>accept</u> God's free gift of salvation.

B.I.B.L.E. (Basic Instructions Before Leaving Earth)

This is an old reminder from my first years as a Christian and the song we sang. Sing it if you know it: *The B.I.B.LE. That's the book for me. I stand alone on the Word of God. The B.I.B.L.E.*

COME! GROW! GO!

This is how I approach ministry in the local church:

COME – Centripetal Force. Drawing the people in.

GROW – Internal Force. Equipping the people here.

GO – Centrifugal Force. Sending the people out.

CORE – COMMITTED – CONGREGATION – CROWD – COMMUNITY

The five groups of people in a local church:

The Core – The inner circle of attenders.

The Committed – The faithful attenders.

The Congregation – The casual attenders.

The Crowd – The occasional attenders.

The Community – The non-attenders.

F.D.W.S.E.D.P.

The marks of a healthy Christian. We need to grow in:

Fellowship: Engaging in loving, need-meeting relationships with others.

Doctrine: Understanding and being able to defend the basic doctrines of the faith.

Worship: Responding in a variety of ways to the infinite majesty of God.

Service: Serving God using my gifts and talents graciously given by God.

Evangelism: Presenting the true gospel by grace alone through faith alone in Christ alone.

Discipleship: Helping others become loving and obedient followers of Christ.

Prayer: Communicating with God in sincere praise, repentance, and petition.

GODISNOWHERE

My perspectives on life's circumstances:

Through eyes of despair: "God is nowhere."

Through eyes of faith: "God is now here."

When she was young, my dyslexic daughter found a third option:

Through eyes of dishonesty: "God, I snow here." (i.e., "Don't lie to God!")

Have a G.R.E.A.T. Day

My daily routine:

G. – Greet the Day with Praise.

R. – Report to the Day with Purpose.

E. – Engage the Day with a Plan.

A. – Analyze the Day with Perspective.

T. – Terminate the Day with Prayer.

HO-JO-AM-OB-JO-MI-NA-HA-ZE-HA-ZE-MA

The first two letters of the twelve Minor Prophets put together as one word. Yes, I actually memorized this as a new Christian. I found out later it was much easier to simply memorize the whole name.

I.C.E.R.

My personal reminders regarding the proper order when counseling someone:

I. – Identification: Identifying the problem.

C. – Confrontation: Confronting the problem.

E. – Exhortation: Exhorting the person.

R. – Restoration: Restoring the person.

JARON

The name of the ministry we founded. Initially: Jaron was the combined name of our names, Jim and Karon. Later, JARON (with capital letters) reflected we are "Jesus's Ambassadors Reaching Out to Nations."

P.O.I.A.P. (or simply POIAP)

How I approach the study of Scripture:

P. – Preparation: Anticipating God's Direction.

O. – Observation: Asking the Right Questions.

I. – Interpretation: Answering the Right Questions.

A. – Application: Applying the Right Answers.

P. – Presentation: Applying the Good News.

P.R.A.Y.E.R.

My version of the Lord's Prayer (cf. Matthew 6:9-13) in summary:

P. – Praising: "Lord, I thank You for…"

R. – Repenting: "Lord, will You forgive me for…"

A. – Asking: "Lord, I ask You for my needs…"

Y. – Yielding: "Lord, if it be Your will…"

E. – Entreating: "Lord, I pray for…(others)

R. – Rejoicing: "Lord, thank You, in advance, for what You are going to do."

P.U.S.H.

My reminder for persevering in prayer:

P.U.S.H. – Pray Until Something Happens!

THE FIVE C'S

What I look for in a fellow minister, missionary, and ministry volunteer:

Character: Is this a person of integrity?

Chemistry: Is this person the right fit?

Competence: Is this person capable of doing the job?

Confidence: Am I confident in this person?

Cost: Is this person worth the price (in terms of time, money, and effort)?

V.H.P. – V.N.P – V.D.P.

Three kinds of people in the local church:

V.H.P. – Very Helpful People.

V.N.P. – Very Needy People.

V.D.P. – Very Draining People.

For Personal Reflection:

1. Pick out a few of the above to memorize and share with others.

2. Make a list of your own acrostics, acronyms and abbreviations you can share with others.

© Dr. James M. and Karon M. Cecy.

Jim's Ministry Devotional #22

Applauding the Offering

> John 17:20-25 "I do not ask on behalf of these alone, but for those also who believe in Me through their word; that they may all be one; even as You, Father, are in Me and I in You, that they also may be in Us, so that the world may believe that You sent Me. The glory which You have given Me I have given to them, that they may be one, just as We are one; I in them and You in Me, that they may be perfected in unity, so that the world may know that You sent Me, and loved them, even as You have loved Me. Father, I desire that they also, whom You have given Me, be with Me where I am, so that they may see My glory which You have given Me, for You loved Me before the foundation of the world. 'O righteous Father, although the world has not known You, yet I have known You; and these have known that You sent Me.'"

Many years ago, I became aware of a small church in our area that was standing alone against its denomination on matters of theology and practice. They chose to stand on what they believed to be the solid teachings of the Word of God. In so doing, their denomination removed them from their association, requiring them to turn over all their assets and facilities. These were precious people who had worked for decades to build, furnish and equip this church.

After many attempts and appeals, their only recourse was to seek legal help to stop what they considered to be an unfair and illegal action on the part of the denomination. In their minds, their local church had not departed from their historically prescribed faith and practice; the denomination had strayed from their charter beliefs. So the battle began. A tiny church against a large, international denomination. Truly, this was a modern-day David versus Goliath story unfolding. However, it seemed obvious Goliath was about to win!

Once I discussed the matter with our church elders, I stood before our congregation and told the story of a church a few miles from us, facing the battle of their lives as a congregation. I cautiously expressed, "Even though they have some slightly different views, we have a responsibility to help our 'sister church' fight this giant battle. I am asking us to dig deeply into our hearts and our wallets to help pay their legal fees."

What happened next was one of the greatest surprises in my ministry. The place broke out into cheers and applause. Applauding an offering. Never before. That is especially remarkable because this tiny church was "not completely in our camp" theologically. It didn't matter. Our brothers and sisters in Christ needed us—and they needed us now!

That next day, we counted the special offering and were shocked at the amount. We had a messenger take the substantial funds to the church with a note expressing how blessed we were by their courage to stand up for what they believed. We told them we will stand with them.

To our amazement, after many months of legal battles, their church won the case and were granted complete ownership of all the properties, facilities, and equipment. Once again, when I announced their victory, our congregation applauded and cheered.

Shortly after their church settled in to rebuilding their new congregation, they merged with a church from another denomination that was also starting to part from the truth. When the two churches merged, they were blessed with a special financial gift from the sale of one of the church's properties. From those funds, they gave substantially to another church from another very different denomination that was fighting their own doctrinal battle. They shared they were "paying it forward" because of the generosity of our church. However, their gift was many times over what we gave to them!

Sadly, the other church did not survive the battle and the denomination removed them from their association, leaving them with nothing—and no place to go. I went to our elders with an idea of allowing this local church to use our facilities rent-free. Once again, as we shared with the congregation, they rejoiced. Their church used our facilities for many years. They have now saved enough money to move to their own facility. We truly miss them!

During this series of joint efforts, our church merged with the first church we helped. Since they had merged with a church, we were now a local church with three different denominational backgrounds. In reality, this is the story of four local churches (three that merged), each floating their unique boats in completely different parts within the River of Evangelicalism. All of us have the same goal—to love God with all of our hearts, souls, minds, and strength and to love one another just as Jesus commanded us. In the timeless words of Saint Augustine: "In essentials, unity; in non-essentials, liberty; in all things charity."

We believe by outwardly expressing our inward unity amidst our diversity, many in this community are coming to know we are truly His disciples who have trusted in Christ alone for our salvation.

Every January, our faith community in the Fresno area joins together for *21 Days of Prayer and Fasting*. The people of God from over one hundred churches participate. Many gather for nightly meetings in various churches where we express our worship to the Lord and extend our love for one another. That is also most worthy of our applause. We are also praying it gets the world's attention:

> John 13:35 "By this <u>all men will know</u> that you are My disciples, if you have love for one another" (My emphasis).

To God be the glory!

For Personal Reflection:

Take an honest look at the "sister churches" in your community. Consider a combined worship service, a joint ministry project, or even a "pulpit swap." Your goal is to celebrate your "unity amidst diversity."

© Dr. James M. and Karon M. Cecy.

Jim's Ministry Devotional #23

Out of the Mouth of Babes

> Matthew 21:15-17 "...when the chief priests and the scribes saw the wonderful things that He had done, and the children who were shouting in the temple, 'Hosanna to the Son of David,' they became indignant and said to Him, 'Do You hear what these children are saying?' And Jesus said to them, 'Yes; have you never read, 'Out of the mouth of infants and nursing babies You have prepared praise for Yourself'?'"

It is our practice as a local church to partake of the Lord's Supper every month. I figure I have led Communion countless hundreds of times in my fifty years of ministry. Admittedly, I have been guilty of just going through the motions in what should be one of the holiest moments of church life.

One particular Sunday, I was standing in front doing my duty as the pastor leading Communion. In the second row was a precious group from our disability ministry. As the plate with the bread was being passed by the ushers, one of the sweet ladies, Karen, who had Down's Syndrome, excitedly grabbed a fistful of crackers. Her friend, who was also mentally disabled, slapped her hand and whispered loudly, "No, just take one!" I stifled my laughter as I saw Karen fill her mouth with crackers. Oh, how she was enjoying the feast! I can only imagine how dry her mouth must have been.

It was now time for the tiny juice-filled cups to be passed. This time Karen began to grab the cups, one-by-one, and fill her cracker-filled mouth with grape juice. I could no longer keep a straight face as I started to giggle. But then my eyes began to fill with tears. In child-like faith, Karen was getting more out of

Communion than I was. In the sweet simplicity of the moment, she was feasting with joy; I was not.

From that day on, I decided to no longer be the only one who leads Communion at our church. That task is now shared with the other pastoral staff. I needed to sit and share in Karen's joy and celebration and the reminder of the goodness and mercy of Christ who gave His life for a sinner like me. When I get to heaven, I will thank sweet Karen for teaching this "professional pastor" such an unforgettable lesson regarding the joy of Communion. I have come to a new appreciation of Jesus's words:

> Matthew 18:3 "Truly I say to you, unless you are converted and become like children, you will not enter the kingdom of heaven."

> Matthew 19:14 "But Jesus said, 'Let the children alone, and do not hinder them from coming to Me; for the kingdom of heaven belongs to such as these.'"

For Personal Reflection:

Share some of the lessons children and precious "child-like people" have taught you.

© Dr. James M. and Karon M. Cecy.

Jim's Ministry Devotional #24

Tiger Stories

> 2 Corinthians 11:26-28 "I have been on frequent journeys, in dangers from rivers, dangers from robbers, dangers from my countrymen, dangers from the Gentiles, dangers in the city, dangers in the wilderness, dangers on the sea, dangers among false brethren; I have been in labor and hardship, through many sleepless nights, in hunger and thirst, often without food, in cold and exposure. Apart from such external things, there is the daily pressure on me of concern for all the churches."

I never thought I would be able to relate to the many challenges faced by the Apostle Paul on his missionary journeys. However, I did come close. The following is an adaptation of a newsletter I wrote over thirty years ago. Every time I read it, I am reminded of God's grace and mercy in the beginning years of JARON Ministries International. To this day, I do not think I have had a more dramatic missionary report.

Here it is:

* *

I'm told that missionaries call dramatic events on the mission field "tiger stories." Well, do we have some tiger stories of our own to share with you! Satan was active in his attempts to thwart our recent ministry in the Philippines. Gratefully, we experienced the sheltering arms of Almighty God protecting us all the way. Read on.

Tiger Story #1

The war in the Gulf started just a few hours before our scheduled departure to Manila. To make matters even more frightening for our families, the first threats of international terrorist attacks against U.S. citizens came from the communists and Iraqi sympathizers in the Philippines. The day we arrived in the Philippines, an Iraqi terrorist tried to bomb one of the U.S. government buildings in Manila. He wasn't very good at it and blew himself up by mistake.

> *"Lord, thank You for Your divine protection from the foolishness of evil men."*

Tiger Story #2

Three of my fellow missionaries and I were excited to learn at the airport we were being given a free upgrade to business class. This meant good service and room to stretch and sleep. God knew we'd need the rest! We arrived in Manila around midnight only to find out we were to travel all night by car to Baguio City, where a group of pastors would gather in the morning to attend a conference I was to teach on "Building Personal Purity."

As we got in the car, we were told there had been several threats on Americans in the region where we were going. We were also told there was no need to worry because one of the men driving with us was a member of the Philippine CIA. He was well-armed and ready to protect us for the next week. At first, I resisted the idea of having a bodyguard. We were soon glad he was around!

After driving all night, we arrived in beautiful (and delightfully cool) Baguio City. After a brief meal, we proceeded to Risen Lord Fellowship where I would teach the conference for seven hours. I was amazed at the energy God gave as I taught. I truly sensed the power of God throughout this whole time. It is difficult to put into words. We also sensed God's Spirit moving mightily among those pastors as they recommitted themselves to live and teach all over northern Luzon the principles regarding personal purity. By the time we hit the pillows that evening, it had been over two days since we had slept.

"Jesus, thank You that in our great weakness Your strength truly shines!"

We were humbled by the response of our host pastor. Besides using my recorded messages, they refurbished a room to serve as a library to house several theological books they are praying we will bring them on our next trip. This resource center will be used by numerous pastors and leaders in the region.

We visited with a military instructor at the Philippine Military Academy in Baguio. He is asking us to provide him with seminary level training so that he might be more effective in his service for the Lord at the academy. Here is a man who can impact the entire country by impacting the present and future top-ranking military officers in the Philippines. He and I talked about the possibility of our coming to teach at the Academy.

"Lord, we pray You would open wide this tremendous door of opportunity for the Gospel in the Philippines."

Tiger Story #3

While driving to the U.S. military base, the guard, believing I looked like an Arab terrorist, and having just been warned of a terrorist threat at the very same base, pointed his assault rifle and commanded us to get out of the car. Our Filipino friends were quick to tell them we were American missionaries. The guards examined our passports and let us pass; not without adding, "You looked like

Gaddafi." Throughout our time in the Philippines scores of people stared at me and said, "Hey, Saddam! You, Iraqi!" It was equally curious for them to see my fellow missionary, a tall, blonde American walking with a "little Arab." We escaped the notice of very few. I couldn't convince them I was Italian. One lady commented to us, "You are very brave to be here at this time." No, we weren't!

> *"Heavenly Father, thank You that You know us as we really are."*

Tiger Story #4

Very early the next morning, as we were driving from Baguio to Rizal to attend our main pastors' conference, our vehicle overheated, and we were forced to stop on a major thoroughfare. We were busy with our heads under the hood, attempting to replace a broken water hose. We found out later that while we were hard at work our bodyguard had to pull his gun on two men coming quickly toward us on a motorcycle. They were carrying a suspicious handbag in a manner our bodyguard, in his expert opinion, felt was "a threat to our safety." The two men saw him reach for his gun and wisely left the scene. This all happened without our knowing what was going on.

> *"We praise You, Lord God, for protecting us even when ·we don't know we are in danger."*

Tiger Story #5

The small car problem turned out to be a major breakdown—a blown head gasket. We were towed to a poorly equipped garage where we waited for ten hours for the car to be fixed. Our bodyguard nervously watched the whole time!

While at the gas station, we watched in horror as a husband beat up his wife. I wanted to help but our bodyguard insisted I stay out of it. "Such things," he said, "are common in the Philippines. Even our police do not involve themselves in such matters." My heart ached for that poor woman!

It was now nighttime, and we were finally on the road again, still many hours from the camp. We had missed the first day of the pastors' conference, and since we had no access to a phone, we fervently prayed that God would give two others of our team members the wisdom to go ahead without us. They did!

"Thank You, God, that You are in control of the details of our lives. Your plans are infinitely better than ours."

Tiger Story #6

After staying the night in Manila, we headed out to the conference center. We were rested and relieved, hopeful things were finally going to run smoothly. Satan had a different plan.

A few miles from the camp, a young man darted out from nowhere and we hit him traveling about thirty miles an hour. In a split second that seemed like an eternity, his body smashed against the front of the car, flew to the hood, and slammed against the windshield which then sent him flying about thirty feet in front of us. Before we could stop, we were on top of him again. The young man staggered to his feet, and we put him in the car and rushed him to a nearby hospital.

While he was in the car, we laid hands on him and prayed (and cried). We got him to the hospital and left him in the hands of the doctors and the Lord. We finally arrived at the camp, obviously shaken up. We asked every pastor at the conference to fervently pray for the young man. God miraculously answered. After staying in the hospital overnight for observation and tests, they treated his amazingly few scratches and released him. Two of the men at the conference were able to share more about Christ with the young man's Catholic family. The family was astounded at what they, too, knew was a miracle.

> *"Thank You, Lord, for Your healing in that young man's life. May he come to know You had Your hand of protection on him."*

Tiger Story #7

Our team members were surprised to hear our stories. Unlike us, they had spent the last few days resting and enjoying the marvelous hospitality of two local missionaries. Little did they know they were about to experience a tiger story of their own.

While I was teaching the pastors, three of my fellow missionaries decided they would like to walk into town, just a few hundred yards from the camp. One of them had the foresight to suggest they should ask our bodyguard to walk with them. As they left the camp, the bodyguard prayed that God would protect them and give him wisdom to know how to react to any situation.

They were walking down the street when the bodyguard calmly announced to our three team-members, "Don't move, the man across the street is pulling a gun on you." At that moment our bodyguard drew his gun to fire. The man with the gun saw him and quickly held his gun with two fingers and shouted, "Do you want to buy a gun?" Whether the man was intending to shoot or to sell his gun, we'll never know. None of our team volunteered to ask!

> *"Thank You, Heavenly Father, for Your specific wisdom in difficult and dangerous situations."*

Tiger Story #8

The conference was going reasonably well as we taught all day on several subjects. However, we sensed very early in the conference a great deal of discouragement in many of the pastors. Concern over the Gulf War had truly impacted them, their churches, and their extended families, many of whom live in the Middle East. Others could not explain why they were depressed. We quickly recognized this to be another of Satan's attacks.

We committed ourselves to specifically pray for God's deliverance and healing from this cloud of unusual despair. The very next morning we saw a tremendous breakthrough. Miracles began to happen in the lives of these men as they joyfully and enthusiastically soaked up all we could teach them.

> *"Lord, continue to give these men wisdom, power, and insight as they teach Your Word to the people of the Philippines."*

Tiger Story #9

Before leaving for Asia, Karon and I had prayed for God's protection for us while we were apart. Her primary concern was for my safety in the Philippines. Little did we know that here at home Karon would face one of the most dramatic events of her life.

Karon and my children, along with another team member's wife, were stopped at a stoplight in our sleepy little town of Scotts Valley. Suddenly, a gunman jumped in front of our van, pointed a pistol at them and shouted. At the precise moment the armed man stepped aside to point his gun at another car, Karon quickly drove past him. She headed for a nearby gas station where she called the police. At that moment, Lupe ran into the gas station to tell Karon that the gunman was still coming at them. They raced back to the van and sped away. A few seconds later, the gunman stole another woman's car and drove away. They considered the incident as over.

Karon was later to find out the armed man had run out of gas, jumped out of his stolen car, and threatened to kill the police, who by this time had surrounded him. He began firing and, in the process, shot a police dog! The police had no choice but to open fire on the man. That night, in the news, Karon learned the man was a mental patient who had stolen the gun and was on a killing frenzy, shouting to everyone in his path, "You're all going to die!"

"Dear God, thank You for Your promise that the Angel of the Lord encamps around those who fear Him. Thank You for not allowing this man to take my family and our friend from me."

Tiger Story #10

Apart from a sprained ankle the day before we left for home, and a dozen thorough security checks at the airport, the rest of the trip was uneventful. Or was it?

We flew home safely, but once again we saw Satan try to throw us into a tailspin. Karon fell down our stairs, breaking her foot in two places. Along with our recent move to Fresno, conferences to teach, doctoral studies, and a pile of work left undone from before the trip, I now had to cook, clean, and take care of the children. Thank God for family and friends who helped tremendously with many of these chores.

Additionally, the other team members faced similar difficulties. One experienced a family crisis. Two experienced unusual bouts of depression and admitted to struggling emotionally and spiritually. What did we expect?

"Heavenly Father, we are grateful for the privilege of ministering to needy people around the world. Keep us in the center of Your will as we serve You in even the most difficult of circumstances. In Jesus's name. Amen."

The Good News

Though there are times of fear, frustration, and discouragement in all of our lives and ministries, Satan need not get the victory. As I reflect on the events of this trip, my mind fills with Scripture references that have become more meaningful than ever before. I hope these will be an encouragement as you face the "tigers" waiting to pounce on you.

• From the Story of King Jehoshaphat:

> *2 Chronicles 20:6, 15, 17 "...O LORD, the God of our fathers, are You not God in the heavens? And are You not ruler over all the kingdoms of the nations. Power and might are in Your hand so that no one can stand against You....thus says the LORD to you: 'Do not fear or be dismayed because of this great multitude, for the battle is not yours, but God's....You need not fight in this battle; station yourselves, stand and see the salvation the LORD on your behalf....Do not fear or be dismayed; tomorrow go out to face them, for the LORD is with you."*

• From the Words of the Apostle Paul:

> *Ephesians 6:10-13,18-20 "Finally, be strong in the Lord and in his mighty power. Put on the full armor of God so that you can take your stand against the devil's schemes. For our struggle is not against flesh and blood, but against the*

rulers, against the authorities, against the powers of this dark world and against the spiritual forces of evil in the heavenly realms. Therefore put on the full armor of God, so that when the day of evil comes, you may be able to stand your ground, and after you have done everything, to stand...And pray in the Spirit on all occasions with all kinds of prayers and requests. With this in mind, be alert and always keep on praying for all the saints. Pray also for me, that whenever I open my mouth, words may be given me so that I will fearlessly make known the mystery of the gospel, for which I am an ambassador in chains. Pray that I may declare it fearlessly, as I should" (New International Version).

I now sing with greater passion the words of the popular chorus written in 1988 by Rich Mullins:

Our God is an awesome God!
He reigns from heaven above.
With wisdom, power, and love.
Our God is an awesome God!

* *

For Personal Reflection:

1. Read some or all of these "tiger stories" to your family and discuss the dangers many face in serving the Lord.

2. Pray for your missionaries. They may not be in as much danger as others but know they are under attack.

© Dr. James M. and Karon M. Cecy.

Jim's Ministry Devotional #25

I'm Glad I'm Not Popular

> Proverbs 14:20 "The poor is hated even by his neighbor, but those who love the rich are many."

> Proverbs 18:24 "A man of too many friends comes to ruin, but there is a friend who sticks closer than a brother."

> Proverbs 28:11 "The rich man is wise in his own eyes, but the poor who has understanding sees through him."

Like many of my youthful peers, I had my share of visions of grandeur. I grew up wanting to become a famous this or a world-renowned that. Later in life, I met some people "at the top of the heap"—the rich and famous and the so-called "cream of the crop." Sadly, I observed too many suffering the pain of popularity. No surprise. The Book of Proverbs warns that it leads to "ruin" (cf. Proverbs 18:24). The Hebrew word *ra'a* means to suffer great displeasure, injury, and to be "broken in pieces." So it seems to be for the rich, famous, or at least, extremely popular.

Here's what I have noticed over seventy years of life. Admittedly, everything on the list is not every popular person's experience, but too many are. Given the following observations, I ask myself why anyone would crave to be widely known. See if you agree:

• Popularity is not a cure for loneliness.

• Popularity makes you question why people befriend you.

• Popularity isolates you from others.

• Popularity requires compromise.

• Popularity requires rarely making a mistake.

• Popularity subjects you to jealous people.

• Popularity gives you undeserved privileges and creates an attitude of entitlement.

• Popularity prevents you from much-needed privacy.

• Popularity is distracting.

• Popularity can be addictive.

• Popularity can make you surround yourself only with those who agree with you.

• Popularity can make you feel used.

• Popularity in one area can make you think your opinions matter in other areas.

• Popularity can create the need to crave any kind of publicity—good or bad.

• Popularity encourages a distorted view of yourself.

• Popularity is rarely admitted.

• Popularity can cause you to strive for fame more than faithfulness.

• Popularity encourages false humility and can infect you with pride.

• Popularity is sometimes based on being measured by externals.

• Popularity generates hyper-scrutiny and causes others to accuse your motives.

• Popularity is sometimes inherited and often undeserved.

• Popularity feeds the ego, not always the mind.

• Popularity is fickle and never enough. It has wings!

So, here's where I am as an older, not-so-famous person—or as I like to say, "I'm a Nobody from Nowhere serving a Great Somebody from Everywhere."

• I would rather be faithful than famous.

• I love being able to say something "half-baked" and not worry about being quoted internationally.

• I am grateful I am not being recognized when I wear grubby, paint-covered clothes to the hardware store.

• I like not having to take myself so seriously that I am panicked over the littlest of mistakes because of my image.

• I am blessed to say I have friends who are not impressed with me but "stick closer than a brother" in spite of me (cf. Proverbs18:24).

Not too long ago I watched a video of a famous singer telling a giant crowd of adoring fans, "I love you all, my friends." I laughed, thinking, "Imagine all these so-called friends asking for her phone number so they can call her when they need a ride home!"

For Personal Reflection:

1. Discuss what makes people well-known. Consider what you most want to be well known for.

2. Discuss what character qualities are worth imitating and which are not.

3. Consider the words of 1 Samuel 16:7 "...for God sees not as man sees, for man looks at the outward appearance, but the Lord looks at the heart."

Jim's Ministry Devotional #26

The Book of Books

> 2 Timothy 2:15 "Be diligent to present yourself approved to God as a workman who does not need to be ashamed, handling accurately the word of truth."

When I was in the Chicago area, I was teaching a community-wide leadership conference. Before one of the sessions, a distraught woman approached me and asked, "Dr. Cecy, can you recommend a book for me? My life is falling apart." I handed her my Bible. She handed it back to me and said, "No, no, I mean a current book that can really address my problems." I handed her my Bible. At this point she was insistent, "Can't you recommend a book that will really help me—maybe one you've written?" Do you know how hard it was to not take that dear woman's credit card and fund my ministry with the sale of a pile of my materials?

However, she did not need my books. She needed the Only Book—the Book of Books—the Word of God—the Holy Scriptures—the Sword of the Spirit—the Hammer of Justice—the Word of Truth—the Lamp unto our Feet—the Light unto our Path—and the Word of Life. She needed the Bible—every one of those sixty-six life-changing books, 1,189 character-building chapters, 31,173 Spirit-led verses, and some 800,000 God-breathed words (depending on which version). She needed that marvelous love letter from God to man, written in three languages (Hebrew, Aramaic, and Greek), by forty different authors (shepherds, judges, priests, kings, prophets, tax-collectors, physicians, etc.), from three different continents (Asia, Africa, Europe) ,over a period of 1600 years. And

God wanted her—as He wants every one of us—to become masters of all it contains!

• From the lips of the wise King Solomon we are told:

> Ecclesiastes 12:11 "The words of wise men are like goads, and masters of these collections (i.e., the Word of God) are like well-driven nails; they are given by one Shepherd" (My addition). "

• And from the pen of the great Apostle Paul we are challenged:

> 2 Timothy 2:15 "Work hard so you can present yourself to God and receive his approval. Be a good worker, one who does not need to be ashamed and who correctly explains the word of truth" (New Living Translation).

There really are just two kinds of books—the Bible and everything else!

For Personal Reflection:

1. Be honest. Do you spend more time reading books about the Bible than the Bible itself?

2. Establish a Bible reading Plan and stick to it.

(Adapted from *"Mastering the Scriptures: A Self-Study Course in Effective Bible Study"* by Dr. James M. Cecy. Available at www.amazon.com and www.jaron.org.)

© Dr. James M. and Karon M. Cecy.

Changing My Methods

> 2 Timothy 2:2 "The things which you have heard from me in the presence of many witnesses, entrust these to faithful men who will be able to teach others also."

I love the story of the stranger walking by a blind man, holding a sign. Noticing the blind man had only a few coins in his cup, he dropped in more coins and, without asking for permission, took the sign and re-wrote it. He quietly returned the sign to the blind man and left.

That afternoon, the kind stranger returned to the blind man and noticed that his cup was full of bills and coins. The blind man recognized his footsteps and asked if it was he who had re-written his sign and wanted to know what he had written on it. The man responded: "Nothing that was not true. I just wrote the message a little differently." He smiled and went on his way. The new sign read: "Today is spring and I cannot see it."

In other words, a new and more personal approach was necessary and quite effective. I am drawn once again to the timeless message of the Apostle Paul:

> 2 Timothy 2:2 "The things which you have heard from me in the presence of many witnesses, entrust these to faithful men who will be able to teach others also."

Notice the four generations:

> Generation #1: The Apostle Paul teaching Timothy and many other "witnesses."

Generation #2: Timothy "entrusting" to "faithful" people what he learned from Paul.

Generation #3: Those faithful people Timothy taught who, in the future, would "be able to teach others also."

Generation #4: The "others" who would then teach the next generations—including us.

Although I am absolutely committed to never changing the ageless message of the gospel, I am constantly aware that I must adapt my older methods and strategies to better communicate that message to a new generation that will be able to teach the following generations. I am holding tightly to the words of the Psalmist:

Psalm 78:6-7 "…that the generation to come might know, even the children yet to be born, that they may arise and tell them to their children, that they should put their confidence in God and not forget the works of God…" (My emphasis).

In this season of my life and ministry, I am especially impressed with the reality that I must be even more effective in mentoring those who will come after me. To revise the words of the kind man to the blind man: "Today is coming and I can see it. It's time to write the message a little differently."

For Personal Reflection:

What are some of the new methods you might consider using to present the timeless message of the Gospel?

Jim's Ministry Devotional #28

Kangaroo Courts

> Mark 13:9, 11 "...be on your guard; for they will deliver you
> to the courts...you will stand before governors and kings
> for My sake, as a testimony to them....When they arrest you
> and hand you over, do not worry beforehand about what you
> are to say, but say whatever is given you in that hour; for it
> is not you who speak, but it is the Holy Spirit."

The Island of Corregidor in Manila Bay is famous for its stories from
World War II. This is the place from which General Douglas
MacArthur said, "I shall return." I have visited the island a few times
and each time I am intrigued by the history.

On one occasion, a young boy offered to sell us some "war
memorabilia." My fellow missionary and I jumped at the chance and
were able to buy some rusted artillery fragments, some old rifle
casings, and a .45 caliber pistol, rusted all the way through.

When I got to Manila Airport to begin my long journey
home, the airline desk agent informed me that those fragments were
fine to take as long as they went in my check-in luggage.

We flew to Hong Kong, the first leg of our journey. While at
the gate, waiting for our flight to San Francisco, my name was
called. I went to the podium and the gate agent politely invited me
to follow her. Then it happened.

I was surrounded by airport security and taken down to a
little room on the tarmac where the plane was being loaded. As I
entered the room, I saw my luggage on a table surrounded by armed
soldiers with assault rifles. They commanded me, "Open your
suitcase." My hands shook as I fumbled for the keys and explained,
"Yes, I have some rusted-out war memorabilia in there." I assumed

their X-rays had spotted the shapes of what they thought were dangerous items.

Upon examination, they saw that all of the items were non-functioning. However, they were not going to let me go. In fact, later I would find out they told my travel partner I was going to jail in Hong Kong!

I looked at the small crowd and said respectfully, "I followed exactly what the gate agents in Manila told me to do. They said everything was fine. I did nothing wrong." One of the police officials responded in English, "This is Hong Kong; we have different rules." I knew I was in trouble. I prayed, asking God for the right words. I looked at the airline representatives and said sternly but respectfully: "You can keep the memorabilia. I have an appointment in San Francisco I cannot miss. If I do, I will report your names to your company and I will insist all of you lose your jobs immediately. Now, let me on that plane now!"

An argument in Chinese began among the police officials and the airline representatives. It felt like an eternity. I was so very frightened. Suddenly, the airline representative said, "You can go!" They ushered me back to the gate and, to my fellow missionary's surprise, I sat next to him on the plane.

It was a sleepless flight to San Francisco. I kept wondering what could have happened. I arrived and immediately decided to "report" to security—the U.S. Customs and Border Protection. I assumed news of my mistake had gone ahead of me and I was in deep trouble here in the U.S. Before I could finish my story, one of the officers burst into laughter: "I bet you were in Hong Kong, right? No worries. It happens all the time. You did nothing wrong."

So, what happened to the war memorabilia? The Border Patrol officer walked me to the luggage carousal and soon a small box with the airline name popped out. He said, "There you go! Welcome home!"

Lesson learned. If I am going to bring things from another country, I make sure I check the rules every place I stop. I like Chinese food, but the thought of eating prison chow mein in Hong Kong leaves something to be desired.

In Acts 25, we go back in time to the trial of "Paul vs. Everybody"—this time before Governor Festus, who replaced Governor Felix. Festus goes to Jerusalem and gets an earful from the jealous Jewish leaders, who want the Apostle Paul dead—and they want him dead now!

The Apostle Paul again declares his innocence and willingness to be executed, if found guilty in anything but their illegal "kangaroo court." He appeals to the Roman Emperor, the highest human authority in Paul's life, yet knowing well the King of the Universe was in charge.

Even though Governor Festus believes Paul to be innocent, he is obligated to declare, "You have appealed to Caesar, to Caesar you shall go" (Acts 25:12). Before that happens, King Herod Agrippa II shows up. With great ceremony, Paul is paraded before the crowds. Later, in chapter 26, he will present the gospel to the "small and great" (Acts 26:22).

As Jesus was presenting the signs of the end times He warned:

> Mark 13:9, 11 "...be on your guard; for they will deliver you to the courts...you will stand before governors and kings for My sake, as a testimony to them....When they arrest you and hand you over, do not worry beforehand about what you are to say, but say whatever is given you in that hour; for it is not you who speak, but it is the Holy Spirit."

It seems to me that if what happened to the Apostle Paul in the first century was a birth pang of the end times, we should be even more prepared for these illegal charges and phony courts two thousand years later especially as we share the Gospel. Are we?

For Personal Reflection:

1. How well do you feel prepared to handle being falsely accused?

2. What does the Apostle Paul mean when he speaks of "persevering in tribulation" (Romans 12:12)?

© Dr. James M. and Karon M. Cecy.

Jim's Ministry Devotional #29

Words I Now Live By

Proverbs 11:14 "Where there is no guidance the people fail, but in abundance of counselors there is victory."

Proverbs 15:22 "Without consultation, plans are frustrated, but with many counselors they succeed."

In Jim's Devotional #35 in Volume One of *"Telling Our Faith Story,"* I listed out some of my *"Words to Live By."* In this volume, I want to share what I consider some of the most memorable things I have heard from fellow ministers and now pass on to you:

• From an older pastor when I first started ministry:

"Let people go! The same Holy Spirit who called them to come may also be calling them to leave."

The Lesson: Be prepared for the ups and downs of people coming in and out of your churches and your lives. Love them when they come and when they go.

• From that same older pastor:

"If you get too far ahead of your people, you will look like the enemy."

The Lesson: Make sure you share your vision and goals in manageable objectives. Not too much too soon.

• From a pastor who wanted me to attend a seminary in a city I hated:

> *"What do you want, a vacation or an education?"*

>> The Lesson: Get the best education and ministry training whenever and wherever it can be found, regardless of the inconvenience.

• From the old quote book collecting dust on my shelf:

> *"Perhaps God gave us two ears and one mouth so we will listen twice as much as we talk."*

>> The Lesson: Be quick to listen (cf. James 1:19).

• From the senior pastor as he left me in charge when he moved to another church:

> *"Make your decisions slowly, but make them."*

>> The Lesson: Don't let fear of failure or disapproval keep you from being decisive.

• From a sign in my office at church:

> *"A ship in harbor is safe, but that is not what ships are built for."*
>> The Lesson: Fulfilling the purpose of God involves risk (cf. Acts 13:36).

• From a young pastor rightly correcting me when I jumped to a conclusion too quickly:

"Don't favor the opinion of the last person you talked to."

> The Lesson: Take notes and weigh all opinions equally.

• From my fellow teaching pastor:

"There is never an excuse for being boring."

> The Lesson: Preach and teach with biblical accuracy but also with enthusiasm, passion, and conviction.

• From a pastor in town:

"Build the church on the backs of strong men."

> The Lesson: Follow the standards laid out in Titus 2:2-6—especially with older, maturing men teaching younger men…to be sensible.

• From another old quote book:

"A word once spoken is forever history."

> The Lesson: "Make sure what you say is good for edification, according to the need of the moment, and is a grace-gift (cf. Ephesians 4:29).

• From an old quote I have never forgotten:

"Only God can use a pencil without an eraser."

The Lesson: Mistakes are inevitable. Own up to them immediately and learn from them.

• From a dear old friend who wrote a book with the same title

"Lead, follow, or get out of the way."

The Lesson: Know your role and fulfill your calling.

• From the many kids lined up at church for a kiss on the top of the head:

I hope they are thinking, *"Pastor Jim, thanks for loving me."*

The Lesson: I want every child to remember a pastor who loved them and saw them as important.

• From my theology professor in seminary:

"Remember, there is a little heresy in us all."

The Lesson: Teach with grace and humility.

• From a sign on the wall at the office of my first dentist:

"Be true to your teeth or they will be false to you."

The Lesson: Take care of things today before they become a problem tomorrow. True even outside the dentist office.

These are just some of the many words of wisdom I have received from a host of mentors in my life. The next devotional, *Mentoring Moments,* presents many bits of counsel I have given.

For Personal Reflection:

List a few of the wise counsel you have received that are worthy of passing on to others:

© Dr. James M. and Karon M. Cecy.

Jim's Ministry Devotional #30

Mentoring Moments

Proverbs 13:10 "...wisdom is with those who receive counsel."

In my previous devotional entitled, *Words I Now Live By,* I presented some of the wise counsel I have received from others, and found worthy of passing on to you. Now it's my turn.

Ask my pastoral staff at Campus Bible Church or anyone on my ministry team at JARON Ministries International. Since we share the same facilities, both groups are bound to agree: "Jim is full of 'sayings.'" My response is simply taken from the writings of King Solomon:

Proverbs 4:20 "… give attention to my words. Incline your ear to my sayings."

The following are some common words of counsel I have given to many over the years. Some would call them *clichés*; I like to call them "mentoring moments." Some are revisions of things I have learned and now have made them mine and humbly think you would be wise to make them yours. See if you agree:

• *"After a thorough study of God's Word be willing to graciously change the opinions you previously held."*

• *"A pat on the back and a kick in the behind are not far from each other anatomically, but there is a world of difference when we consider the impact."*

• *"As a leader you are always responsible; not always to blame."*

• *"As a leader your door is always open."*

• *"Ask yourself often, 'Do people see Jesus in me?'"*

• *"Be F.A.T.—Faithful. Available. Teachable."*

• *"Be a faith-builder, knowledge-promoter, change-maker, team-player, and generation-equipper"* (cf. Titus, Chapter 1 and 2).

• *"Be a player-coach."*

• *"Be the first to arrive and the last to leave."*

• *"Be honest with your fellow leaders when you are not doing well."*

• *"Be quiet...really quiet...the night before you preach or teach."*

• *"Be thorough the first time."*

• *"Be willing to share all your best ideas and teaching materials. After all, God shared His."*

• *"Beware of jealousy and selfish ambition. Both will destroy your ministry."*

• *"Delegate; don't abrogate your responsibilities."*

- *"Develop your own paradigms—the rules and standards by which you live and do ministry."*

- *"Do not assume everyone knows you. Introduce yourself to as many as possible."*

- *"Do not demand people trust you. Earn their trust."*

- *"Do not golf or fish if you are not willing to learn humility and patience."*

- *"Do not invite someone to a restaurant and not expect to pay."*

- *"Do not let others' failure to plan constitute your emergency."*

- *"Do not let your God-given creativity turn into man-pleasing novelty."*

- *"Do not pilfer time or materials. If it's not yours, it's not yours!"*

- *"Do not 'sad sack' by hinting and expecting favors because you are a minister."*

- *"Do not quit or give up, even in the secret places in your heart."*

- *"Do not take yourself so seriously."*

- *"Do not waste sleepless nights. Pray. Reflect. Read."*

• *"During certain seasons, it takes twice as long to do half the work."*

• *"Equip your people to grow healthy in fellowship, doctrine, worship, service, evangelism, discipleship, and prayer."*

• *"Everybody's hurt is always the worst."*

• *"Expect to get hurt."*

• *"Expect your people to 'Come! Grow! Go!'"*

• *"Failure need not be fatal; not learning from it is."*

• *"Forgiveness is to be immediate; reconciliation takes time."*

• *"Get your sermons and lessons done well in advance in order to be prepared for emergencies."*

• *"God doesn't need us; He uses us."*

• *"Greet as many people as possible."*

• *"Greet the day with praise."*

• *"Grow old gracefully."*

• *"If I whisper in your ear, will you leave this position well so we can bless you well?"*

• *"If it's good enough to preach once, it is good enough to preach again—even better.*

• *"If you stick your head above the crowd, expect someone may throw a brick at it."*

• *"If you tell someone about a conflict, make sure you also tell them about the resolution."*

• *"Independence does not rule out the important need for interdependence."*

• *"Inspect what you expect."*

• *"It is much easier to put people in leadership than it is to take them out."*

• *"Keep a record and call people on the anniversary of the death of their loved ones."*

• *"'Land the plane on time.' Finish your message when you say you are about to finish."*

• *"Laugh more, especially at yourself."*

• *"Lead your flock in giving generously, sacrificially, and cheerfully of your time, talent, and treasure."*

• *"Learn to be a 'one-minute manager' rather than a 'killer lecturer.'"*

• *"Learn well how to memorize names. It's the first way to make a lasting connection."*

• *"Look in people's eyes when you greet them. Give them your full attention, even if for just a few seconds."*

• *"Manuscript all your messages and file your research. As your memory fades, you will thank yourself in the future."*

• *"None of us have ever preached a perfect sermon or taught a perfect lesson."*

• *"Own your mistakes."*

• *"Pay special attention to the kids, the elderly, and the disabled."*

• *"Practice the timeless words of Augustine of Hippo: 'In essentials, unity; in non-essentials, liberty; in all things, charity.'"*

• *"Pray. Discuss. Decide. Don't get those out of order."*

• *"Protect from criticism those who serve under you."*

• *"Purity, integrity, and unity are the hallmarks of an effective ministry."*

• *"Put Christ first; everything else is second."*

• *"Ready! Aim! Fire! Don't get those out of order."*

• *"Reward your family if you use them in a sermon."*

• *"Say, 'Will you forgive me?' more than 'I'm sorry.'"*

• *"Sermon preparation involves opening your veins and bleeding all over the paper."*

• *"Spend time with the Lord apart from studying for lessons."*

• *"Strive to finish well."*

• *"Strive to fulfill the purpose of God in your generation"* *(cf. Acts 13:36).*

• *"Strive to listen with God's heart and speak with His words."*

• *"Take to heart the old expression: 'People don't care how much you know until they know how much you care.'"*

• *"Take a sabbath every morning, as well as every week."*

• *"Take more of your share of the blame than the credit."*

• *"Take the risk to have friends in the church but remember you are their pastor first."*

• *"Teach people; not sermons. We are in the people business; not the ministry business."*

• *"Tell your congregation you love them often."*

• *"The more menial the task, the more love is demonstrated."* (e.g., Thank the nursery workers and the janitors.)

• *"To survive these days you need hupomone (endurance); not a heap of money."*

• *"Understand the difference between contentment and fulfillment. Your lack of contentment is on you. Your lack of fulfillment may be God moving you."*

• *"Unum diem ad tempus–One day at a time."*

• *"Use the words 'we' and 'us' more than 'you' and 'them.'"* *Be on the same ship with the people (i.e., fellowship).*

• *"Use your own material and cite sources of borrowed notes. Plagiarism is the new immorality in the ministry."*

• *"Waiting is a form of worship."*

• *"When you are deciding to hire and fire, look for character, chemistry, competence, confidence, and cost."*

• *"You are not so important to keep you from picking up the garbage."*

• *"You can't teach the people you don't love. You don't love the people you won't teach."*

• *"You do not always have to give your reasons for saying, 'No.'"*

• *"You exist to serve others."*

• *"Your attitude and actions toward negative people are your choice; not theirs."*

• *"Your goal is to make the people who work for you great. You exist to serve them."*

And the last one…

- *"You must be on guard for the daily joy-stealers."*

> Joy-Stealer #1: "I don't have enough time to do all I need to do today."
>
> Joy-Stealer #2: "I am holding on to frustrations and hurts from yesterday or the days before."
>
> Joy-Stealer #3: "This is going to be a horrible day."

For Personal Reflection:

1. Mark the key "Mentoring Moments" you choose to adopt as your own.

2. Add your own to the list.

© Dr. James M. and Karon M. Cecy.

Jim's Ministry Devotional #31

More of "Papa Jim's" *Clichés*

> Proverbs 1:8-9 "Hear, my son, your father's instruction…. Indeed, they are a graceful wreath to your head and ornaments about your neck."

> Proverbs 4:1 "Hear, O sons, the instruction of a father, and give attention that you may gain understanding…"

In the two previous devotionals, I listed some of the wise counsel I received and then added my own words of advice, should you want to adopt any of them as your own. Now let's have some fun with some more words of advice that, as far as the people who know me are concerned, fall in the category of what some of my staff call *"Papa Jim's Clichés."*

The word *cliché* is a French term that means to produce in stereotype. A stereotype was a printing plate used to create multiple versions of the same design. Printshop workers would hear the printer make a *clicking* sound which resulted in the word *cliché.* It has come to refer to a stale, commonplace phrase that, because of overuse, may have lost its original meaning or impact. These platitudes are said to lack originality, novelty, and freshness. If we are not careful, this can especially happen when we pray. So said Jesus:

> Matthew 6:7 "…when you are praying, do not use meaningless repetition as the Gentiles do, for they suppose that they will be heard for their many words."

The longer we walk this earth, the more we will be prone to repeat ourselves. Over the decades I certainly have my own list of well-used, perhaps hackneyed, phrases. However, I still believe some of them are worth repeating. You decide if that's true.

By the way, some of these are quotes or revisions of quotes, whose authors are long forgotten. Now their words or thoughts have become a part of me and those who listen to me. I trust this is recognition enough:

- *"Dear God. Your will. Nothing more. Nothing less. Nothing else."* (Quoting renowned baseball player, Bobby Richardson.)

- *"Don't shoot first and draw the circle later."*

- *"Give me your wallet so I can give like I always wanted to give."*

- *"Good morning, Beloved. You are the agapetos tou theou...the Beloved of God."*

- *"If a Band-Aid works, don't do surgery."*

- *"Five more minutes!"* (Said whenever and wherever our kids asked, *"Are we there yet?"*)

- *"I am just a nobody from nowhere serving a Great Somebody from Everywhere."*

- *"I am mostly dead."*—to adapt a phrase from the movie, *The Princess Bride*.

- *"I am not a spiritual dump station for your ideas. You get to help make things happen, too."*

• *"I am not responsible for my ancestors, but I can influence my descendants."* (Said to those who ask about my relationship to my distant relative, Al Capone.)

• *"I am so full of medicine; every time I sneeze I cure a dozen people."*

• *"I am too short to play Holy Spirit."*

• *"I feel so bad I think I will have to get well to die."*

• *"If Christianity were a crime, would there be enough evidence to convict you?"*

• *"If you are happy, inform your face."*

• *"It doesn't take a majority of salt to season a stew nor a majority of light to dispel darkness."*

• *"It's your egg; you hatch it."*

• *"Just because people don't believe in hell doesn't make it one degree cooler."*

"My Cousin Guido, the Enforcer, can take care of that for you."

• *"No one takes your joy; you give it away!"*

• *"See you here, there, or in the air!"* (Earth. Heaven. Or on our way.)

- *"Stop smiling; put on your church face instead."*

- *"The greatest thing you can do for your children is to love their mother."* (Said to fathers.)

- *"The longest journey in the world is eighteen inches, from your head to your heart."*

- *"There are two kinds of people: Italians and those who wish they were."*

- *"To know Him is to love Him. To love Him is to obey Him. To obey Him is to serve Him."*

- *"Too many gave up a long time ago; they just haven't told anybody."*

- *"Yes, I will pray for you, but you pray for you, too."*

- *"You can't make me not love you."* (Said to my foster children.)

- *"You can't outgive God."*

- *"You have the power of being little."*

- *"You're my favorite!"* (Said to <u>every</u> grandchild.)

- *"Why wait; let me pray for you right now."*

- *"Worship is more like 'wow-ship'–the adoring response of us as creatures to the infinite majesty of the One who is Our Creator."*

There are more of "Papa Jim's" *clichés* to come. Just ask the people who know me. My rationale for every *cliché* comes from the words of Lucius Annaeus Seneca the Younger, the ancient Roman philosopher: "That is never too often repeated, which is never sufficiently learned"

However, may I suggest that some things never get too old or overused, like:

- Praising God at a sunset, with the well-used words, "Wow, isn't that incredible?"

- Reciting Psalm 23 "The Lord is my shepherd…" and John 3:16 "For God so loved the world…"

- Saying, "I love you" and "I am proud of you" to loved ones.

- Singing *"How Great Thou Art"* and *"Holy! Holy! Holy!"*

These have never lost their meaning or impact, no matter how *cliché* they have become. They do not, in my opinion, need a major revision or a sprinkling of novelty. And all of God's people said, "Amen"—again and again and again.

For Personal Reflection:

What are the things you often say to your family and friends? Ask them.

© Dr. James M. and Karon M. Cecy.

PART TWO

KARON'S
MINISTRY AND MISSION
LESSONS

Karon's Ministry Devotional #1

His Story is Better than Ours

The following is a similar story to what I wrote in *Volume One*, only this time it has as its focus on our ministry lives. Besides, it is one of my favorite love stories—ours! It begins with one of our favorite passages of Scripture:

> Psalm 37:3-5 "Trust in the LORD and do good. Dwell in the land and cultivate faithfulness. Delight yourself in the LORD and He will give you the desires of your heart. Commit your way to the LORD. Trust also in Him and He will do it."

In 1971, I devoured these verses! They directed me in my relationship with the Lord, reminding me I could depend on God. I certainly was done trying to depend on humans. My human relationships up to this point had been complex and disappointing, to say the least. As a twenty-one-year-old, I was done with dating. I decided to dedicate my life to singlehood. Ministry satisfied my needs for companionship and I was convinced I wanted to be single for life. I held tightly to the words of the Apostle Paul:

> 1 Corinthians 7:32-35 "But I want you to be free from concern. One who is unmarried is concerned about the things of the Lord, how he may please the Lord; but one who is married is concerned about the things of the world, how he may please his wife, and his interests are divided. The woman who is unmarried, and the virgin, is concerned about the things of the Lord, that she may be holy both in body and spirit; but one who is married is concerned about the things of the world, how she may please her husband. This I say for your own benefit; not to put a restraint upon you, but to

promote what is appropriate and to secure undistracted devotion to the Lord."

Undistracted devotion to the Lord. That's what I wanted most!

A year later, working as a receptionist at Twin Lakes Baptist Church in Santa Cruz, California, I looked up to see our Campus Pastor walking into the church lobby with a young man who wore a leather jacket and boots. (I remember the knife on his hip; he doesn't.) To complete the tough-looking outfit, his hair was cut in a big bushy "afro." I remember thinking his eyes did not match his tough persona—they had the light of a new believer! Sure enough, I found out he had accepted Christ recently and his name was Jim Cecy.

Fast forward a year. Although Jim and I were in the same college group at church, we didn't know each other well. That was about to change. Our Campus Pastor asked both of us to lead a college Bible study, starting in September. It would be held at the house I rented with two other women. The living room looked out over one of the Twin Lakes and was within walking distance of the ocean. It was such a beautiful location.

Jim and I began to meet once a week to prepare for the study. Afterward, we would often walk along the lake or the nearby ocean to debrief. We enjoyed talking about ministry and prayed together for the needs of our fellow college-aged attendees. Pretty soon we met two or three times a week.

Our times together were full of deep conversation, fun, and laughter. Jim loved pulling me out of my shell of shyness. His passion for the Lord was stimulating and contagious. And, yes, he was rather cute. (Jim added this line to my story!)

On November 30th, the woman who was discipling me asked if I had fallen in love with Jim. To my shock, I quietly admitted I had indeed fallen in love with him—a man with whom I had never dated, at least in a romantic way. However, he was my best friend. I surprised myself when I said, "If, in the long-distant future, Jim asked me to marry him, I would have to say 'Yes!'" The next day, on December 1ˢᵗ, Jim asked me to marry him!

No, he had not received a message from this woman telling him what I had admitted the day before. He had spent a couple of days in the mountains praying about his feelings about me. Without any prompting, except from the Lord, he was compelled to ask me to spend the rest of our lives together. He admits he was petrified. After all, early in our relationship, he had also expressed a willingness to be single. Now he had surprisingly fallen in love with me, his best friend and ministry partner. Apparently, God had a different and much better plan for both of us:

> Proverbs 16:1 "The plans of the heart belong to man, but the answer of the tongue is from the LORD."

We were married on February 17, 1973, just five months after we began teaching together. Our dedication to singleness was overruled by God's matchmaking. He had planted in our hearts the seeds of a growing love that has bloomed for over fifty years as intimate friends and lifelong companions.

Throughout our five decades of marriage and a century of combined ministry, Psalm 37 has guided our lives. It has called us to:

• Trust in the Lord, not our own plans.

• Do the right thing, no matter what.

• Dwell in the place God puts us, no matter where.

• Cultivate faithfulness in every situation.

• Delight in the Lord, no matter how hard.

• Expect He will match the desires of our hearts with His.

• Commit our daily activities and our lifelong plans to Him.

• Trust Him to do the rest.

The rest is history—His story—so much better than ours!

For Personal Reflection:

1. Make a list of the most important decisions facing you.

2. Read Proverbs 16:1-3 "The plans of the heart belong to man, but the answer of the tongue is from the Lord. All the ways of a man are clean in his own sight, but the Lord weighs the motives. Commit your works to the Lord and your plans will be established."

3. Reflect on the following statements from Psalm 37:3-5:

• Trust in the Lord, not my own plans.

• Do the right thing, no matter what.

• Dwell in the place God puts us, no matter where.

• Cultivate faithfulness in every situation.

• Delight in the Lord, no matter how hard.

• Expect He will match the desires of my heart with His.

• Commit my daily activities and my lifelong plans to Him.

• Trust Him to do the rest.

© Dr. James M. and Karon M. Cecy.

Karon's Ministry Devotional #2

God Leads Us

> Psalm 25:4-5 "Make me know Your ways, O LORD. Teach me Your paths. Lead me in Your truth and teach me. For You are the God of my salvation. For You I wait all the day."

> Acts 5:29 "We must obey God rather than men."

Our seminary days were a real financial strain. While Jim studied full-time in seminary, I worked full-time as an executive assistant. Because of Jim's prior military service, we also received financial assistance from the G.I. Bill. Besides living expenses, the tuition for seminary put our budget to the test. Jim worked between semesters and during the summer to supplement our income.

Close to the end of Jim's second year, he asked to chat about our summer plans. Much to my surprise, he told me he felt led by God to donate his entire summer as a volunteer at our local church. He expressed he needed to get more pastoral experience. My first response was, "We cannot afford it!" Then I got really frustrated and rather unkind: "I am working full-time, all year round, and you want the summer off!"

We finished the conversation somewhat cordially and agreed to pray about it. A few days later I told my husband, "Fine. You go ahead and volunteer at church for the summer while I keep working full-time, but I still do not agree with you!"

Jim once again insisted God had pressed upon him that he should volunteer. A couple weeks later, I felt God's conviction heavy on my heart. After much prayerful confession, I also sincerely asked Jim to forgive me for not being willing to follow what he sincerely believed was God's leading. I was, however, still not convinced.

Every day in the summer, Jim dressed up in a shirt and tie and worked all day in the church office. He counseled people and did the duties of "The Pastor of the Day." Very early in the summer, I could see evidence God was using this experience to develop and grow Jim into the pastor he hoped to one day be. Toward the end of summer, Jim was receiving affirmation for his diligence and commitment from the pastors and elders of the church. I was so proud of him! The Executive Pastor even reported that Jim, who was an unpaid volunteer, was putting in more hours than some of the paid staff.

In September, Jim was informed by the elders that they had decided to pay for Jim's entire last year of seminary as a gift for his service to the church. There was no way we could ever have earned that much if he had worked a summer job!

Not only was I thrilled for my husband, but in a quiet moment of praise to the Lord, I was deeply humbled. I was so thankful Jim had listened to God's leading even though his wife did not. He had also won the church's respect as well as mine. I learned a personal lesson expressed in the words of the Apostles:

Acts 5:29 "We must obey God rather than men."

For Personal Reflection:

1. Reflect on your childhood playing "Follow the Leader." Draw some analogies on how God wants you to follow Him.

2. Read Psalm 25:4-5 at least five times: "Make me know Your ways, O LORD. Teach me Your paths. Lead me in Your truth and teach me. For You are the God of my salvation. For You I wait all the day."

3. Write it on a card and post it in a prominent place.

© Dr. James M. and Karon M. Cecy.

Karon's Ministry Devotional #3

Pastor's Wife to Missionary Mentor

> Hebrews 13:17 "Obey your leaders and submit to them, for they keep watch over your souls as those who will give an account. Let them do this with joy and not with grief, for this would be unprofitable for you."

I was delighted when my new husband felt called by God to become a pastor. He and I had no idea what was ahead. Both of us were late converts so as we stepped into the role as leaders we were woefully unprepared. As a new pastor's wife, I was ignorant and naïve. No other pastor's wife stepped in to help me navigate through my unexplained role. I had to figure it out on my own. Thankfully, this was God's assignment, and He provided the experiences needed to grow me up quickly.

As the ministry years ticked by, I learned the basics—often the hard way. Being a leader opened my eyes to the great need for leaders' wives to mentor other leaders' wives. This began my lifelong ministry to pastors' wives and leaders' wives locally and around the world through my added role as a JARON missionary. I named this branch of JARON Side-By-Side Ministry. (More detailed information about this ministry is in the Appendix.)

Through this ministry, I have offered a listening ear, counsel and encouragement to local pastors' wives, university professors' wives, para-church organization leaders, missionaries, and even a member of the Parliament of the United Kingdom.

Ministry to women in leadership throughout twenty different countries has led me to the conclusion that their needs are often buried and neglected. They are expected to be without struggles and they must hide it well in order to protect their reputation. All too often they have no one in whom it is safe to confide. It is no wonder many are friendless, lonely, and can even become angry and bitter.

God inspired me to give to these women what I did not have as a young, inexperienced pastor's wife: mentoring, counseling, encouragement and even a much-needed hug. To motivate leaders to open up to me, I had to learn to be transparent about my own past struggles as a pastor's wife. Under God's tutelage, I relied on the experiences, struggles, and even failures in my life as a leader to help these women. Often when I share with leaders' wives, their eyes light up. "Finally, someone understands me!"

God has lavished me with wonderful people who have blessed my life with friendship, joy, and love. Many of them are pastor's wives and some are not. I am so grateful to God for giving me everything I need to do the work of the ministry, despite my inadequacies. Yes, the moment I realized I would be a pastor's wife, I had no idea that one day God would use me to bring comfort and encouragement to some amazing women in leadership. Praise the Lord. His way is always the best!

For Personal Reflection:

1. Trust God to reveal to you His purpose for your life. Pray about it and be ready to be surprised.

2. Ask God to turn your inadequacies into opportunities to show God's power in your life.

3. Pray for your leaders and their spouses. Seek ways to show them you appreciate their hard work. Don't be too hard on them if they don't do ministry the way you wish.

© Dr. James M. and Karon M. Cecy.

Karon's Ministry Devotional #4

That Special Day of Prayer

> Philippians 4:6-7 "Be anxious for nothing, but in everything by prayer and supplication with thanksgiving let your requests be made known to God. And the peace of God, which surpasses all comprehension will guard your hearts and your minds in Christ Jesus."

What do you do when you wake up with a feeling of anticipation that something important is going to happen today? Fear and uneasiness often creep in. Overwhelmed by the magnitude of unexplained change, the only thing to do is have a day of prayer.

A momentous experience happened in 1990 when my husband was away at a men's retreat. Deciding to dedicate an entire day to pray was not a normal thing for me. Raising three young girls made the concept of a whole day of prayer daunting and seemingly impossible. "How do I homeschool the kids today?" "What about their meals?" "Surely there will be a few conflicts that need intervention." The driving force of my heart pushed me beyond those obstacles. "I must pray all day!"

I remember gathering my girls together, explaining my plan, and giving homework instructions. I asked them to help me stay focused on prayer and take care of each other.

So, I began. I settled in my bedroom with my Bible. I began with a prayer to our Mighty God, asking for His direction for my day. My routine was natural. I prayed, read the Bible, and had moments of quiet listening to the Holy Spirit's direction. At noon, as I was debating whether I should also fast from lunch, the girls proudly brought me a tray of "kid food." So sweet! I guess fasting was not needed.

All day the kids were angelic. The hours ticked by as my heart responded to the experience. Fear and uneasiness were banished. Instead, there seeped into my soul calm and peace.

At the end of the day, my husband returned from the retreat. The purpose of my day of prayer became apparent when he announced he was considering stepping down as the Senior Pastor. He described how God moved him to find a private place to pray at the retreat—a custodial closet. In that quiet place, God was impressing Jim that it was time for a change—time to start a new ministry of training pastors and ministry leaders, which later became known as JARON Ministries International.

Like most wives I know, I thrive on security. Being faced with this change would normally cause fear and confusion to take over my thinking. However, none of that happened. God had prepared me. I was at peace and ready to support my husband for taking this brave step into an unknown future. The future was not unknown to God. In fact, it was His plan about which He had not given us much notice. We were forced to trust Him for the details to come.

That journey of discovery began in 1990. Now, some thirty-five years later, I look back with gratitude and wonder at all the works of God. JARON Ministries International has ministered to countless pastors, missionaries, chaplains, government leaders, churches, schools, para-church organizations, police, firemen, politicians, and ministry leaders all over the world. Their teaching, medical, and construction teams have provided invaluable assistance globally. They have even ventured into a substantial ministry in the film industry.

God began this ministry by giving us a special call to prayer—on the same day! I have since learned to listen to God when He calls me to be quiet and pay attention to His leading. I expect His peace to guard my heart and mind as His plans unfold. I am learning to, in the words of Proverbs 31:25, "smile at the future."

For Personal Reflection:

1. Prayer is our intimate connection with God. Allow Him to guide your thinking through prayer.

2. If you ever feel moved to pray for a day or part of a day, please do it. God may be preparing you for big changes.

3. Trust Him to bring you His peace and to cause you to "smile at the future" (Proverbs 31:25).

© Dr. James M. and Karon M. Cecy

(Note: See the Appendix for more information about the history and ministries of JARON Ministries International, Inc.)

Karon's Ministry Devotional #5

Great and Awesome Things

> 2 Samuel 7:23 "And who is like your people Israel, the one nation on earth whom God went to redeem to be his people, making himself a name and doing for them great and awesome things..." (English Standard Version).

> Proverbs 13:12 "Hope deferred makes the heart sick, but desire fulfilled is a tree of life."

This morning as I was reading my Bible, I began thinking about my lists. No, I am not talking about my grocery list nor my endless "To-Do" list as a busy wife, mother, grandmother, women's counselor, missionary, and children's ministry director. I have lists that go with lists—though not quite like my "listaholic" husband.

I want to share a list that inspires my hope in God—a list of all the great and awesome things He has done in my life. This is motivated by my reading of 2 Samuel when God declares His covenant with David:

> 2 Samuel 7:8 "Thus says the LORD of hosts, I took you from the pasture, from following the sheep, that you should be prince over my people of Israel. And I have been with you wherever you went and have cut off all your enemies from before you. And I will make for you a great name like the name of the great ones of all the earth" (English Standard Version. My emphasis).

We pick up part of David's prayer of gratitude a little later in the chapter:

2 Samuel 7:23 "And who is like your people Israel, the one nation on earth whom God went to redeem to be his people, making himself a name and <u>doing for them great and awesome things</u> by driving out before your people, whom you redeemed by yourself from Egypt, a nation and its gods" (English Standard Version. My emphasis).

I am fascinated with the fact that when God speaks of what He will do in the future, He often brings attention to His mighty works of the past. I have a list of many of the "great and awesome things" God has done in my life. Surprisingly, the list includes even the "great and awesome" little things. Here are a few:

• While my husband was in seminary, we were as poor as the proverbial "church mice." One week, we ran out of groceries and my paycheck was not due for a week. We prayed to the Lord to meet our need for food but accepted the possibility that God may want us to fast for a week. A short time later, we were startled with a knock on the door. Opening the door, I saw our neighbor with two bags of groceries in her arms. She explained she was leaving out of town and did not want this food to waste. She asked, "Can you use these?" God met our immediate need in such a loving way.

• Our kids were growing out of their clothes. Knowing our financial pressure, I prayed to the Lord about this. The next day a few bags of kids' clothes were on my doorstep. "Thank You, Lord, for Your provision."

• Most recently, I needed to find a teacher for Sunday School. After many, many calls, I gave up and prayed. I should have prayed sooner. A name popped in my head. I called and they were delighted to say, "Yes!" to which I prayed, "Thank You, Lord, for Your answer to prayer."

A lifetime of stories could be posted here. Instead, I simply pray:

"Thank You, Lord, for...well...everything! We are blessed with a long list of the great and awesome things You have done. We are the recipients of Your promises so graciously given."

For Personal Reflection:

1. Reflect on the meaning of hope and how important it is.

2. One of the ways we build our hope is making a list of the "great and awesome things" our faithful God has done for us.

3. Often rehearse the words of Psalm 46:1 "God is our refuge and strength, a very present help in trouble."

© Dr. James M. and Karon M. Cecy.

Karon's Ministry Devotional #6

Preparing to Sleep Well

> Proverbs 3:24 "When you lie down, you will not be afraid.
> When you lie down, your sleep will be sweet."

Sleep captures me every night. I can drink coffee or watch a movie to delay sleep, but sleep will come over me like a fog rolling into a valley. Sleep always wins. God gave us this turn-off switch to nourish our bodies and minds. However, because we live in a sin-filled world, our sleep can be plagued by nightmares. Sometimes the nightmare is real.

My husband traveled frequently to start our new ministry, now called JARON Ministries International. Shortly after beginning this ministry, there was a six-month period of time when I had a stalker. He only came when Jim was gone on a ministry trip. He usually came after midnight and stood outside my bedroom window. A couple of times he waited in the bushes in front of my house and called out to me.

The Fresno Police and our neighbor who worked in the Fresno County Sheriff's Department worked hard to catch him. The stalker always eluded them. They only saw his footprints. Our church put up motion lights around our house to supplement our inside alarm system. Many of our fellow Christians joined in praying for our safety.

Jim was so worried he began to question whether he should be traveling. He and I decided we did not want evil to thwart JARON. We were convinced God was leading us to start up this ministry. We recognized the Lord had provided our friends, our church family, our neighbors, and the police to protect us and our family.

Whenever Jim was gone, I was on high alert, ready to make the calls for help. However, I was thoroughly exhausted from the lack of sleep. One morning, after an especially difficult night, I cried out to God: "Please Lord, help me sleep tonight and have an angel wake me up if the stalker comes. I choose to trust You."

That night I slept like a baby, until 2 a.m. when I awoke with clarity. I "knew without knowing"—the stalker was back. As I phoned the police and my sheriff neighbor, I thanked the Lord for waking me up. We did not catch the intruder that night, although the evidence was there, including his footprints. Eventually, the stalker stopped coming. We don't know for sure how, but God delivered us.

When Jim was gone, sleeping soundly until the Lord awakened me became my routine. This living nightmare taught me to trust God. It also led me to start a nightly routine. Let's call it:

Karon's "Preparing to Sleep Well" Plan

1. I praise the Lord who will deliver me from all my fears.

2. I declare my trust in the Lord to watch over me when I am sleeping.

3. I confess any known sin or compromise.

4. I put my physical, emotional, and spiritual safety in the hands of the Lord.

5. I fill my mind with Scripture-based, Christian music.

6. I fill my heart with Scriptures, such as:

Psalm 4:8 "In peace I will both lie down and sleep, for You alone, O LORD, make me to dwell in safety."

Psalm 34:4 "I sought the LORD, and He answered me, and delivered me from all my fears."

Psalm 56:3-4 "When I am afraid, I will put my trust in You. In God, whose word I praise. In God I have put my trust; I shall not be afraid. What can mere man do to me?"

Proverbs 3:21 "My son, do not let wisdom and understanding out of your sight..." (New International Version).

Proverbs 3:24 "When you lie down, you will not be afraid; when you lie down your sleep will be sweet."

And when I do these things, I am ready for a good night's sleep.

For Personal Reflection:

1. Try my "Preparing to Sleep Well" Plan for seven days. It works!

2. Encourage your family to talk about their nightmares. Remind them God is more powerful than their bad dreams. Pray with them for deliverance.

© Dr. James M. and Karon M. Cecy

Karon's Ministry Devotional #7

A Brief Lesson on Prayer

Proverbs 15:8 "...the prayer of the upright is His delight."

The most important prayer of my life was the day I prayed to receive Christ! My life was forever transformed. However, I admitted, as a new believer, prayer confused me. I asked myself often:

"Why did I need to pray when God already knew my thoughts?"

"Does God really want me to tell Him what He already knows?"

God was patient with my ignorance and taught me through the years that prayer was really about developing a relationship with our loving and mighty God. I remember one day when I felt particularly overwhelmed with the burdens of ministry and the condition of the world in general. I felt like I was living in a swirling, destructive hurricane. The world felt so chaotic, evil, and powerful.

I fell on my knees and poured out my heart to God. My noisy, clashing, crushing thoughts became silent. In the eye of the hurricane, I felt God's presence, His quiet, and His peace. Through cleansing tears, I soaked up His comfort and drank in His strength. My thoughts were refreshed with purpose and direction. I was encouraged in my spirit and empowered by Almighty God.

When my prayer time was finished, I stood up with a new perspective. The chaos was still raging outside, but I was different inside. God had spoken to my heart like I had rarely experienced before in my life. Prayer had enabled me to do what God called me to do. As a result, He changed and refreshed my spirit and my thinking to align with His purpose. Amid the storms, I was holding on to:

> Isaiah 41:10 "Do not fear, for I am with you. Do not anxiously look about you, for I am your God. I will strengthen you, surely I will help you. Surely, I will uphold you with My righteous right hand."

> I Thessalonians 5:16-18 "Rejoice always, pray continually, give thanks in all circumstances; for this is God's will for you in Christ Jesus" (New International Version).

I was resting in the eye of the hurricane, knowing even my most fear-prone prayers bring My Heavenly Father joy:

> Proverbs 15:8 "...the prayer of the upright is His delight."

Truly, our Heavenly Father delights when we talk to Him!

For Personal Reflection:

1. Reflect on the words of Proverbs 15:8 "...the prayer of the upright is His delight."

2. Post a list of prayers and their answers in a visible area in your home. Teach your family to celebrate "Yes," "No," or "Wait" answers to prayer.

3. Reflect on Philippians 4:6-7 "Do not be anxious about anything, but in every situation, by prayer and petition, with thanksgiving, present your requests to God. And the peace of God, which transcends all understanding, will guard your hearts and your minds in Christ Jesus" (New International Version).

© Dr. James M. and Karon M. Cecy.

Karon's Ministry Devotional #8

The Evil Child

Proverbs 22:15 "Foolishness is bound up in the heart of a child. The rod of discipline will remove it far from him."

I have had such an amazing life serving kids:

- As a parent.

- As a foster parent.

- As a grandmother.

- As a childcare owner and worker.

- As a spiritual mentor.

- As a pastor's wife.

- As a youth leader and Bible teacher.

- As a missionary.

- As a children's ministry director.

I have been around so many different kinds of kids. Most of them have been a joy. Then there are those "other" kids! Those Terrible Twos. Those Mouthy Adolescents. Those Wayward Teens. Those Rebellious Young Adults who still act like children.

Raising a child of any age to become a mature, responsible, and godly human being is not easy. I know; I've tried. I have had some successes and too many failures. This is not new.

Shortly after King Solomon, the last monarch of the United Kingdom of Israel, passed into history, a set of kings followed, serving in the Divided Kingdom, north and south. Some of these kings were placed on the throne at a very young age. Let me tell you the story of one:

Around 600 B.C., King Jehoiachin (also called Jeconiah and Coniah) was just eight years old when he became King of Judah. Just eight years old! He reigned three months and ten days in Jerusalem—a hundred days!

He was carried captive to the City of Babylon by King Nebuchadnezzar and imprisoned for thirty-seven years. Eventually, he was freed and lived in the Babylonian king's palace until he died (cf. Jeremiah 52:31-34).

So young to be a king! Such a short reign! Such a long thirty-seven-year imprisonment! But here's the saddest news of all. Even before being captured, this eight-year-old is recorded as one who "did evil in the sight of the LORD" (2 Chronicles 36:9).

How does an eight-year-old get branded in Bible history as evil? What bad choices had he made at such a young age? Where were his mentors? His parents? How much damage had he done to the overall spiritual life of God's people that young Child-King Jehoiachin would be the one captured by the Babylonians, beginning the seventy-year "spanking" God gave His people? Perhaps some of the lessons are to be found in the ancient Wisdom Literature. From the Book of Proverbs we observe:

Proverbs 22:15 "Foolishness is bound up in the heart of a child. The rod of discipline will remove it far from him."

Proverbs 29:15 "The rod and reproof give wisdom. But a child who gets his own way brings shame to his mother."

Apparently, in this case, the Child-King brought shame to an entire nation! King Solomon also presents the solution:

Proverbs 22:6 "Train up a child in the way he should go. Even when he is old he will not depart from it."

Here in Proverbs 22:6 the word train (Hebrew: *kanak*), in essence, means to break the wild nature and stimulate righteousness. One wonders how history might have changed if someone had done that with young Jehoiachin.

But that's all in the past. What about the present? How do we break the wild nature of a child whose very nature is foolish (cf. Proverbs 29:15)? How do we stimulate righteousness in a child who was born a sinner (cf. Psalm 51:5)? The answer is found throughout the Book of Proverbs—all thirty-one chapters. I also love what King Solomon wrote at the end of his life and at the end of the Book of Ecclesiastes:

Ecclesiastes 12:11-14 "The words of wise men are like goads, and masters of these collections (i.e., the wisdom literature like Proverbs) are like well-driven nails; they are given by one Shepherd. But beyond this, my son, be warned: the writing of many books is endless, and excessive devotion to books is wearying to the body. The conclusion, when all has been heard, is: fear God and keep His commandments, because this applies to every person. For God will bring every act to judgment, everything which is hidden, whether it is good or evil" (My addition).

As simplistic as it may seem, no matter what role you play in a child's life, you must strive to be a Proverbs Man or a Proverbs Woman if you want a chance to be successful in making these children "well-driven nails." You can run to scores of other books on child-raising. King Solomon warns it will be "wearying to the body." I say it will also be "a burden to your wallet."

So, if you who have been called to equip children, what are your waiting for? Make a commitment to become a "master of these collections." Start with Proverbs and move on from there. Maybe you will help prevent the next "child-king" from being a shame to an entire nation. I will settle for the children I train to bring honor to the Lord. In the words of the Apostle John:

> 3 John 1:4 "I have no greater joy than this, to hear of my children walking in the truth."

For Personal Reflection:

1. Begin reading Proverbs one chapter at a time, underlining key passages, and reflecting on how it applies to growing in wisdom.

2. Make a subject list of issues related to "training up a child in the way he should go" (Proverbs 22:6). As you read through Proverbs, catalog those that fit with the subject.

3. Reflect on 3 John 1:4 "I have no greater joy than this, to hear of my children walking in the truth."

© Dr. James M. and Karon M. Cecy.

Karon's Ministry Devotional #9

Others

> Hebrews 10:24-25 "…let us consider how to stimulate one another to love and good deeds, not forsaking our own assembling together, as is the habit of some, but encouraging one another; and all the more as you see the day drawing near."

As I read this passage, the word "consider" jumps out at me. Reading on, more direction is given. I need to "consider" how to stimulate (i.e., stir up one another) to love and good works towards others. I get it; it's about others! I "consider" how much of my life is about me? What delicious morsel am I going to eat? What do I want to wear and how will I spend my time? How much of my life is truly spent on others? My heart is convicted. I ask myself:

> *"How am I going to stimulate others to love and good deeds?"*

> *"How am I going to connect with others to encourage them while I have the opportunity?"*

Like you, I have so many answers. Let me offer a few that come to mind:

> • "I can gather for worship or join on-line groups if I am unable to attend."

> • "I can text or call someone on my phone."

> • "I can arrange to drop by someone's house."

• "I can send a note of encouragement."

• "I can communicate a message of love by doing something for them."

God wants me to put love into action for others with the same attentiveness I give to my own personal needs and desires. Another Scripture fills my mind:

Leviticus 19:18 "...love your neighbor as yourself. I am the LORD."

My husband loves to tell the story of an elderly widow who was such a great example to us in our early years of ministry. She had led a life full of suffering and sorrow. Her husband deserted her. One of her sons, a World War II pilot, was shot down in the Pacific Ocean. She suffered greatly from a debilitating disease that required her to crawl on the floor when she first got out of bed to "warm up her bones."

She lived in a simple apartment above a garage and would often invite my husband, as a young pastor, for chicken pot pie. He hated chicken pot pies but he loved spending time with this "honored widow." She was an amazing prayer-warrior who spent hours every day bringing the needs of many before the Lord. In fact, on her shelves were binders filled with the names of the countless people she prayed for. It was often said, "She prayed so many of us into ministry!"

The walls of her humble apartment had few decorations but a sign hung prominently next to her front door. It was a small, framed white sheet of paper with just one word—a word that described her life. It simply said, "Others." She was, to us, a living example of one who knew how to "stimulate" and "encourage" others until God called her home to Heaven (cf. Hebrews 10:24-25).

Practically speaking, what does ministering to others "this side of Heaven" look like? Let me have us ponder some of the many "one another" verses in the Bible:

- Accept one another (Romans 15:7).

- Bear one another's burdens (Galatians 6:2).

- Be hospitable to one another (1 Peter 4:9; Romans 12:13).

- Be kind to one another (Ephesians 4:32).

- Be tender-hearted toward one another (Ephesians 4:32).

- Build up one another (1 Thessalonians 5:11).

- Comfort one another (1 Thessalonians 4:18).

- Contribute to the (financial) needs of one another (Romans 12:13).

- Encourage one another (Hebrews 3:13; 10:24-25; 1 Thessalonians 5:11).

- Forgive one another (Colossians 3:13; Ephesians 4:32).

- Give preference to one another (Romans 12:10).

- Love (self-sacrifice for) one another (Romans 12:9-10; 1 Peter 4:8; John 13:34; etc.).

- Pray for one another (James 5:16).

• Regard one another as more important than yourself (Philippians 2:3).

• Teach and exhort one another (Colossians 3:13, 16).

• Use your gifts to serve one another (1 Peter 4:10; Galatians 5:13).

"Consider" a few of these today!

For Personal Reflection

1.Memorize the simple but lifechanging words of Leviticus 19:18 "Love your neighbor as yourself." (Post it around the house)

2. Make a sign that simply has the word OTHERS and hang it in a prominent place.

3. Make a list of "other" people you want to love and encourage.

4. Review the above list of "one another" verses. Write out how you might apply them in your life today.

© Dr. James M. and Karon M. Cecy.

Karon's Ministry Devotional #10

Promise-Keeper

> Psalm 56:4 "In God, whose word I praise, in God I have put my trust; I shall not be afraid. What can mere man do to me?"

I remember the fear that consumed my heart when, during a deluge of very heavy rains, the hillsides near our home fell in. Many houses were buried and whole families were killed in the "avalanche of mud." The memory still disturbs my heart. So much has happened since then.

Daily our news reporters insist we have something more to worry about locally, nationally, and globally. We are filled with anxiety as we reflect on our problems physically, emotionally, relationally, financially, socially, and spiritually. It feels like an impending "avalanche of chaos" ready to bury us alive.

Yet, in the midst of the prevailing bad news, God has promised He will take care of His children—that He will supply all our needs "according to His riches in glory in Christ Jesus" (Philippians 4:19). No wonder the Apostle Paul could say earlier in that same epistle:

> Philippians 4:6 "Be anxious for nothing, but in everything by prayer and supplication with thanksgiving let your requests be made known to God."

Of course, Matthew 6:8 reminds us that our Heavenly Father knows our needs even before we ask Him. Also, remember 1 Peter 5:7 telling us we can cast all our cares on Him. Why? Because He cares for us. These are not just hollow platitudes and *clichés*. These are promises from the God of Integrity—the God who cannot lie and the One who does everything He promises. 2 Peter 3:9 reminds us the Lord is not slow about those promises—i.e., they happen in His perfect timing and in His perfect way; not ours. So, we either choose to trust Him to take care of what we fear or not. The Bible is clear:

Psalm 11:11 "You who fear the LORD, trust in the LORD...."

All of us need to hold on tightly to the words of the Psalmist:

Psalm 56:4 "In God, whose word I praise, in God I have put my trust; I shall not be afraid."

It makes me want to break out into the old song written in 1886 by Russell Kelso Carter: *Standing on the Promises.* It is a beloved hymn of the faith for a reason—the people of God have always needed the reminder. Our Loving Heavenly Father is a Faithful Promise-Keeper. Thus, we sing with confidence:

Standing on the promises of Christ my King,
Through eternal ages, let his praises ring.
Glory in the highest, I will shout and sing,
Standing on the promises of God.

For Personal Reflection:

1. Review some of the ways our Promise-Keeping God has ministered to you.

2. Post some of the promises in the Word of God in a prominent place, such as 1 Kings 8:57 "May the LORD our God be with us, as He was with our fathers, may He not leave us or forsake us."

© Dr. James M. and Karon M. Cecy.

Karon's Ministry Devotional #11

Where You Lead Me, I Will Follow...

Acts 18:21 "...I will return to you again if God wills."

Over my many years in ministry, I have had the opportunity to travel to more than twenty countries. As one can imagine, international travel can come with difficulties. However, unlike many of my fellow missionaries, most of my challenges have been about inconveniences. Unlike them, I have not faced major illness, injury, prison, or the threat of death. Some call them "Tiger Stories" while others take a lighter approach: "Lord, where You lead me, I will follow; what You feed me, I will swallow."

Even for us who have been inconvenienced, missionary work is not about getting stuck in airports, eating foreign food, sleeping in strange beds, or fighting traffic in rickety vehicles. It is about doing what it takes to reach people with the gospel and training them to serve Him.

In Acts, Chapters 16 through 18, we read the report of the Apostle Paul's second missionary journey to places where churches were already established. He is then prompted by the Holy Spirit to go to Macedonia to preach the gospel.

It is easy to get caught up in the travel details, but don't miss the real news—his "Tiger Stories." Let me break it down into some bite-sized morsels, especially of the things the Apostle Paul had to "swallow."

"Where You lead me, I will follow..."

The Apostle Paul allowed the Holy Spirit to provoke his spirit and move him to places he had not planned to go (cf. Acts 16:9-12). Throughout the trip, he reasoned from the Scriptures; not his own opinions, speaking to anyone who was present, anywhere they gathered—by rivers, in homes or synagogues, in the marketplace, in the famous Areopagus in Athens, and the judgment seat in Corinth.

"What You feed me, I will swallow."

Acts records that the established churches were strengthened in the faith and were increasing in numbers. In other places many received the word with eagerness and were immediately persuaded, choosing to trust in Jesus Christ as Lord and Savior. Others wanted to study further. Many people were converted almost everywhere Paul and his ministry companions went. He even had some in Athens respond positively to the message and became believers. Many were baptized. That's the tasty food to swallow.

However, in some places the response was not so tasty. After delivering a demon-possessed slave-girl, her masters dragged Paul and Silas into the streets where they were beaten with rods and imprisoned. After miraculously being delivered from jail, they departed. In another place, the Jews became jealous, formed mobs, started a riot, and attacked the new believers. The missionaries were once again forced to leave town.

Place after place, the Jews stirred up the crowds against Paul and Silas. Even in Athens, although some responded well, others just sneered. In Corinth, Paul was brought before the judgment seat and witnessed them beating the leader of the synagogue. That's the hard-to-swallow, bitter fruit!

God is on the move, as much today as He was then. Is the Holy Spirit provoking us to minister in places we had not planned— or refuse to go? I expect I will be seeing more countries and facing more inconveniences for the gospel, but is it worth it? Yes, it is! Where He leads me, I will follow; what He feeds me, I will swallow."

For Personal Reflection:

1. Read Acts 16-18 about the Apostle Paul's Second Missionary Journey and underline portions of his "Tiger Stories."

2. Be honest about what and where you would be <u>unwilling</u> to do or go in ministry for the Lord. It is not that God will call you to do those things or go to those places. It's more about the willingness than it is the doing or going.

3. See Jim's Ministry Devotional #24 entitled, *"Tiger Stories."*

© Dr. James M. and Karon M. Cecy.

Karon's Ministry Devotional #12

Hospitality: Loving Strangers

> Leviticus 19:34 "The stranger who resides with you shall be to you as the native among you, and you shall love him as yourself, for you were aliens in the land of Egypt; I am the LORD your God."

> 1 Peter 4:9 "Offer hospitality to one another without grumbling" (New International Version).

> Romans 12:13 "...practicing hospitality..."

Frequently traveling internationally as JARON missionaries, my husband and I have been blessed by many people's hospitality. We have stayed in some very humble homes. Whether it was a mat on the floor or a simple couch, we were grateful. The food was often unfamiliar. Soup with floating fish heads for breakfast, mystery meat for lunch, and unrecognizable vegetables for dinner. Yet, we were blessed by our hosts as they gave sacrificially of themselves.

I think fondly of the time in Europe when a young couple invited us to dinner. We crowded around their small table in the tiny kitchen. We were treated to a plate of sausages and Spam with a few potatoes and carrots. We felt loved and cared for because we knew this meal was very expensive for them.

A family hosted us in Northern Ireland. They made sure our needs were met, even giving us their own bed while they moved to the attic. The family drove us everywhere and packed us lunches to enjoy while we traveled. Their kindness will not be forgotten.

These families gave what they had—simple or elaborate. They made us feel loved and accepted as they offered their friendship and fellowship. To them and us, hospitality is about the heart—not fancy foods or a perfect house. I suppose we might get that by staying in a hotel. However, we prefer to enjoy the love we find in the hearts of God's people.

We see in the Scriptures that hospitality is commanded by God, especially for church leaders (cf. 1 Timothy 3:2; Titus 1:8). But what is hospitality? Hospitality is not primarily opening our homes to family and friends. Quite literally the New Testament word *philoxenos* means to be "a lover of strangers."

Christ revealed the ultimate example of hospitality when he greeted the woman at the well. She was a woman. Rabbis were not supposed to talk to women. She was a Samaritan. Jews in Jesus's day hated Samaritans, considering them "half-breeds." She was an outcast, shamed by her blatant immorality and her many broken relationships. Here she is collecting water all alone, in the middle of the day when it was scorching hot! Yet, Jesus tenderly reached out to her, loving and accepting her, not as a stranger, but as a precious child in the eyes of God. His offer to her was so very welcoming:

> John 4:14 "...whoever drinks of the water that I will give him shall never thirst; but the water that I will give him will become in him a well of water springing up to eternal life."

Just like that woman, when we were strangers, Christ met our greatest need—salvation. He invited us to quench our thirst with the living water. He sacrificed Himself for us while we were strangers (cf. Romans 5:8, 10).

Hospitality is sacrificing for a stranger. It is offering what we have to give and more. As Christ did with the outcast woman, hospitality is showing by our actions that we value people—any people—with the value God places on us:

> 1 John 4:19 "We love, because He first loved us."

For Personal Reflection:

1. Read the story of the woman at the well (John 4:7-26). Reflect on what Jesus was offering the woman. It wasn't just water; it was eternal life.

2. Pray about inviting someone you don't know to your home.

© Dr. James M. and Karon M. Cecy.

Karon's Ministry Devotional #13

Hunger

> Deuteronomy 8:3 "He humbled you and let you be hungry, and fed you with manna which you did not know, nor did your fathers know, that He might make you understand that man does not live by bread alone, but man lives by everything that proceeds out of the mouth of the LORD."

Traveling is not easy. Beyond the airport hassles, lost luggage, and exhausting ministry schedule comes the challenge of maintaining a regular eating schedule. In my experience:

- Europeans have a heavy breakfast and a late dinner.

- Asians eat very early and very late.

- Italians eat whenever and wherever—"*Mangiare!* Eat up!" (My husband had me throw that in!)

Hunger is defined by Webster's Dictionary as "a craving or urgent need for food or a specific nutrient." It is that uneasy sensation occasioned by a prolonged lack of food. Here is what I have noticed about my own seasons of spiritual hunger.

It is easy to recognize when I need spiritual food, but I do not always seek to be fed. Sometimes, I ignore the symptoms and let it go, making me more and more miserable. I experience "spiritual hunger pains." Here are my symptoms:

- I suffer with an unsettled and uneasy feeling—a deep-seated hunger in my spirit.

• I experience loneliness—an emptiness that cannot be filled by friends and family.

• I struggle with temptation (e.g., complaining, anger, etc.).

• I succumb to sin—which temporarily separates me from my awareness of God's presence.

Jesus spent forty days fasting in the wilderness. At the end of those long days, He was obviously hungry. Who wouldn't be? The devil saw this as an opportunity to tempt Jesus:

Matthew 4:3 "If You are the Son of God, command that these stones become bread."

Jesus knew that the Tempter was not just appealing to His physical hunger; he was trying to get Jesus's eyes off His Heavenly Father and Jesus knew it. In answer, He quoted the latter part of an Old Testament verse found in the Book of Deuteronomy.

Deuteronomy 8:3 "...man does not live by bread alone, but man lives by everything that proceeds out of the mouth of the LORD" (cf. Matthew 4:4; Luke 4:4).

I know what to do when the symptoms of spiritual hunger happen:

• I am to pray and ask the Lord for forgiveness for ignoring my craving for His Word.

• I am to thank God He is always ready to fill me with His Spirit.

• I am to make myself sit down and chew on the Word of God.

• I am to ask God to help me come eagerly to His table tomorrow—and the next day and the next.

And when I do, my spiritual hunger will be satisfied!

Matthew 5:6 "Blessed are those who hunger and thirst for righteousness, for they shall be satisfied."

"Dear God, please help me recognize when I am hungry for You. Help me see that my uneasiness, my loneliness, and my sin are because I need Your Word to feed my soul."

For Personal Reflection:

1. Reflect on a time when you were hungry for God and He provided the spiritual refreshment.

2. Pray and ask God to create a hunger in you for His Word.

© Dr. James M. and Karon M. Cecy.

Karon's Ministry Devotional #14

The God of Details

> Hebrews 9:11-12 "But when Christ appeared as a high priest of the good things to come, He entered through the greater and more perfect tabernacle, not made with hands, that is to say, not of this creation; and not through the blood of goats and calves, but through His own blood, He entered the holy place once for all, having obtained eternal redemption."

It finally happened! Reading through the Bible, I now arrived at Leviticus. In the past I found great difficulty reading this particular book. Consequently, I decided to pray and ask the Holy Spirit to reveal something new to me: "Lord, help me to understand You more." Faithfully, I trudged through all the details, chapter after chapter.

The day came when I read the last chapter. I finally understood. Almighty God was calling His people to be holy as He is holy. He gave boundaries and distinct instructions about how He is to be worshiped. The minute details had a greater purpose—to teach the people that our Creator is a God of Specifics who cares about every detail of our lives.

The New Testament reminds us all these details were a "mere shadow" of what Jesus Christ came to do for us as our High Priest and as the Lamb of God who takes away our sin (cf. Colossians 2:16-17; John 1:29). We also find more specifics regarding Jesus as our Perfect Atoning Sacrifice in the New Testament Book of Hebrews (cf. Hebrews 9:11-12; 10:1, 10), and regarding Christ as the Propitiation (i.e., the Satisfaction) for our sins in the First Epistle of John (cf. 1 John 2:2; 4:10). These great doctrines draw my attention back to the Book of Leviticus: The Book of Details.

My role as a Children's Director in a local church requires I spend a great deal of time selecting curriculum for several age groups and children's clubs. The task is daunting, especially trying to coordinate a balance between Old and New Testament books and basic doctrines. I also admit not all the Books of the Bible are at the top of my list. So, imagine my surprise when I read that, according to Jewish history, Leviticus was the very first book taught to children. Wow!

I understand now the value of unearthing the gold from the Book of Leviticus for myself and the children. We learn from Leviticus the specifics about our Holy God who hates our sins and calls His creation to be holy. The Apostle Peter repeats the age-old call of God on all of our lives. In explaining this, he quotes the Book of Leviticus:

> 1 Peter 1:15-16 "...like the Holy One who called you, be holy yourselves also in all your behavior; because it is written (i.e., in Leviticus 19:2; 20:26). 'You shall be holy, for I am holy'" (My addition).

What did I learn from the Book of Leviticus? Holy God, the God of Details who is nearby, cared about every part of our lives, provided the Perfect Lamb of God to take away our specific sins, and gave us all the detailed blessings of an abundant life (cf. John 10:10).

It is quite understandable why the lessons from the Book of Leviticus should be some of the first things we teach our children— followed by a look at the Book of Hebrews. They both contain details none of us can afford to miss.

Now on to the Book of Numbers...

For Personal Reflection:

1. Use a trusted Bible history resource to explain the relationship of the Old Testament Book of Leviticus with the New Testament Book of Hebrews, explaining how the Messiah (Christ) is our Perfect Sacrifice (e.g., Hebrews 9:11-12).

2. Read the Books of Leviticus and Hebrews together. Highlight the word "holy" in both books.

© Dr. James M. and Karon M. Cecy.

Karon's Ministry Devotional #15

My Reset Button

Hebrews 10: 24-25 "...let us consider how to stimulate one another to love and good deeds, not forsaking our own assembling together, as is the habit of some, but encouraging one another; and all the more, as you see the day drawing near."

I push the little red button on the black box and the magic begins. The Wi-Fi is reset, the glitches are corrected, the connections are refreshed, and all is well, at least for the moment. I love the reset button!

There is an even more wonderful reset button—my local church! A feeling of anticipation comes over me whenever I walk into the auditorium and wait for the worship service to start. I know this experience will reset my life. It will renew me and correct any glitches in my thinking.

It is marvelous to be among a group of believers. We all have very different backgrounds, challenges, hurts, victories, and failures. But in this church gathering the wondrous truth is that we are all one, enjoying "unity amidst diversity." Review with me these familiar reminders:

Galatians 3:28 "There is neither Jew nor Greek, there is neither slave nor free man, there is neither male nor female; for you are all one in Christ Jesus."

Ephesians 4:4-6 "There is one body and one Spirit, just as also you were called in one hope of your calling; one Lord, one faith, one baptism, one God and Father of all who is over all and through all and in all."

Colossians 3:15 "Let the peace of Christ rule in your hearts, to which indeed you were called in one body; and be thankful."

Church is where I worship our great God with others. He does a work in our hearts through Bible teaching, music, fellowship, service, as well as the celebration of the ordinances of baptism and communion. I also go to church to grow in fellowship, doctrine, worship, service, evangelism, discipleship, and prayer.

Some people might think church is man's idea, but this reset experience is God's plan. In fact, He tells us it is vital for our survival in these last days before Christ's return. I take to heart these timeless words:

Hebrews 10: 24-25 "…let us consider how to stimulate one another to love and good deeds, not forsaking our own assembling together, as is the habit of some, but encouraging one another; and all the more, as you see the day drawing near."

Sometimes when I sit in church and soak up the blessings, I think of Heaven. I believe church is one of God's ways of giving me a preview of things to come:

Revelation 19:6 "Then I heard what sounded like a great multitude, like the roar of rushing waters and like loud peals of thunder, shouting: 'Hallelujah! For our Lord God Almighty reigns.'"

My local church is my place of joy and praise. I am convinced that if I do not attend regularly, I am missing out on something special. It renews, corrects, refreshes, and restores me. Praise God for the great reset button!

For Personal Reflection:

1. Reflect on why it is a joy and privilege to go to church. Be honest about why it is not.

2. If you are resisting going to church, ask yourself why you feel this way and suggest a plan on how to solve the problem. Who do you need to talk to about this?

3. Plan on attending church even if you do not want to. Being a part of a local church is God's plan and can be a special part of your life.

4. Most likely, you live in a community with many local churches. Keep searching until you find one you feel the Holy Spirit is calling you to attend.

5. And remember: There is no perfect church. (Besides, the moment you attend, it will stop being perfect!)

© Dr. James M. and Karon M. Cecy.

Karon's Ministry Devotional #16

Never Alone

Matthew 28:20 "…I am with you always, even to the end of the age."

So many people I talk to are struggling with loneliness. These conversations have prompted me to share an experience I had as a JARON missionary in the Czech Republic in 2019. I hope my experience can be an encouragement.

Click! Clack!. Thud! My suitcase is quite noisy as I drag it along the cobblestone streets of Prague. I have just finished teaching a group of ministry leaders and pastors' wives. I have been to many countries around the world. However, this is the first time my husband and I have ministered in separate locations.

Hana, my new friend and interpreter from the retreat, is guiding me to the hotel where I will spend the night. We turn into an alley, my suitcase complaining all the way. Upon entering the hotel lobby, Hana makes arrangements with the desk clerk. I don't understand a word of their language. Hana says goodbye and I make my way across the lobby as my suitcase hums across the smooth floor.

I step inside my room and lock it snugly. A quick glance tells me I have all I need. Pulling aside the window drapes, I see the alley. I am struck with the reality I am truly alone! I hear my heartbeat. My only companion is my suitcase. I lift it to a bench and zip it open flat. The sound of being alone is loud. Every simple movement I make seems to scream, *"I am really alone!"* I finally admit to myself how afraid I am: *"What if something happens and I need help?"*

There is a phone in my room, but the desk clerk does not speak English. I swiftly grab my mobile phone and plug it into the wall. I whisper to myself: *"Good, I have a phone! In an emergency,*

I could call my dear husband...but he is so far away. He really could not come to my rescue here. I could call Hana...but what if she doesn't answer?"

I take my Bible out and it makes a plopping sound on the bed. Sitting down on the edge of the bed, I feel sheer panic begin to rise. Verses begin to pop into my mind like popcorn popping on a hot stove.

Pop! Philippians 4:13 "I can do all things through him who strengthens me."

Pop! Psalm 56:3 "When I am afraid, I put my trust in You."

Pop! Matthew 28:20 "I am with you always, even to the end of the age."

Pop! 2 Corinthians 12:9 "My grace is sufficient for you, for power is perfected in weakness."

Finally, I acknowledge the presence of God in my room:

"Thank you Holy Spirit for bringing to my mind your Word! I am not alone!"

I chuckle out loud as I remember one of the topics I just taught to the women was on loneliness. As I snuggle under the covers and my head drops to the pillow, another verse comes quickly into my mind.

Pop! Proverbs 3:24 "If you lie down, you will not be afraid; when you lie down, your sleep will be sweet."

I wake refreshed and victorious in the morning. Hana arrives on time, and we wave to the hotel clerk and step outside. My long journey home has begun. Hana and I chat pleasantly as we walk down the cobblestone alley. My suitcase sings behind me:

Click! Clack! Thud! I am not alone. God is with us.

For Personal Reflection:

1. Reflect on something you did that was really frightening and how you overcame your fear with God's help.

2. Embrace adventure, knowing you will always have God with you.

3. In the midst of fearful situations, repeat the words of Jesus in Matthew 28:20 "I am with you always...." and Psalm 46:1, 10 "God is our refuge and strength, a very present help in trouble....Cease striving and know that I am God."

© Dr. James M. and Karon M. Cecy.

Karon's Ministry Devotional #17

On the One Hand...

> Proverbs 12:25 "Anxiety in a man's heart weighs it down, but a good word makes it glad."

Recently, my husband and I watched one of our favorite movies, *Fiddler on the Roof*. We were once again reminded of the delightful way the main character, Tevye, argued with himself:

> "On the one hand....On the other hand..."

The Bible actually uses this format as a way of getting our attention. For example, let me re-phrase the familiar words of Romans 6:23:

> On the one hand, the penalty of sin is death—eternal separation from God. On the other hand, the free gift of eternal life is made possible by grace alone, through faith alone, in Christ alone!

These feelings of "on the one hand...on the other hand" has been a pretty good description of many of our lives, hasn't it?

> • On the one hand, we have those who say these days are worse than we thought they would be. These are the worst of times and it is only going to get worse. On the other hand, we have those who say these are the best of times, and it is going to get better.

> • On the one hand, we have people insisting our pastors, ministry directors, and church leaders are not being as

effective as they should be. On the other hand, we have many who are thankful for the faithfulness of their spiritual leaders.

• On the one hand, all these conflicting opinions can weigh us down. On the other hand, we have a good word for us that makes us glad—the Word of God.

> Psalm 19:8 "The precepts of the LORD are right, rejoicing the heart…"

• On the one hand, we are living in anxiety-producing days. On the other hand, as born-again children of God, we can choose to hold on to the Promises of God:

> Psalm 40:16 "Let all who seek You rejoice and be glad in You..."

> Proverbs 3:5-6 "Trust in the LORD with all your heart and do not lean on your own understanding. In all your ways acknowledge Him, and He will make your paths straight."

My prayer during these challenging days is simple but heartfelt:

> *"Lord, fill me with gladness that can only come by knowing You. You are still on Your throne."*

On the other hand…

Wait…there is no other hand!

For Personal Reflection:

1. Try making an "On the one hand…. On the other hand…." list regarding your life and ministry.

2. Take Romans 6:23 to heart:

   • On the one hand…"For the wages of sin is death (i.e., separation from God)…"

   • On the other hand…"…the free gift of God is eternal life in Christ Jesus sour Lord."

3. Read portions in the Book of Proverbs with contrasting proverbs where the second line uses the word "But…" (e.g., Proverbs 28:1 "The wicked flees when no one is pursuing, but the righteous are as bold as a lion.")

© Dr. James M. and Karon M. Cecy.

Karon's Ministry Devotional #18

Rain! Rain! Inevitable Rain!

James 1:2-4 "Consider it all joy, my brethren, when you encounter various trials, knowing that the testing of your faith produces endurance. And let endurance have its perfect result, so that you may be perfect and complete, lacking in nothing."

"The way I see it. If you want the rainbow, you gotta put up with the rain" (Dolly Parton).

The year is 2021. After a busy time of ministry, my husband and I are touring in Northern Ireland for the first time. It is raining non-stop and I am complaining to myself: *"It's everywhere. Above me, below me, beside me, on me! Water, water, and more water. Does it have to rain today?"*

My clothes are soaked. My face and my hands are dripping with rain. We are walking along an uphill pathway. I'm prepared with a warm parka, waterproof boots, and an umbrella—a necessity here in this beautiful land. On my right are wild, empty, rolling hills. The rain is soaking into the ground. As I step around the puddles on the path, I look to my left at the roaring sea. The waves crash against the rocks, sending dancing sprays high into the air. Each wave seeks to go higher and higher like one great contest. My attitude has changed: *"This is breathtaking!"* I embrace the rain. If it did not rain, Ireland would not look so gloriously green. I take a moment to reflect: *"Just as the rain on the fields of Ireland create gloriously green hills, so trials produce glorious results in my life."*

I then recall the ancient words of James 1:2-4, written by James, the brother of our Lord. I memorized them decades ago. These timeless verses challenge me to embrace trials because the results are worth it. My All-Knowing, All-Wise, Heavenly Father uses them to produce lifelong results. I reflect more: *"Trials grow me up. Suffering teaches me. Difficulties change me inside for the better."* I move in my thinking to reflect on the rest of the passage:

> James 1:4 "And let endurance have its perfect result, so that you may be perfect and complete, lacking in nothing."

I need to embrace the downpour of trials that will most certainly drench me. They were designed by God to show evidence I am maturing in Christ. I am learning not just to <u>go</u> through trials but to <u>grow</u> through them. I pray quietly:

> *"Thank You, Lord, for the rain…the inevitable downpour of cleansing and purifying trials that make me more like Jesus."*

However, the next time I come to Northern Ireland, I think I will bring a heavier coat and a better umbrella. The inevitable trials I can handle; the wet clothes are avoidable.

For Personal Reflection:

1. Read James 1:2-4 at least seven times.

2. Teach your kids trials come in many shapes and sizes. Keep it simple. (e.g., a skinned knee). Perhaps you can explain them this way:
"Without rain, we would not have beautiful flowers, or vegetables to eat. Many kinds of trials can rain down on us at once, but they can produce beautiful results in our lives."

© Dr. James M. and Karon M. Cecy.

Karon's Ministry Devotional #19

Serving in the Midst of Pain

> John 13:4-5 , 14-15 "…so he got up from the meal, took off his outer clothing, and wrapped a towel around his waist. After that, he poured water into a basin and began to wash his disciples' feet, drying them with the towel that was wrapped around him….'Now that I, your Lord and Teacher have washed your feet, you also should wash one another's feet. I have set you an example that you should do as I have done for you'" (New International Version).

Vacation Bible School is in full swing. We are blessed to see the children full of joy. It is such an important event in the life of a child. There is another aspect of VBS that captivates my attention at the moment. The Volunteers! Many of them are giving loving service during times of intense personal pain.

Jim has taught me his five conditions for finding volunteers. I have found them to be very helpful and, in the rush of ministry, have suffered the consequences when I have ignored them:

• Character: Are they people of integrity?

• Chemistry: Are they the right fit?

• Competence: Are they capable of doing the job?

• Confidence: Am I confident in them?

• Cost: Are they worth the price (in terms of time, money, and effort)?

Presently, I am blessed to have a team that meets all those qualifications. However, many are suffering. Permit me to share a word of testimony:

I am asked to pray with a volunteer for her family. She has tears in her eyes as she turns to serve the kids. Another volunteer's husband is fighting cancer. The joy flowing out of her is a miracle. I know another volunteer is so stressed with the troubles of her life— I was not sure she would be here. But she is here, joyfully moving the kids along to their next station. Another volunteer's adult daughter was in the Emergency Room last night. Yet, she is here serving.

As I look around the auditorium I know it holds people with many burdens and heartaches. Why are they serving? I sense their desire to spend time with the kids and their willingness to follow Christ's example of loving service despite the pain of knowing what was ahead for Him:

> Hebrews 12:2 "...fixing our eyes on Jesus, the author and perfecter of faith, who for the joy set before Him endured the cross, despising the shame, and has sat down at the right hand of the throne of God."

Back to Jesus in the Upper Room:

> John 13:14-15 "Now that I, your Lord and Teacher have washed your feet, you also should wash one another's feet. I have set you an example that you should do as I have done for you" (New International Version).

I imagine Jesus gripping each foot and gently wiping down the muck and mire—cleaning between each toe. Oh, the smell. The splatter. All the while He was thinking of his upcoming, agonizing sacrifice.

I imagine Jesus looking deep into each disciple's eyes, conveying His perfect love for them while they are dirty with sin. When He was done washing their feet, He had their dirt on His hands and embedded in His fingernails. His clothes held the spray from their mucky feet.

He washed their feet with water but He knew that soon He would wash their hearts. His body would hold the splatter of His own blood and the weight of their sin-encrusted souls. Jesus wanted them clean, not just on the outside. He embraced the painful cross for them (and us) because of His great love.

The Volunteers have finished well today. They have served in love despite their personal trials and pain. Jesus is pleased. His challenge is to all of us:

John 13:15 "I have set you an example that you should do as I have done for you" (New International Version).

Now, go wash someone's feet!

For Personal Reflection:
(Especially for your children)

1. The next time you wash your children's feet, tell the story of Jesus washing the disciples' feet in John 13. Remind them you love them which is why you wash them and take care of them. So does Jesus.

2. Let your kids play in a mud puddle and get really dirty. While you are washing the mud off, talk about how Jesus washed all our dirty sin from us when He died on the cross, so that our hearts can be clean.

© Dr. James M. and Karon M. Cecy.

Karon's Ministry Devotional #20

Goliath Battles

> I Samuel 17:45, 47 "You come to me with a sword, a spear, and a javelin, but I come to you in the name of the LORD of hosts, the God of the armies of Israel, whom you have taunted....and that all this assembly may know that the Lord does not deliver by sword or by spear; for the battle is the LORD's and He will give you into our hands."

Who is not inspired by the account of the ill-equipped shepherd, David, slaying the seasoned, giant warrior, Goliath, who, according to some historians, was almost ten feet in height! Yet David—a teenager most likely a little over five feet high—did not shrink in fear before this behemoth! David knew God was bigger and more powerful than a mere giant! I love the declaration David shouted to Goliath before he slung the stone:

> 1 Samuel 17:45 "You come to me with a sword, a spear, and a javelin, but I come to you in the name of the LORD of hosts, the God of the armies of Israel..."

We all are faced with Goliath Battles from time to time. Your gigantic monster might be finances or a broken marriage, or even a physical battle with disease or injury. Even our children may be in a battle with colossal problems at home, massive difficulties in learning, or facing an oversized bully.

I still remember vividly one of my Goliath Battles that happened years ago. Jim tells the same story from his perspective in his devotional entitled *"Tiger Stories."*

I was on the way to drop off my friend at her home. My three daughters were in the back seat of our van, chatting away as we drove through the sleepy town of Scotts Valley, where my uncle was the Chief of Police.

I came to a stop before the crosswalk and waited for a pedestrian who was completely dressed in white. He walked to the front of my van and stopped between my two headlights. Turning to look at me, he raised a gun. I could see the shape of the barrel now pointed towards me and my daughters seated behind me. I was later told the gunman was screaming, "You're all gonna die!" I held my breath and prayed, *"Oh God!"* My van was trapped on the left by a concrete divider, a car on the right, and a car behind me. *"Do I run him over?"*

Just as my mind raced for an escape, the gunman waved the gun towards the car to my right and stepped towards it. Immediately, I stomped on the accelerator and sped to the nearest gas station. Screeching to a halt, I jumped from the van and raced to the phone in the office. (No cell phone in those days!)

Yelling to people in the gas station office that there was a gunman on the loose, I called 911. It was busy! I called again—still busy! Turning to look at my van, in horror, I saw the gunman across the street, creeping towards the gas station. Multiple police officers were tracking behind him. *"My kids and friend are right in his path!"* In a panic, I raced to my van, jumped in, and sped away to safety.

A couple of hours later, while listening to the news, I learned the gunman had stolen the car parked next to mine at the gas station. He led the police on a chase through the small town and onto the freeway—until he ran out of gas. A shoot-out with the police resulted in a police dog being shot and, consequently, the gunman being shot to death.

As I emotionally processed this terrifying event over the next few days, I was so very thankful God was with us through it all. Fortunately, my kids were not fully aware of all that was happening.

Since this event, I have had other Goliath Battles—not quite so dramatic, thankfully—but battles, nonetheless. We live in a sin-sick world and look forward to the day we are delivered from the presence of sin in Heaven.

Whatever Goliath Battles you or your loved one's face, whether you are delivered here on Earth or end up with the Lord in Heaven, God is always with you (cf. Matthew 28:20). He is bigger and mightier than any giant. Thus, we can say what David said to his giant:

1 Samuel 17:47 "…for the battle is the LORD's…"

For Personal Reflection:

1. Read the story of David facing Goliath (1 Samuel 17:1-58). Reflect on the size difference between David and Goliath. Consider why David was so courageous when facing the giant. It was far more than youthful courage!

2. Talk to others about the battles they may be facing, reminding them that the God of David is mightier and stronger than any giant they will ever face.

Karon's Ministry Devotional #21

Preparing for Sundays

> Acts 2:41-47 "So then, those who had received his word were baptized; and that day there were added about three thousand souls. They were continually devoting themselves to the apostles' teaching and to fellowship, to the breaking of bread and to prayer. Everyone kept feeling a sense of awe; and many wonders and signs were taking place through the apostles. And all those who had believed were together and had all things in common; and they began selling their property and possessions and were sharing them with all, as anyone might have need. Day by day continuing with one mind in the temple, and breaking bread from house to house, they were taking their meals together with gladness and sincerity of heart, praising God and having favor with all the people. And the Lord was adding to their number day by day those who were being saved."

Jim and I love this passage for so many reasons. We marvel at the thought of our first-century brothers and sisters in Christ gathered for worship. We think about:

• The people receiving the word (i.e., the Gospel).

• The many baptisms—testimonies of the grace of God.

• The over three thousand souls who had come to Christ and many that followed.

• The devotion to the apostle's teaching.

• The sincere fellowship—meeting one another's needs.

• The breaking of bread (i.e., communion) house to house.

• The fervent prayer.

• The sense of awe.

• The many signs and wonders through the apostles.

• The togetherness and commonality.

• The sacrificial selling of their properties and possessions in order to give to needy people.

• The daily gathering "with one mind" in their place of worship.

• Taking their meals together in gladness and sincerity of heart.

• Praising God "together."

• Having favor with all the people—even outside in the community.

• Then…watching God add to their number day by day those who were being saved.

Wow! Imagine putting all of that in a report regarding what is truly happening in my church or yours. In the words of the old hymn: *What a fellowship. What a joy divine…*

Practically speaking, I also believe it took lots of preparation for these many people to gather for fellowship, teaching, communion, and worship. Many things had to be done "decently and in order" (cf. 1 Corinthians 14:40, King James Version) to allow for such undistracted worship to occur so that everyone could feel "a sense of awe" (Acts 2:43).

• Somebody had to help get the families situated.

• Somebody had to set up the gathering place for the crowd of people.

• Somebody had to prepare the meals.

• Somebody had to prepare the place for baptism and communion.

• Somebody had to plan for some control of the smaller kids.

And don't miss this!

• The wives and mothers had to prepare their families beforehand.

Anybody who has been in ministry for any length of time knows what can happen on a Saturday night or Sunday morning before church:

• Broken vehicles.

• Sick kids and pets.

• Kid fights (e.g., *"Hey, that's my sweater!"*).

• The unexpected.

We had a large family with three daughters and sometimes two foster children at any one time. Needless to say, it had its chaotic moments. So, here's what I used to do:

The night before church:

> • I prepared and laid out all our clothing.

> • I set the breakfast table with items that wouldn't spoil.

> • I reminded my husband to make sure our vehicles had gas.

> • I had a backup plan ready because stuff happens!

> • I prayed for all who were preparing for church tomorrow.

> • I chose not to schedule events on Saturday nights.

On the day of worship:

> • I got up early to be the first to get dressed and have some time to pray.

> • I prepared breakfast, as I woke the kids up.

> • I kept the noise to a minimum so Dad could pray and review his sermon notes and I could review my Sunday School lesson.

> • As we left for church, I reminded the kids of what our expectations and plans were.

• On the way to church, I often reflected on the words of Acts 2:41-47, as well as:

> Hebrews 10:24-25 "…let us consider how to stimulate one another to love and good deeds, not forsaking our own assembling together, as is the habit of some, but encouraging one another; and all the more as you see the day drawing near."

For Personal Reflection:

1. Develop a specific plan and backup plan for preparing for church. Share it with your family.

2. Read Acts 2:41-47 and Hebrews 10:24-25 to your family.

3. Take time to prepare your heart to gather for worship.

4. If you are teaching or ministering, review Jim's Ministry Devotional #15: *"Preparing My Heart for Effective Ministry."*

© Dr. James M. and Karon M. Cecy.

Karon's Ministry Devotional #22

Power Source

John 14:16-17, 26 "I will ask the Father, and He will give you another Helper, that He may be with you forever; that is the Spirit of truth, whom the world cannot receive, because it does not see Him or know Him, but you know Him because He abides with you and will be in you....But the Helper, the Holy Spirit, whom the Father will send in My name, He will teach you all things, and bring to your remembrance all that I said to you."

Acts 1:8 "...you will receive power when the Holy Spirit has come upon you..."

Once again, I wait patiently for my ministry friend to log on. How amazing it is that I can connect with someone in Bucharest, Romania.

"She's here!" I click the button to let her in my chat room and her beautiful face appears on the screen. We first met in Poland several years ago at the European Leadership Forum. She signed up for a mentoring appointment with me. Little did we know it would begin an intercontinental friendship.

After several years of thirty-minute conversations once a week, we know a lot about each other. We share a heart for ministry. We share victories over the challenges God has brought us through. She knows my family; I know hers. I marvel at her job as a research scientist—specializing in Quantum Theory. *"Wow, is she smart!"*
The best part about her is that she has become my true sister in the Lord.

What a wondrous world we live in that makes our relationship possible. When we think of communication in friendships we usually mean "in person" but my experience is that even a long-distance, global connection can be enjoyed through the power of modern technology. This is equally as true in my role as a missionary for JARON Ministries, as I mentor ministry leaders in many countries. It also applies on the home front.

One day, I got a desperate call from our daughter, "Can you please talk to my kids? They are not listening to me! I'll get them seated on the couch and I will open a video chat with you." Soon after, my husband and I have a close-up view of our wide-eyed grandkids lined up on the couch, not quite ready to receive their "Pa and Grammy Talk." I still remember my husband saying to the kids, "How dare you treat your mother—my daughter—my baby girl—with such disrespect." We proceeded, with the permission of their mother, to "lay down the law." It worked! Soon, the dishes were done, and their bedrooms were clean. *"Zip! Zop! All was quiet—for now!"* What an amazing time in which we live, where we can even discipline our grandchildren from a distance. My window to the world—near and far—is opened through the power of the internet.

The wonders of long-distance communication have especially caused me to reflect on the Holy Spirit's role in my life. Instantly, the connection is solid because He lives in me (cf. John 14:16-17, 26). I don't have to battle with a lost connection. There is no static. Perfect clarity. He speaks to my heart; I speak to His. He is with me wherever I go. I don't have to plug into an outlet. He gives me advice, convicts me, comforts me, and helps me to make decisions. The Holy Spirit motivates me to keep on the right path.

I am sad to admit sometimes I try to shut His voice down and unplug the connection. When that happens, He wakes me up in the middle of the night to speak to my heart. He pursues me when I am stubborn. He loves me enough to work with my weakness through His strength. He never gives up on me. And the best part of all—His connection to me is never broken. He is my constant Power Source.

For Personal Reflection:

1. Work on staying connected to loved ones far away through any means possible.

2. Use the illustration of electronic platforms that allow face-to-face communication to explain the Holy Spirit's intimate role in your life. Reflect on how the connection cannot be broken permanently when you are a child of God.

3. Read John 14:16-17 in your favorite version as you discuss the Holy Spirit's role in your life.

© Dr. James M. and Karon M. Cecy

Karon's Ministry Devotional #23

Life Lessons from Karon: "A Mother to Many"

> Proverbs 1:8-9 "Hear, my son, your father's instruction and <u>do not forsake your mother's teaching</u>. Indeed, they are a graceful wreath to your head and ornaments about your neck " (My emphasis).

> Proverbs 31:26 "She opens her mouth in wisdom, and the teaching of kindness is on her tongue."

> Titus 2:3-5 "Older women likewise are to be reverent in their behavior, not malicious gossips nor enslaved to much wine, teaching what is good, so that they may encourage the young women to love their husbands, to love their children, to be sensible, pure, workers at home, kind, being subject to their own husbands, so that the word of God will not be dishonored."

I am intrigued by the influence of women, especially the older women in the Bible. I am curious about why Deborah, the Prophet and Judge was, like no other woman, called "a mother in Israel" (cf. Judges 5:7). What qualified her for such a noble title? Was it her strength, her wisdom, her caring nature, or a host of other "motherly qualities" that attracted people to her? We certainly know her devotion to the Lord and how He mightily used her to deliver Israel (Read Judges, Chapters 4 and 5).

There have been many occasions in recent years when I have been called "a mother to many." I am not sure how well-deserved this title is. Most likely it is due to almost seventy-five years of life and fifty years of marriage and ministry. In that amount of time, one would hope I have learned some valuable lessons to pass on to others, especially those who are fellow Skilled Helpers. I am sure none of these are profound nor are they necessarily "quotable quotes" but they do come from my heart to yours.

My husband presented me with the categories; I added a few principles in hopes these will be helpful. Of course, I draw your attention to the Book of Proverbs and other Scriptures where the only truly "inspired" wisdom comes from (cf. 2 Timothy 3:16).

Lessons from Karon to All of Us

- *"Better to have someone love you for who you really are than for who you pretend to be."*

- *"Don't go to bed angry. Try to resolve your hurt before you close your eyes."*

- *"Don't let others reduce you to sin."*

- *"Don't let the disappointment of other's sin change who you are."*

- *"Truth is your friend."*

- *"You have to choose the kind of person you want to be."*

Lessons from Karon to All Wives

- *"Settle it in your heart of hearts; nagging doesn't work."*

- *"Stop trying to understand your husband; just love him."*

- *"Your husband needs you to tell him you are proud of him."*

Lessons from Karon to All Husbands

- *"A true gift costs you something—yourself!"*

- *"Don't buy your wife a gift that has a cord."*

- *"Just because she is emotional doesn't mean she is wrong."*

- *"Lead your wife by example, especially spiritually."*

- *"Listening to your wife is a gift to her."*

- *"Love your wife as Christ loves the Church" by giving yourself up for her* (cf. Ephesians 5:25-30).

- *"Love your wife the way she wants to be loved."*

- *"Of course, your wife wants you to go out of your way. In her mind, the 'long walk' is part of the gift."*

- *"Return to doing those courtship courtesies you used to do for her—like opening her door."*

- *"She may be different physically and emotionally, but she is the same spiritually. Treat her as a 'fellow heir of the grace of life'"* (cf. 1 Peter 3:7).

- *"Show your children that pleasing your wife, not them, is your highest priority."*

- *"Stop trying to fully understand your wife; just love her."*

- *'Tell her you love her every day. She will never tire of hearing it."*

- *"Treat her like she is still your girlfriend; not just your wife."*

- *"Try to get things done around the house <u>before</u> she asks."*

And, please, please, please...
- *"Put the toilet seat down!"*

Lessons from Mom to Her Children

- *"Make the Book of Proverbs your Life Book."*

- *"The best way to attract the friends and the kind of spouse you need is by walking in the Spirit and manifesting the fruit: love, joy, peace, patience, kindness, goodness, faithfulness, gentleness, and self-control."*

- *"When we tell you we love you, believe it."*

- *"Your friends are the biggest encouragement and the biggest threat to your maturity. Choose them wisely."*

Lessons from Mom to Her Adopted Children

- *"It was God's plan for you to be ours."*

- *"You may not look like us physically, but we desire for you to look like us spiritually."*

- *"You were not raised <u>under</u> my heart but <u>in</u> it."*

• *"We will speak well of your birth parents and family."*

• *"You will not offend us if you have a healthy relationship with your birth family. Of course, we will be a little sensitive when you tell us about your birth family, but tell us nonetheless."*

Lessons from Foster Mom ("Mommy Karon") to Her Foster Children

• *"Don't try so hard to be loved."*

• *"Our home is your home; our family is your family."*

• *"We will speak well of your parents."*

• *"We will expect you to abide by the same rules as the rest of the family."*

• *"You are safe here in our home."*

• *"You can eat anything as long as you ask. No hoarding."*

• *"You can't make us not love you"*
     (Bad English; life-giving point!)

Lessons from "Grammy" to Her Grandchildren

• *"Of course, when any of you ask, we will say <u>you</u> are our favorite."*

• *"Your Grammy and Pa raised your parents; everything they do is not their fault. Blame us if you want; they do."*

- *"'Truth is your friend!'—the same thing I told your parents when they were your age."*

- *"You can always count on us; we are here for you."*

And, as Pa likes to say:

- *"If we had known how much fun it is to have grandchildren, we would have found a way to have you first."*

Karon's Ultimate Lesson to All of Us

- *"Trusting in Christ and walking in obedience to Him is my single greatest desire for you. You are God's children; act like it!"*

> 3 John 1:4 "I have no greater joy than this, to hear of my children walking in the truth."

In the next devotional, I will focus on lessons to ministry wives. See you there!

For Personal Reflection:

1. Mark any of my life lessons that most impact your thinking.

2. Write down some life principles you can share with your family and friends. Feel free to use any of mine and make them your own.

3. Make a plan to read the Book of Proverbs one chapter at a time, underlining your favorites. Share them with your loved ones.

© Dr. James M. and Karon M. Cecy.

Karon's Ministry Devotional #24

To My Fellow Ministry Women

Isaiah 35:3 "Encourage the exhausted, and strengthen the feeble."

Acts 11:23 "...Then when he arrived and witnessed the grace of God, he rejoiced and began to encourage them all with resolute heart to remain true to the Lord..."

1 Thessalonians 5:11 "Therefore encourage one another and build up one another, just as you also are doing."

Hebrews 3:13 "...encourage one another day after day, as long as it is still called 'Today,' so that none of you will be hardened by the deceitfulness of sin."

In the last devotional, I shared some life lessons to wives, husbands, children, and grandchildren. The following life lessons are especially for ministry wives. Many of these can be applied to men, as well. Please accept these from my heart to yours:

• *"Beware of gossip and slander. Gossip is telling that which may be true to those who do not have the need to know. Slander is telling that which is false to anyone."*

• *"Beware of jealousy; it will destroy your joy and contentment. Instead, use this God-given emotion to stimulate your zeal to imitate people and their strengths."*

• *"Beware of seeing the ministry as a threat to your joy."*

• *"Choose carefully the ones with whom you pour out your heart, but make sure you have someone in whom you can confide."*

• *"Deal with expectations and hurts before the day is over so today's anger does not become tomorrow's unresolved conflict."*

• *"Determine, in advance of the need, who to go to if your marriage and family are in trouble."*

• *"Don't compare yourself to others. Just be the woman God made you to be."*

• *"Don't sacrifice your family on the altar of ministry."*

• *"Establish a habit of prayer for your spouse and children."*

• *"Give people your full attention, even if only for a few seconds."*

• *"Identify and watch out for the joy-stealers in your life."*

• *"If you are not a part of the solution, you may be part of the problem."*

• *"Keep all confidential information to yourself. Don't allow prayer requests to turn into 'sanctified gossip.'"*

• *"Learn from experience and other mature ministers how to properly deflect praise and handle criticism."*

• *"Learn how to deal with people who try to get to your ministry partner through you."*

• *"Learn how to respond to unrealistic expectations."*

• *"Learn how to turn into praise the unexpected ministry hours your spouse works."*

• *"Learn what to do when resentment invades your heart."*

• *"Learn what to do when your spouse or family is not doing well."*

• *"Learn when to speak up and when to give constructive criticism."*

• *"Look people in the eyes when you talk to them."*

• *"Make a list of your successful stress-relievers."*

• *"Make friends in your ministry. Yes, you may get hurt but it is worth the risk."*

• *"Meet often with other ministry wives and families to encourage and be encouraged."*

• *"Of course, you will get lonely in ministry. Draw close to the Lord, your family, and your close friends. Then minister to others who may be lonely."*

• *"Practice asking questions and being more interested in what others have to say."*

• *"Practice finding fulfilment using your own unique gifts and talents."*

• *"Practice memorizing names. This is your first step to showing people how important they are."*

• *"Practice seeing people as God sees them; not as you or others do."*

• *"Redirect people who are complaining to you about the ministry or another person."*

• *"Remember, 'hurt people hurt people.' Offer them grace, mercy, and understanding."*

• *"Remember, when you worship, focus on your priority to pay attention to God—your 'Audience of One.'"*

• *"Review often the rewards of seeing God use you in ministry."*

• *"Set clear boundaries for very draining people."*

• *"Take the time daily to refresh yourself physically, emotionally, and spiritually."*

• *"Tell someone you trust when you are losing your passion and drive for ministry."*

• *"The word 'No' can be a beautiful word if graciously expressed. However, you do not always have to give your specific reasons."*

- *"Understand 'living in a fishbowl' and 'under a microscope' is normal in ministry families. Turn it into an opportunity to be a major influence in the lives of others."*

- *"When you are not content and become critical, hear God telling you to stop it and stop it now."*

- *"When you are unfulfilled and empty, it may be God moving you to another place or type of ministry."*

- *"You will not be effective if you are empty and dried out."*

So much more could be listed. Why not add your own words of counsel?

For Personal Reflection:

1. Read the above words of counsel, marking the ones that are most important for your reflection and application now.

2. Write out your own words of counsel for yourself and others. Pass them on.

© Dr. James M. and Karon M. Cecy

(For further help, order "The Accountable Life: Protecting Myself and Others" by Dr. James M. Cecy. Available at www.amazon.com and www.jaron.org.)

Karon's Ministry Devotional #25

The World is Still Waiting for Us

> Psalm 71:18 "And even when I am old and gray, O God, do not forsake me, until I declare Your strength to this generation, Your power to all who are to come."

Jim and I began ministry in 1974. He was "officially" licensed to the Christian ministry on June 12, 1976. I joined in as his "sidekick" and "chief supporter."

I suppose it could be said that after five decades together—a century of combined ministry—he and I should be winding down and passing the baton to the younger folks. Certainly, the time has come to be even more committed to training the next generation of Christian leaders. That has always been our passion. Jim loves to say it as simply as he knows how, "I ain't dead...yet!"

General Booth, the Founder of the Salvation Army, who ministered until he died at eighty-four years old, said it well:

> "Your days at the most cannot be very long, so use them to the best of your ability for the glory of God and the benefit of your generation."

His wife, Catherine Booth, was considered to be "the mother of the Salvation Army." She often charged her nine children with something similar and equally as powerful:

> "You are not here in the world for yourself. You have been sent here for others. The world is waiting for you!"

The world is still waiting for us. I love that, don't you? So, rather than asking God to slow us down, we need to be asking Him

225

for greater strength. My prayer comes from the desire of the Apostle Paul for all of us:

> 2 Thessalonians 2:16-17 "Now may our Lord Jesus Christ Himself and God our Father, who has loved us and given us eternal comfort and good hope by grace, comfort and strengthen your hearts in every good work and word."

> Ephesians 6:10 "Finally, be strong in the Lord and in the strength of His might."

Jim often says to people,

> "It's not over until someone at your funeral squeezes your dead cheek and says, 'You're done.'"

Until then...

For Personal Reflection:

1. Why has God given you life? Might it be to be used by Him to share the Good News of the Gospel with others before you die?

2. Make a list of the ten people about whom you will pray God gives you an opportunity to point to Jesus. Do it before it is too late. The world is waiting for you!

© Dr. James M. and Karon M. Cecy.

PART THREE

JIM'S LESSONS
FROM A MILITARY
VETERAN

Jim's Veterans' Devotional #1

I am a Veteran

> 2 Timothy 2:1-4 "You, therefore, my son, be strong in the grace that is in Christ Jesus. The things which you have heard from me in the presence of many witnesses, entrust these to faithful men who will be able to teach others also. Suffer hardship with me, as a good soldier of Christ Jesus. No soldier in active service entangles himself in the affairs of everyday life, so that he may please the one who enlisted him as a soldier."

In 1969, as an enlisted man, I made the following Oath of Enlistment:

> *I, James Michael Cecy, do solemnly swear that I will support and defend the Constitution of the United States against all enemies, foreign and domestic; that I will bear true faith and allegiance to the same; and that I will obey the orders of the of the United States and the orders of the officers appointed over me, according to regulations and the Uniform Code of Military Justice. So help me God.*

I served six years in the U.S. Navy, first as a Naval Reservist and then on active duty during the Vietnam War, serving in the war zone on board the attack carrier *U.S.S. Kitty Hawk.* After my return from foreign service, I served briefly at Balboa Naval Hospital and ended active duty in November 1971. I returned to reserve status which also including a short period of full-time Temporary Active Duty at the Naval Reserve Center in Santa Cruz, California. I ended my military service in 1975.

I recently read two quotes that got my attention:

"My oath of enlistment has no date of expiration; my pledge of allegiance is for a lifetime."

"I took a DNA test. God is my Father. Veterans are my brothers"—and sisters, I might add.

According to the U.S. Department of Veterans Affairs, since the American Revolution in 1775, more than 42 million Americans have served in the military during a time of war. Over 650,000 Americans have been killed in battle serving our country around the world. Therefore, I am blessed to make the following declarations:

"I am a Military Veteran."

• I will salute the flag every time it "passes in review."

• I will show respect to service members of all branches of the military. Although our uniforms may have been different, the flag we saluted was the same. We will always be "brothers and sisters in arms."

• I will continue to minister to needy veterans and vote for their much-deserved support.

• I will remind our children and grandchildren of family members who proudly served in the past.

My wife's great, great, great uncle was a Medal of Honor recipient, fighting for the Union in the Civil War. Her grandfather was in the Army in World War I. My father was a member of the Canadian Army in World War II, serving with the Lincoln-Welland

Regiment. Their motto was *"Non nobis ned patriae"—"Not for ourselves but for our country."* My wife's father was a U.S. Navy medic on the *U.S.S. Dorothea Dix* during the 1944 Allied invasion of Normandy. Her uncle later served as a Navy Corpsman with the First Marine Division. That uncle's wife served in the Marine Corps. My older brothers were Vietnam Era sailors—one stationed at a missile base, the other at the Navy's TOPGUN Training School.

"I am a Navy Veteran."

• I served on the Attack Aircraft Carrier, *U.S.S. Kitty Hawk (CVA-63)*, and am now a proud member of the *U.S.S. Kitty Hawk Association*. Our ship was the first carrier to receive the Presidential Unit Citation and, during my time onboard, earned the Navy Unit Commendation.

• I will pray for my fellow sailors who are serving at sea, on land, or in the air—whether in a war zone or not.

• I will grieve over every ship that is decommissioned, dismantled, and sold for scrap. For a season, every one of those ships was someone's beloved home. *The Hawk*, recently scrapped, was mine.

• I will hold on to the unofficial and official Navy mottos:

• *Semper Fortis*—"Always Courageous."
• *Non sibi sed patriae*—"Not self but country."
• "Forged by the Sea."
• "Honor, Courage, Commitment." (Adopted by the U.S. Navy in 1992.)
• *Semper Paratus*—"Always Ready." (U.S. Coast Guard)

• I will shout with respect, *Oorah,* as I greet any Marine—in memory of our shipboard Marine Detachment (MARDET), with whom I was proud to serve alongside as they demonstrated their commitment to "improvise, adapt, and overcome."

• I will stand in silence at the statue of the Lone Sailor in Washington, D.C., the iconic symbol of the men and women of the Sea Service who proudly wore our Navy's uniform.

"I am a Vietnam War Veteran."

• I will never forget the countless lives of those who made the ultimate sacrifice.

• I will acknowledge every wounded warrior who suffers physically and emotionally.

• I will not minimize the efforts of those who did not (nor do not) fight on the front lines of battle. "All gave some; some gave all!"

• I will regularly visit the Vietnam War Memorial in Washington, D.C., where the names of over 58,000 who gave their lives are etched in black marble—including some of my *Kitty Hawk* and *Carrier Task Force 77* shipmates.

• I will allow my "survivor's guilt" to stimulate me to live and serve in such a way that brings honor to those who gave their lives.

• I will humbly accept the designation from the Veteran's Associations as a "combat veteran" even though I did not experience the bullets flying over my head. Such are my true heroes.

"I am a Veteran for Life."

• I am a proud member of *"The Thin Green Line"* that represents veterans and active service veterans of the U.S. Military, protecting our nation from all threats.

• I will render, for as long as I live, a handshake, a pat on the back, or an appropriate salute to all of my fellow veterans.

• I will honor the many sacrifices of fellow veterans and ministers–mighty men and women of valor–who went ahead of me and those who come behind me.

"I am a Christian Veteran."

On November 17, 1971, the very day I left for home after serving on active naval service, I trusted in Jesus Christ alone for my salvation. On that day I became a Soldier of the Cross and, without really understanding it at the time, a Minister of the Gospel. My standing orders have been clear for over fifty years. They are worth repeating often:

2 Timothy 2:1-4 "You, therefore, my son, be strong in the grace that is in Christ Jesus. The things which you have heard from me in the presence of many witnesses, entrust these to faithful men who will be able to teach others also. Suffer hardship with me, as a good soldier of Christ Jesus. No soldier in active service entangles himself in the affairs of everyday life, so that he may please the one who enlisted him as a soldier."

I love the words of the song:

> *I pledge allegiance to the Lamb,*
> *With all my strength,*
> *With all I am.*
> *I will seek to honor His commands.*
> *I pledge allegiance to the Lamb.*

> *(Shepherd Boy Music, Word Music, LLC.)*

"My Christian Oath of Enlistment is Dear to My Heart."

• I will be strong in the grace and mercy found in Jesus Christ (2 Timothy 2:1).

• I will learn from past generations of disciples and prepare the next generation of faithful and Skilled Helpers to do the same (2 Timothy 2:2).

• I will willingly suffer hardship as a good soldier of Jesus Christ (2 Timothy 2:3).

• I will keep my focus on Jesus and not get entangled in the affairs of everyday life (2 Timothy 2:4).

• I will have as my life goal to please the One who is my Commanding Officer and enlisted me as a Soldier of the Cross (2 Timothy 2:4).

"I am a Soldier in the Army of My God."

The following comes from an anonymous source. I wish I knew the author so I could thank him or her. I have benefited greatly from reading this from time to time. It helps me regain my perspective. I hope you feel the same:

I am a soldier in the Army of God. The Lord Jesus Christ is my commanding officer. The Holy Bible is my code of conduct. Faith, Prayer and the Word are my weapons of warfare. I have been taught the Word of God, trained by experience, tried by adversity, and tested by fire. I am a volunteer in this army, and I am enlisted for eternity. I will retire in this army at times end or die in this army; but I will not sell out, be talked out or pushed out.

I am faithful, reliable, capable, and dependable. If my God needs me, I am there. If he needs me in Sunday school, to teach children, work with youth, help adults or just sit and learn, he can use me, because I am there. I am a soldier. I do not need to be pampered, petted, primed up, picked up, or pepped up. I am a soldier. I am not a wimp. I am in place, saluting my King, obeying his orders, praising his name, and building his kingdom. No one has to send me flowers, gifts, food, cards, candy, or give me handouts. I do not need to be cuddled, cradled, cared for, or catered to.

I am committed. I cannot have my feelings hurt bad enough to turn me around. I cannot be discouraged enough to turn me aside. I cannot lose enough to cause me to quit. When Jesus called me into his army, I had nothing. If I end up with nothing, I will still break even. I will win. My God will supply all my needs. I am more than a conqueror. I will always triumph.

I can do all things through Christ. Demons cannot defeat me. People cannot disillusion me. Weather cannot weary me. Sickness cannot stop me. Battles cannot beat me. Money cannot buy me. Governments cannot silence me and hell cannot handle me. I am a soldier. Even death cannot destroy me, for when my commander calls me from this battlefield, he will promote me to live with him. I am a soldier, and I'm marching, claiming victory! I will not give up. I am a soldier! I will not turn around. I am a soldier marching heaven-bound! Here I stand. Will you stand with me? (Author unknown).

Fellow Veterans, let me ask you:

Will you stand with me?

Fellow Christians, let me also ask you:

Will you stand with me?

For Personal Reflection:

1. Approach a veteran or anyone on active military duty and <u>sincerely</u> express, "Thank you for your service." Teach your children to do the same.

2. What does it mean to you to be enlisted by your Supreme Commander, the Lord Jesus Christ, as a Soldier of the Cross?

3. In what ways are you "entangled" in the affairs of everyday life?

© Dr. James M. and Karon M. Cecy.

Jim's Veterans' Devotional #2

"The Hawk" Was My Home

> 2 Corinthians 5:8 "We are of good courage, I say, and prefer rather to be absent from the body and to be at home with the Lord."

"The Hawk" was My Temporary Home

As a young man, the *U.S.S. Kitty Hawk (CVA-63)* was my temporary home for almost two years. I remember my first view of this massive ship. How intimidating to realize this was now my home. Let me tell you about *The Hawk*:

- It was a conventional, non-nuclear powered, attack aircraft carrier, commissioned in 1961 at a cost of about $265 million (about 3 billion in today's dollars).

- The ship was a floating city for up to 5,000 sailors and airmen, as well as a Marine Detachment.

- *The Hawk* was over 1080 feet long and about 280 feet wide. If you stood it on end it was about as high a 110-story building (i.e., higher than the Empire State Building).

- The flight deck itself was about four and a half acres.

- The engines created about 280,000 horsepower and it could travel at over thirty knots (about thirty-five miles per hour).

- *The Hawk* had a two-million-gallon fuel capacity.

• Each of its four propellers were twenty-one feet wide.

• The ship had two thirty-ton anchors, each of the links weighing 360 pounds.

• Its four restaurants served over 17,000 meals daily (e.g., up to 12,000 eggs daily).

• The *U.S.S. Kitty Hawk* was a floating airport for about nine air squadrons totaling about eighty aircraft with nicknames like Skyhawks, Intruders, Phantoms, Crusaders, Vigilantes, Skywarriors, Prowlers, Corsairs, and Hawkeyes, We also carried Sea Hawk and Huey helicopters. Our most popular airplane, the COD (Carrier Onboard Delivery), delivering 2500 pounds of mail daily.

• The ship was equipped with four steam-powered catapults that launched aircraft day and night.

• It had two hangar bays, totaling 1.6 acres and equipped with four elevators to the flight deck.

• While at sea, *The Hawk* was protected by an armada of cruisers, destroyers, escorts, and submarines while being serviced by various supply ships.

At the time, the *U.S.S. Kitty Hawk—"The Battle Cat"*—was considered to be "the most dangerous 4.5 acres in history." When we first boarded we were given a matchbook with the title, *"The Hawk is My Ship."* It truly was.

The Hawk was decommissioned in 2009 as one of the longest-serving aircraft carriers in the history of modern naval warfare. As a fellow shipmate, I was invited to be on her last cruise to her "resting station" in Bremerton, Washington. I was not able to go due to an unexpected medical issue at the time. I admit I was deeply affected when she was later sold for a penny to a dismantler. I wept as I saw the videos of this once-mighty warship dragged into port by tugboats. She is now scrap metal. However, she will always be remembered as *My Home*!

Fresno is My Present Home

In my first eleven years in Toronto, Canada, we lived in several apartments in York Township. Over the rest of my life (with the exception of my Navy days), I lived in California in places like Santa Cruz, Felton, North Hollywood, San Mateo, Irvine, and Scotts Valley. We eventually moved to Fresno—the place where I have lived for almost thirty-five years and the place where I hope to be buried. Let me tell you about my Fresno home:

> • It's a multi-ethnic city of over 500,000 people in a county of over a million.

> • It is a part of the San Joaquin Valley, known for being a place of the most abundant and productive agriculture. Some say it deserves the title as "bread basket of the world."

> • There are over 400 churches—"Branch Offices of the Body of Christ."

I truly love Fresno even where the temperature can reach 110 degrees Fahrenheit (i.e., over 43 degrees Celsius). I often tease and tell people it makes preaching about hell a lot easier. I quickly add that it's not the end of the world but I can see it from here. Actually, I love Fresno because it is an amazing community of warm and welcoming people. It is an honor to live and minister here.

Heaven is My Forever Home

It is sometimes said the people of God have always been "a people in search of a place." In the Old Testament, they were in search of the Promised Land, the land "flowing with milk and honey" (Exodus 3:8). In the New Testament, Jesus points us even higher:

> John 14:1-3 "Do not let your heart be troubled; believe in God, believe also in Me. In My Father's house are many dwelling places; if it were not so, I would have told you; for I go to prepare a place for you. If I go and prepare a place for you, I will come again and receive you to Myself, that where I am, there you may be also."

Something happened in 1971 when I trusted in Jesus Christ alone for my salvation. I was promised eternal life in a forever home called Heaven. Let me tell you about my Heavenly Home:

• It is a real place Jesus Himself is preparing for us (John 14:1-3).

• It is a place indescribable in human terms (1 Corinthians 2:9).

• It's a place where there will be no more tears and pain (Revelation 21:1-4).

• It's a place where I will be with my believing family (1 Thessalonians 4:17).

• It's the place where I will meet Jesus face to face (Revelation 22:4).

• It's the place I will call *home*—forever! (2 Corinthians 5:8)

The Hawk was my temporary home. Fresno is my present home. Heaven is my forever home. Nothing compares! Thus, my homebound spirit sings the popular children's song by O.A. Lambert:

> *Heaven is a wonderful place*
> *Filled with glory and grace.*
> *I wanna to see my Savior's face.*
> *Cause Heaven is a wonderful place.*
> *(I wanna go there!)*

> *(R.J. Stevens Music, LLC.)*

For Personal Reflection:

1. How do you describe your early home and your heavenly home?

2. As a born-again Christian, what do you look forward to most about your future home in Heaven?

© Dr. James M. and Karon M. Cecy.

Jim's Veterans' Devotional #3

Be the Captain of My Ship

> 1 Timothy 1:17 "Now to the King eternal, immortal, invisible, the only God, be honor and glory forever and ever. Amen."

I was born in 1950 at a Salvation Army hospital in Toronto, Canada. As an underdeveloped, premature baby, I was not expected to live. My mother told me a group of Salvation Army officers laid hands on my incubator and prayed God would save this shriveled-up little boy and prepare him for Christian service. So, by God's grace, here I am.

I have lived to experience almost seventy-five Christmases and New Year's celebrations. Many carry with them some special memories of slinkies, hula hoops, transistor radios, and reel-to-reel recorders.

Admittedly, some of those holidays were rather painful. In 1961, I left Canada to live with my father and my stepmother in Santa Cruz, California. It was hard for an eleven-year-old to be separated from his mother and the Canadian white Christmases. It was also difficult, at the age of nineteen, to face the holidays in 1969, just weeks after my father died of a heart attack at the age of forty-nine.

However, there is one holiday season, in particular, that especially sticks out in my mind—the Christmas of 1970. Before my father's death in 1969, I had joined the U.S. Naval Reserve. Eventually, I was assigned to serve on active duty aboard the attack carrier, the *U.S.S. Kitty Hawk (CVA-63)*. I started out assigned as a damage controlman, manning a fire curtain control station during battle readiness. I ended up working daily in the ship's personnel office, partially with the Legal Department.

In November of 1970, at the age of twenty, we headed out for a nine-month West Pacific tour of duty to Southeast Asia. Our main mission was to provide air support for our troops in Vietnam, Laos, and Cambodia. More on this in other devotionals.

However, I especially want to talk about that first Christmas at sea in 1970. I regularly hung out at the back of the ship; the aft portion of the ship called the stern. This was the area where they tested the jet engines, where the dirty mops were cleaned, and the ship's garbage was tossed. It happens to also be an area called the poop deck and not for reasons you think. In some ways, it was my "quiet place" if there is such a thing on a warship. In some senses, it became my church.

There were twenty-one worship services held every week on the ship. I never went to one. What's significant is that church services were held at the front, the forward bow of the ship, in a place called the Forecastle (pronounced foc'sl), where the anchor was stored. I hung out at the back of the ship where the garbage was kept and as far away from the "spiritual section" of the ship as possible. In fact, at the time I mocked anyone who tried to persuade me to get right with God.

There was one particular shipmate who was a devout Christian who read his Bible every night. I gave him such a bad time for refusing to go out and get drunk with us on shore leave. Yes, getting drunk had become my way of dulling the pain and pretending I had my life in control. What a lie that was!

At one point we spent fifty-seven days at sea, without seeing land. Oh, how small I felt on that vast ocean. Oh, how lonely I felt, even with 4,700 guys on the ship. One day a navy photographer took my picture as I was staring off into the distance. It captured what was going on in my heart. Later, in the cruise book, he placed a caption at the bottom of my picture that said, "...Cecy...sometimes feels like 'the loneliest man in town'..." And it was so true...I did feel that way!

During that lonely holiday season, I often took a break from work and sat at the back of the ship. I was consumed by the thought that my family and friends were on the other side of the world—some in California; some Canada. On one particular night, we were at battle readiness and the ship was dimly lit with hard-to-see red lights. It was surreal.

In the darkness, I felt especially alone, reflecting on the emptiness of my life and the uncertainty of my future. I concluded there was really nothing left to live for! I stared at the churning water and amazing power of the four twenty-one-foot-wide propellers, leaving a wake a mile long. I thought to myself:

"No one would know if I just slipped into the sea and got chewed up by these giant propellers. Then my mother would get twice my insurance for me being lost in a war zone."

I grabbed the safety chain and flicked my cigarette over the side. I still remember the sound—*ppffffit*—and the smell of the ocean spray. It stopped me for a moment as I gazed at the phosphorescent water churning with the eerie green light given off by millions of floating microscopic plankton. It was then I began to get a bit philosophical, maybe even a bit theological.

"God, if You are real and if You can use these tiny creatures to reflect light, why can't You use me?"

It was then I stood and looked to the sky and whispered:

"God, if You are real, show me!"

I expected an angel or something to show up or some church bell to ring, but nothing happened. I went back to my sleeping quarters and laid on my rack (i.e., my bed). I dug through my locker and found a Bible I got when one of my "drinking buddies" talked me into going with him to a church in San Diego. (I still have it. It's a *Brother Jimmy Roper's Dial-a-Prayer Bible, set forth in the King James Version.*)

I began flipping through the pages, not knowing what to read. Remember that guy I mocked for reading his Bible? He saw me with a Bible in my hand, which was quite a shock to him! He asked, "What's going on, Spider?" (Yes, that was my horrible nickname, given to me because I was small but had a nasty sting! That's a whole other story.)

I told my shipmate that I was just searching in the Bible for some answers. He turned in my Bible to Matthew 7:7-11 and said, "Why don't you start with this?" The following are the exact words I read from that exact Bible over fifty years ago. In fact, I whispered them out loud as I read:

> *Ask, and it shall be given you; seek, and ye shall find; knock, and it shall be opened unto you: For everyone that asketh receiveth; and he that seeketh findeth; and to him that knocketh it shall be opened. Or what man is there of you, whom if his son ask bread, will he give him a stone? Or if he ask a fish, will he give him a serpent? If ye then, being evil, know how to give good gifts unto your children, how much more shall your Father which is in heaven give good things to them that ask him?" (Matthew 7:7-11, King James Version).*

Because I had studied a bit of Shakespeare in college, the King James English didn't seem so strange. However, these words struck my heart as nothing I had ever read before.

That night, I began reading other Scriptures and pondered for months what it would mean to become "born-again" and follow Christ. I asked myself:

"What would I have to do to become a follower of Jesus? Where would He lead me? What would I have to give up?"

It wasn't long before I realized I would have to give up ME! My pride. My insistence on running my own life—being the captain of my own ship!

We finished our nine-month tour of duty in Vietnam and arrived back in San Diego in July of 1971. I eventually ended up at Balboa Naval Hospital to have surgery for yet another broken nose. (I seemed to stick it too often in other people's business!) It was just months away from the end of my active duty, so I stayed on working at the hospital. It was there I met Eddie, a heroin addict. Surprisingly, he told me he was a Christian, which fed my idea that Christianity was full of hypocrites.

One night, before he put a needle in his arm, he threw me a copy of a book, entitled *The Late Great Planet Earth* by Hal Lindsay. It was there in the pages of that book I realized I was on the wrong team. I was headed for hell and understood for the first time how to receive Christ. However, I still needed time to think. I knew I was a phony. A con man. A sneak. A game-player. An abuser and user of people. Yes, I was well-deserving of the nickname "Spider." But this time I needed to be sure this "following Jesus thing" was really worth it.

The more I prayed, and the more I read Scripture, the more convinced I became. God was calling me to be a disciple of Jesus Christ even before I had figured out what it all meant. It was what my older brother, Brian, had been trying to tell me even before I shipped out. He and his wife had both become born-again Christians.

So, on Wednesday, November 17, 1971, on the very day I was released from active naval duty, God prepared my heart for the best decision I have ever made. It was 2 o'clock in the afternoon at 32nd Street Naval Station in San Diego. I was standing on a sidewalk in my dress blue uniform with release orders in hand. I knew it was time to start a new life—a life of following Christ.

I tried to pray but couldn't. Then I stood in the gutter. It seems odd now, but it wasn't then. Given my pride, it just felt right. I don't remember all of the exact words I quietly prayed but they went something like this:

> *"Jesus, if You are real, help me. Thank You for dying for my sin. I don't know how You could forgive me but if You are real, I give You my life."*

Then I whispered some words I do remember—words that were to be the constant battle of my life from that day forward:

> *"Jesus, be the Boss of my life."*

I knew even then how much I needed Him, not just to forgive my sins, but to run my life. I had made such a mess of it. I needed to resign as General Manager of the Universe. It was shortly after God brought to my mind a hymn by Ignaz Franz I first sang as a young child in church. It now expressed the words of my heart as never before—words that said, "You are the Lord of my life!"

> *Holy God, we praise Thy Name;*
> *Lord of all, we bow before Thee!*
> *All on earth Thy scepter claim,*
> *All in Heaven above adore Thee;*
> *Infinite Thy vast domain,*
> *Everlasting is Thy reign.*

I had moved back to my hometown of Santa Cruz, California. I cannot tell you how wonderful that first Thanksgiving and Christmas were, now as a born-again believer. Suddenly, the familiar old Christmas songs had great meaning:

Joy to the World,
The Lord is come.
Let Earth receive her King.

Words of the Apostle Paul became my battle cry:

Romans 10:9-10 "…if you confess with your mouth Jesus as Lord, and believe in your heart that God raised Him from the dead, you will be saved; for with the heart a person believes, resulting in righteousness, and with the mouth he confesses, resulting in salvation."

Here I am over fifty Christmases later, having been in pastoral ministry for most of them. In the words of the old sailor,

"Save a wretch like me. He shall never hear the end of it."

And in the words of a song I began to sing as a new believer in 1971:

I have anchored my soul in the Haven of Rest.

And now my soul cries out to the One who is the Captain of My Ship. May I bring Him honor and glory forever.

For Personal Reflection:

Read Romans 10:9-10. In what area of your life do you have the most difficulty submitting to Christ's lordship?

© Dr. James M. and Karon M. Cecy.

Jim's Veterans' Devotional #4

"Man Your Battle Stations!"

> Jude 1:3 "Beloved, while I was making every effort to write you about our common salvation, I felt the necessity to write to you appealing that you contend earnestly for the faith which was once for all handed down to the saints."

One day, off the coast of Vietnam, we had gale force winds, and our ship, an attack aircraft carrier, was pitching deep in the water. Because of the high waves, an enemy boat with a single torpedo could have snuck past our air and sea defenses, as well as our radar. It could have easily headed straight for us, torpedo-armed, and be within range to blow us out of the water. All 4,700 of us would have been in grave danger.

Although I did not know the details, the scuttlebutt (i.e., the Navy rumor mill) spread like wildfire. We were under attack at a very vulnerable time. I remember the announcement well:

> "General Quarters. General Quarters. All hands man your Battle Stations. This is not a drill. This is not a drill!"

As the waves crashed against the sides of the ship, I was tossed back and forth. My battle station was a fire control room where my job was to close the hangar bay doors and light off the fire curtains when ordered by the Combat Information Center to do so.

After we were released from General Quarters, the scuttlebutt continued among the crew with the account of one of our helicopters, armed with machine guns, finally able to take control of the danger. Frankly, I believe the story to be true.

There has been a dangerous battle going on for centuries—a battle to make sure people have the right view of who Jesus Christ really is and what He came to do. You and I know the internet is filled with theological torpedoes and heretical missiles threatening to sink Christianity. In essence, we are all being given a call to arms:

"General Quarters. General Quarters. All disciples to your Battle Stations. This is not a drill."

One of the ways the early church combated continual threats of false teaching was to design formal statements of beliefs. They were called creeds, from the Latin verb *credo*, which means "I believe." These creeds—these "I believe" statements—generally emphasized the biblical doctrines opposing those errors thought to be the most dangerous at the time. For example, in the fourth century, the Nicene Creed was first adopted by the Council of Nicaea in A.D. 325. It was finally edited and approved by the Council of Constantinople in A.D. 381. It was presented primarily to affirm the full deity and full humanity of the Incarnate Son of God, Jesus Christ:

We believe in one God, the Father almighty, maker of heaven and earth, of all things visible and invisible. And in one Lord Jesus Christ, the only Son of God, begotten from the Father before all ages, God from God, Light from Light, true God from true God, begotten, not made; of the same essence as the Father. Through him all things were made. For us and for our salvation he came down from heaven; he became incarnate by the Holy Spirit and the virgin Mary, and was made human. He was crucified for us under Pontius Pilate; he suffered and was buried. The third day he rose again, according to the Scriptures. He ascended to heaven and is seated at the right hand of the Father. He will come again with glory to judge the living and the dead. His kingdom will never end. And we believe in the Holy Spirit, the Lord, the giver of life. He proceeds from the Father and the Son, and with the Father and the Son is worshiped and glorified. He spoke through the prophets. We believe in one holy catholic and apostolic church. We affirm one baptism for the forgiveness of sins. We look forward to the resurrection of the dead, and to life in the world to come. Amen.

With so many threats to sound doctrine, may this ancient "I believe" statement become the present-day creed of our lives.

For Personal Reflection:

1. Read the Nicene Creed more carefully, underlining the portions that strike you most.

2. Why not join the millions of Christians throughout the ages and memorize the Nicene Creed? As a minimum, make a copy and plan on reading it once a month.

© Dr. James M. and Karon M. Cecy.

Jim's Veterans' Devotional #5

Leave No Man Behind

> Luke 19:10 "For the Son of Man has come to seek and to save that which was lost."

> Matthew 18:12-14 "What do you think? If any man has a hundred sheep, and one of them has gone astray, does he not leave the ninety-nine on the mountains and go and search for the one that is straying? If it turns out that he finds it, truly I say to you, he rejoices over it more than over the ninety-nine which have not gone astray. So it is not the will of your Father who is in heaven that one of these little ones perish."

"Man overboard! Man overboard! This is not a drill." I was around twenty years old when I first heard these words while on the way to "Yankee Station"—the place off the coast of Vietnam where we launched our aircraft to assist the troops. Apparently, one of our shipmates was blown off the flight deck during flight operations. We searched for days. He was never found.

That was over fifty years ago, but I will never forget the helpless feelings as the hours and days passed in our sweeping searches. I remember the ache when the rescue and recovery operations were called off and we moved on. Yes, we left a man behind!

I have often wondered what might have been if we had searched just one more day, in one more effort to find him. It still brings sadness to my heart, especially as I try to imagine what his family feels when they see his name etched on a memorial wall in Washington, D.C. *"Why didn't they keep searching? Why did they leave him for lost?"*

My mind reflects often on the many passages of Scripture about God's rescue operations to deliver us as spiritually drowning people. My heart rejoices in His amazing grace that causes me to sing, *"I once was lost, but now I'm found..."* My spirit is also challenged to never give up praying for and participating in God's Search and Rescue Team to the "dying shipmates" in my family, neighborhood, country, and world.

May the Lord always keep us on the lookout for the lost He came to save (cf. Luke 19:10). May our hearts break over the things that break His heart. May we make the most of every opportunity God gives us to rescue souls (cf. Colossians 4:5).

One more day! One more effort! One more life saved!

For Personal Reflection:

1. Take some time to list the names of family members and friends who are "lost" and do not have the hope that comes through a personal relationship with Jesus Christ.

2. What is your plan to do your best to "leave no one behind"?

3. Read the Parable of the Lost Sheep (Matthew 18:11-14; Luke 15:3-7)

© Dr. James M. and Karon M. Cecy

Jim's Veterans' Devotional #6

"Abandon Ship!"

> Acts 27:23 "For this very night an angel of the God to whom I belong and whom I serve stood before me..."

> Acts 28:30-31 "And he [Paul] stayed two full years in his own rented quarters and was welcoming all who came to him, preaching the kingdom of God and teaching concerning the Lord Jesus Christ with all openness, unhindered."

There was one grueling two-month period of time at sea during which we could not see land for fifty-seven long days. Not one mountain. Not one shoreline. Nothing but seawater.

When we were not in combat operations, we were in training. There was one drill often not taken seriously:

> "Abandon Ship! Abandon Ship! This is a drill! This is a drill."

In our inexperience, I mocked the exercise, *"This will never happen. Look at the size of this ship. What a waste of time!"* However, no "salty" sailor ever wanted to hear those dreaded words.

> "Abandon Ship! Abandon Ship! This is <u>not</u> a drill! This is <u>not</u> a drill."

It meant we were sinking and there was nothing that could be done. None of us were ready to "go down with the ship." Our first thoughts were, *"Where's the nearest lifeboat?"* An even more frightening thought was, *"Forget the lifeboats, where do I jump?"*

During Navy Boot Camp, recruits go through a number of drills to prepare them in case they have to abandon ship. We were trained to look for oil fires on the water, jump from an open deck with our arms open to dispel the oil, dive deep, and come up flailing our arms to spread the fiery oil before it sticks to our skin. We were taught to swim away from the vortex of water from a sinking ship that could suck us below the surface. We also practiced treading water while we removed our wet clothes and tied them in knots. Thus, the bell bottoms and tunic could be filled with air and used as "water wings." Even the little white "dixie cup" hat sailors wear could be used as a flotation device—so they said. It worked in Boot Camp, but it was certainly not something I wanted to test in a real life-or-death situation.

By the way, I cheated on my Navy swim test, so there was not much hope for me. My survival strategy was to find a swimmer who paid attention in Boot Camp and hang onto him until help came. Hopefully, he also was bigger and more attractive to sharks! My ultimate plan was to suck in as much water as possible and take up residence in Davy Jones' Locker a few hundred fathoms below. In my mind, a shipwreck was certain death for an ill-equipped sailor. Then again, survival adrenaline and the will to live might have had their way of keeping me alive.

In Acts 27, we read the record of the first part of the Apostle Paul's journey to Rome in the fall of A.D. 60 to stand before Caesar, as God had promised (cf. Acts 23:11). It is a risky time to travel by ship and Paul warns of the danger. The Roman centurion, however, listens to the ship's pilot and the captain instead. Bad call!

A violent storm threatens the ship and all on board. An angel of God appears to the Apostle Paul and assures him God has granted all 276 of them will arrive safely in Rome, but not without running aground. They arrive on the island of Malta, as the story continues in Chapter 28.

Before we get there, let's consider some "Lessons from a Shipwreck." First, it is wise to take advice from someone who can speak of God "to whom I belong and whom I serve" (Acts 27:23)— who speaks to God and hears from God. Secondly, sometimes the promises of God involve violent storms and a few shipwrecks. Ultimately, He will lead us to where He promised.

Later in Acts 28, we find the Apostle Paul and the entire shipwrecked crew safely on the Island of Malta. It is now the spring of A.D. 61—six months after they left Caesarea for Rome. Paul is healed from a deadly snake bite and heals many of the island people of their diseases. Boarding a third ship, off to Rome they sail, landing in Puteoli (Naples, Italy). Chained to his guards, Paul meets a few Christian brethren there and later travels to Rome.

For two years he lives under guard but nonetheless preaching about Christ "with all openness, unhindered" (Acts 28:31)—for now. Many believe it was during this time he wrote some of the epistles. Thus ends the Book of Acts. Yet, there is more to the story. Let's call it:

Acts 29: The Next Chapter in Church History

Did the Apostle Paul stand before Caesar? Many think he did (cf. Philippians 4:22). Did Caesar release him? Many believe so and he continued his missionary service for a few more years. However, sometime following the great fire in the City of Rome in A.D. 64, Paul was arrested, imprisoned in Rome, and eventually beheaded. There's even more to the story. On to the next devotional!

For Personal Reflection:

Take the time to read and reflect on Acts 27-28.

© Dr. James M. and Karon M. Cecy.

Jim's Veterans' Devotional #7

Suffering Our Own Shipwreck

> 1 Timothy 1:18-19 "This command I entrust to you, Timothy, my son, in accordance with the prophecies previously made concerning you, that by them you fight the good fight, keeping faith and a good conscience, which some have rejected and suffered shipwreck in regard to their faith."

The Apostle Paul was shipwrecked not just once but at least three times! Listen to his testimony:

> 2 Corinthians 11:25 "...three times I was shipwrecked, a night and a day I have spent in the deep."

In our last devotional, we shared the details of the Apostle Paul and 276 others who were shipwrecked yet, by God's grace and mercy, were able to safely make it to the island of Malta (cf. Acts 28:1). It is obvious he and the rest of the crew had passed "Shipwreck Survival School."

Let's move on to what some preachers like to call "*Acts 29: The Rest of the Story.*" No need to check, there is no Acts 29. However, if there had been, I believe it would not be about the Apostle Paul. It would be about us—the people to whom he passed the baton of responsibility to share the good news to fellow "shipwrecked people" concerning the Lord Jesus Christ and to do so "with all openness, unhindered" (Acts 28:30-31)—at least, for now.

But what keeps it from happening? Our own shipwrecks! No, not the deep-sea kind. There is a kind of shipwreck that, in the mind of the Apostle Paul, is far worse—those who "suffered" shipwreck (i.e., who were stranded; Greek: *nauageo*) in regard to their faith" (1 Timothy 1:19).

Many historians point out that the Apostle Paul may also have been referring to the deadly crashes during chariot races (in Latin: *naufragia*)—the land-based shipwrecks. Both are graphic descriptions:

A shipwrecked life is a life that is:

> • Burned by the sticky fires of lust and sin (cf. Proverbs 6:27-29; James 1:15).

> • Crushed by the consequence of neglect (cf. 1 Timothy 1:18-19).

> • Driven and tossed in the surf of doubt (cf. James 1:6).

> • Falling prey to the false-teaching brood of poisonous vipers (cf. Matthew 3:7).

> • Sucked into the vortex of division (cf. 1 Corinthians 12:25).

> • Suffering from an unquenchable spiritual thirst (cf. Psalm 42:1-3).

> • Tossed around by the waves and carried about by the winds of false doctrine (cf. Ephesians 4:14).

It's time to pay attention to the Holy Spirit's "Shipwreck Survival School." You will never know when you will need it most. What does that course of action look like?

• Learning how to admit, confess, and turn from deceitful lust and sin (cf. 1 John 1:9).

• Learning how to fight the good fight, keeping the faith and a good conscience (cf. 1 Timothy 1:18-19).

• Learning how to seek the Lord with all your heart (cf. Matthew 6:33).

• Learning how to stand on solid ground and resist the devil (cf. Ephesians 4:14-15, 6:10; 1 Peter 5:9).

• Learning to trust the authority of the reliable Word of God (cf. 2 Timothy 3:16).

• Learning how to trust the Lord and not fickle feelings (cf. Proverbs 3:5-7).

Where do we find that kind of training? Just ask your pastors, elders, and spiritual leaders. We do not need to be a victim of any emotional, moral, or spiritual shipwreck. Help is just a step away— once we make the S.O.S. call for help. By the way, S.O.S. means "Save Our Souls." How appropriate is that?

The Anchor Holds is a song written by Lawrence Chewning in 1992, after losing his father and baby in what he calls "a year of sorrows." The song has ministered to many who have suffered a dark night of the soul, a deep season of discouragement, and their faith being shipwrecked. May it do so for you:

I have journeyed,
Through the long, dark night,
Out on the open sea.
By faith alone,

Sight unknown,
And yet His eyes were watching me.

The anchor holds,
Though the ship is battered.
The anchor holds,
Though the sails are torn.

I have fallen on my knees,
As I faced the raging seas.
The anchor holds,
In spite of the storm.

In the darkest storms, we hold on to the promise:

> Hebrews 6:19 "This hope we have as anchor of the soul,
> a hope both sure and steadfast…"

For Personal Reflection:

1. In what ways, specifically, has your life "suffered shipwreck" in the past?

2. If it is a present struggle, to whom do you need to reach out with an S.O.S.?

© Dr. James M. and Karon M. Cecy.

Jim's Veterans' Devotional #8

A Fireman or Not?

2 Thessalonians 3:13 "But as for you, brethren, do not grow weary of doing good."

My wife comes from a long line of public servants—cops, medics, and firefighters. Her grandfather was a firefighter in Indiana. Some family members say he was a fire chief or a captain. One of my favorite cousins was a firefighter in the City of Toronto.

My own experience with firefighting was cut short but not without some major lessons and a great deal of respect for all the members of the community of firefighters. My days in the U.S. Navy began my lifelong season of respect for members of the Fire Service.

Fire is the most feared thing on a ship. There is no place to run, and any fire can quickly require "all hands on deck." Since the fire disaster on the *U.S.S. Forrestal* in 1969, every U.S. Navy sailor is required to attend a short course in Shipboard Firefighting. Mine was held in 1969 at the Damage Control School in San Diego. I later attended a second time while serving on the *U.S.S. Kitty Hawk*. Fundamentally, our training was based on the axiom: "A good firefighter knows how; an educated firefighter knows why." It was at this training school I learned some things I have never forgotten:

• **The basics of fire science.** Oxygen. Fuel. Heat. The Fire Triangle. Of course, this led to what fundamentally every sailor needed to know instinctively: "Stop, drop and roll."

• **The different classes of fires**—A, B, C, D, and especially K—oil fires on ships and aircraft. At Boot Camp, every sailor was also trained in "abandoning ship" in such a way as to sweep floating oil fires away before they stick to your skin.

• **The nature, purpose, and use of a variety of fire suppression tools and equipment.** I will never forget the importance of checking fire extinguishers—and today, smoke alarms and carbon monoxide monitors.

• **The power and dangers of mishandled firehoses.** Under pressure a unattended, flying hose can, in an instant, cut a human body in half!

• **The techniques for handling nozzles and the specific role of every member of a nozzle team.** Everyone wanted to be in the front or second in line where the spray and protection of the cool water could be felt.

• **The necessity of a working OBA (Oxygen Breathing Apparatus)**—a closed circuit oxygen rebreather, now replaced by the Self-Contained Breathing Apparatus.

• **The use of powder (called Purple-K), not water, to suppress the immense intensity of a magnesium fire.** An enflamed magnesium helicopter engine can, quite literally, blow a hole in a ship, if improperly treated with water or thrown into the sea. Hydrogen molecules and flames are a deadly combination. Today they pair the powder with foam as more effective twin agents.

On my first day in firefighting school, I was assigned to the second nozzleman position as our team entered a burning, oil-drenched metal building at the training facility. Even though that was fifty-five years ago, I still remember the oppressive heat, the choking smell of smoke, and the claustrophobic experience of not being able to see in front of my facemask.

Shortly after Boot Camp, I reported to the *U.S.S. Kitty Hawk* as a "fireman"—a general term used to speak of those who serve below decks. My first specific assignment was to be a Damage Controlman (in my case, a firefighter). My permanent station was changed to working in the Personnel Office aside the Legal Department. However, during General Quarters, I was still considered a firefighter. I was "locked" in a fire control station overlooking one of the Hangar Bays. When commanded to do so by the Combat Information Center, I was to close the giant Hangar Bay door on our end of the ship and engage the water systems.

I was supposed to have a well-trained teammate, but I was, as a young sailor, left all alone. My training was limited, for sure. My job was, in the words of the angry officer I called for advice, to "just push the - - - - buttons." Enough said!

After we returned to San Diego, I attended another course on Shipboard Firefighting. I thought it would be easy. Not so. Just before entering the building engulfed in flames, the drill instructor noticed I was becoming very faint. I began to crumble. He wisely pulled me out and discovered my oxygen rebreather (i.e., my OBA) was not working and I was breathing my own carbon dioxide—a life-threatening issue had I entered the burning building with my fellow ill-equipped trainees.

It was, frankly, a career-changing experience, not because of fear, but because God had different plans for me. For the last fifty years, I have been serving as a pastor, missionary, and counselor. I am not a firefighter—or am I? In one sense, I am not one of you in the Fire Service. In another sense, I, too, am involved in "relational fire prevention." There are so many ministry principles I learned in my very limited fire-fighting experience:

• As a pastor and missionary, I am called to do my best to preach the Gospel and prevent people from an eternity in the fires of hell. Considering the summer heat of where I live, I often tease, "Welcome to Fresno—it makes preaching about hell a lot easier."

• As a counselor, I work hard to teach families the vital principles for preventing the fires of conflict and chaos. Accusations that 'add fuel to the fire' are often no-win situations. Like arsonists, some people are addicted to the flames of anger.

• As a seminar teacher, having taught our *"Purity War"* seminars for decades, I often say to the participants what I learned in those brief firefighting courses, "It is much easier to prevent a fire than it is to fight one." Being proactive works in all areas of life.

• As a senior pastor, it is imperative I teach my staff that like a magnesium fire, some situations require special training to prevent an explosion that creates a giant crater capable of sinking a family or a ministry.

• As a local church pastor, I need to remember that some ministry fires require "all hands on deck." They cannot be handled alone, no matter how experienced I am.

• As a seasoned shepherd, I have learned it is not easy to convince people to sound the alarm when they first smell smoke instead of waiting until the situation is ablaze with consuming emotions.

• As a fellow Christian, I remind people that every room in our hearts needs a smoke alarm.

Maybe I am a firefighter—or so it often feels! I have the greatest respect for the Firefighting Community. You are members of the *"Thin Red Line"* and, in my eyes, more than first responders—you are "first in, last out." You in the Fire Service are some of my greatest heroes. I love the quote: "Save one life, you are a hero. Save hundreds of lives, you're a firefighter."

May you know you have our prayers and support. We will fight to make sure you have what you need to protect and serve at a moment's notice. Your tireless efforts give new meaning to the words of the Apostle Paul:

2 Thessalonians 3:13 "But as for you, brethren, do not grow weary of doing good."

Long before radios and telephones, fire departments used the telegraph. In Morse code, five measured dashes, then a pause, then five measured dashes and another pause, then five more dashes—555—means a firefighter has died in the line of duty. It is universally known as the Tolling of the Bell—a time-honored tradition of honoring all firefighters who made the ultimate sacrifice. We "toll the bell" for your fallen comrades!

Now, my fellow firefighters (if I may respectfully say that), make sure your oxygen-breathing apparatus is working. And while you are checking your other life-saving equipment, why not take some time to check the condition of your heart. That way you will be better suited in every arena of life to face every physical, emotional, and spiritual fire—to be "all in, all the time!" Because you know as well as I do: "The only easy day was yesterday!"

That's why we wrote this book. Every devotional is meant to draw you closer to the life-saving ministry of the Lord Jesus

Christ. We are convinced He will suppress the fires in your life and prevent many others.

I can summarize my ministry and yours in familiar firefighting terms:

Semper Paratus—"Always Ready!"

Ut Vivant Alteri—"So Others Might Live!"

For Personal Reflection:

1. To those of us who are not in the Fire Service, we ask you to write a note of appreciation to your local fire station.

2. To those of you who are in the Fire Service, we ask you to write a note of appreciation to other first responders (e.g., police, emergency medical personnel, etc.). It would also be great if you thanked veterans for their service. Remember, their oath of enlistment never expired.

3. Thank someone in ministry for their tireless efforts at spiritual and emotional fire-prevention and firefighting.

4. Put the words "Do not grow weary of doing good" (1 Thessalonians 3:13) somewhere where you can see them often.

© Dr. James M. and Karon M. Cecy

Jim's Veterans' Devotional #9

Hinneh Mah Tov: A Soldier's Unity

> Psalm 133:1 "Behold, how good and how pleasant it is for brothers to dwell together in unity!

Soldiers who are a part of the Israeli Defense Forces often sing the words of Psalm 133:1 as a reminder of the unity. Soldiers of the Cross should do the same:

In Biblical Hebrew:

הִנֵּה מַה טּוֹב וּמַה נָּעִים שֶׁבֶת אַחִים גַּם יַחַד

In Romanized Hebrew:

Hinneh mah tov umah na'im shevet achim gam yachad.

Translated into English:

Psalm 133:1 "Behold, how good and how pleasant it is for brothers to dwell together in unity!"

Put into Practice:

Oh, how I love the unity among my fellow pastors in Fresno County. We pray together, serve together, and share the bliss and blisters of ministry together. We also laugh together, even about our minor doctrinal differences.

The following is my actual text chain with my pastor-friend, after asking him for prayer because I was in bed with pneumonia:

My text: *"Pray for me; I am really sick!"*

Bob: *"Pray for me too. I'm golfing poorly."*

Bob continues: *"Jim, you've got some Pentecostals praying for you! You're gonna make it!"*

My response: *"Sadly, you have a Baptist praying for your golf game. You don't have a chance!"*

Bob: *"That's my problem! STOP!"*

My response: *"Maybe I should become a Pentecostal now that I have both your golf score and my healing as my motivation."*

Bob: *"Haha. Love you, my friend!"*

My response: *"Laughter is a good medicine."*

Pastor Bob continues to pray for me as his "on fire" brother he lovingly refers to as a "Seatbelt Pentecostal." This baptistic pastor considers it a complement.

Hinneh mah tov. How good it is!

For Personal Reflection:

Write a note to a pastor in another church and express your appreciation.

© Dr. James M. and Karon M. Cecy.

Jim's Veterans' Devotional #10

Facing Myself at the Wall

1 Corinthians 6:20 "For you have been bought with a price: therefore glorify God in your body."

I remember my first visit to the Vietnam Veterans Memorial in Washington, D.C, listing over 58,000 fellow sailors, marines, soldiers, and airmen who paid the ultimate price. *"Semper Fidelis—Always Faithful."*

As I stood at attention and saluted, unable to control the tears, I could see my own reflection behind the etched names on the polished black granite. I asked myself that all-too-common question many war veterans who are experiencing "survivor's guilt" ask: *"Why not me, Lord?"*

Unlike some of my buddies who were assigned to life-threatening riverboat duty in Vietnam, I was assigned to a relatively less dangerous duty station on a ship off the coast of Vietnam. Sadly, some of the names on the wall were fellow shipmates who had paid the ultimate price.

A few years later, I returned. This time, however, I was in the middle of my doctoral research related to why Christian leaders fall morally. As I stood again at the memorial, I imagined the names of too many of my fellow Soldiers of the Cross who fell in the battle with sexual immorality. As I reflected on the consequences, I thought: *"What a horrible price to pay for a few minutes of sinful pleasure."*

There, in that solemn moment of dedication and remembrance of all Christ had done for me, I stood at attention and reflected on the Apostle Paul's words:

1 Corinthians 6:20 "For you have been bought with a price: therefore glorify God in your body."

My life goals are simple:

Life Goal #1. When someone tells my children and grandchildren they are just like me; they will stick out their chests, and not their tongues.

Life Goal #2. When Jesus meets me at the Gates of Heaven, He will say to me:

> Matthew 25:21 "Well done, thou good and faithful servant: Thou hast been faithful over a few things, I will make thee ruler over many things: enter thou into the joy of thy lord" (King James Version).

Much of what I am today, I owe to those fellow ministry veterans and Skilled Helpers who have faithfully given their lives to serve the Lord Jesus Christ. Some of them lost their lives; most of them gave their hearts to serve.

For Personal Reflection:

Take some time to consider those who have sacrificed in their service for the Lord. In what ways are they an example to you?

(Adapted from *"The Purity War: A Biblical Guide to Living in an Immoral World"* by Dr. James M. Cecy. Available at www.amazon.com, www.jaron.org and www.puritywar.com.)

© Dr. James M. and Karon M. Cecy.

Jim's Veterans' Devotional #11

Saluting Our Supreme Commander

> 2 Timothy 2:3 "Suffer hardship with me, as a good soldier of Christ Jesus. No soldier in active service entangles himself in the affairs of everyday life, so that he may please the one who enlisted him as a soldier."

What is it about saluting?

From my short stint as a boy scout to my time during and after my Navy days, I have always loved saluting. The rules for saluting differ according to each branch of the service or agency. However, the purpose is the same. It is intended to be a sign of honor and respect. Historically, an open-handed salute also shows you do not have a weapon.

Whereas it was once required for us to be in uniform, Congress passed a law allowing honorably discharged military veterans to render a salute, when appropriate (e.g., when the flag is hoisted or is passing in review). In fact, on my way out, I sometimes salute the flag hanging on my house. I love it!

Saluting our Commander

In the Fall of 2003, I was invited to South Africa to speak at the Pan-Africa Christian Police Association Conference (PACPAC). On the first evening, hundreds of participants marched into the auditorium in a wide assortment of police uniforms.

While a shortened version of each country's national anthem was played, each squad saluted their country's flag. About a dozen countries were represented that night, mostly from Africa. I was impressed with the many multi-colored flags and unique national anthems. I had never seen so many different styles of salute. I was struck by the beauty of their diversity. I was also deeply impacted by the words of Mike Harris, chairman of the PACPAC board: "We have to be revived before we can be a part of revival; we have to be changed before we can make change."

I spent the next days speaking about a revival of personal purity among evangelical leaders as a major part of God's answer to the many problems in Africa. On my last day of teaching, I shared how impressed I was with the first night's ceremony. "However," I continued, "I am even more impressed with the Christian unity I have seen among you, even amidst so many cultural differences." I asked if they would be willing to stand united with me, not to salute a national flag, nor a human superior officer, but to salute the King of kings and Lord of lords. I will never forget that crowd of Christian police officers, now dressed in civilian clothes, joining me in saluting our Sovereign Lord and Savior, Jesus Christ.

God has a mighty army of His people, unified by His Spirit and empowered by the Word of God, who will stand with us in this battle for personal purity and holiness. Together, we salute His authority and follow His orders. Together, we guard our minds, guard our bodies, and guard each other. Together, we help each other to never get entangled in the web of impurity. Our mutual goal is to please the One who enlisted us to be a part of His army (2 Timothy 2:3-4) and to say with the Apostle Paul:

2 Timothy 4:7 "I have fought the good fight, I have finished the course, I have kept the faith."

Onward, Christian soldiers! March on, Soldiers of the Cross.

For Personal Reflection:

Take a moment and stand at attention. Render a salute–military style or place your hand over your heart. In your own words acknowledge the One who is your King of kings and Lord of lords.

(Adapted from *"The Purity War: A Biblical Guide to Living in an Immoral World"* by Dr. James M. Cecy. Available at www.amazon.com, www.jaron.org and www.puritywar.com.)

© Dr. James M. and Karon M. Cecy.

Jim's Veterans' Devotional #12

The Left-Handed Wrench

> John 14:26 "But the Helper, the Holy Spirit, whom the Father will send in My name, He will teach you all things, and bring to your remembrance all that I said to you."

I was a typically naïve, young sailor on his first training day on a ship at sea. I was ready for the salty crew to treat us with their typical disrespect. I stood back as one of my fellow *newbies* was told to look under a battle helmet for what the old sailors called a sea bat. Curious to see this strange creature, he bent down and lifted the helmet. At that moment, an old sailor hit him on the butt with a broom and shouted, *"See Bat!"* I thought, *"What a fool!"* Then it was my turn.

I was called down to the engine room where I was assigned to assist a Petty Officer. He shouted to me, "Hey you, get me a left-handed wrench." Afraid to disobey anything that sounded like an order, I jumped to it.

Being the mechanic I am not; I went about the area looking for that wrench. After minutes of searching, I finally admitted to my visibly surprised superior, "Sorry, I can't find a left-handed wrench and no one will help me." He just rolled his eyes and walked away.

There are times when we are asked to do things about which we know nothing. We don't get away with the new mantra, "Fake it until you make it!" Although it may be hard to eat a bit of "humble pie," it is best to admit our ignorance and get some help.

The Indwelling Holy Spirit is rightly called our Helper—the One who comes alongside us, especially in times when we do not know what to do. Let me remind us:

• He leads us.

> Romans 8:14 "For all who are being led by the Spirit of God, these are sons of God."

> Galatians 5:18, 25 "But if you are led by the Spirit, you are not under the Law....If we live by the Spirit, let us also walk by the Spirit."

• He shows us the way to go.

> Psalm 32:8 "I will instruct you and teach you in the way which you should go; I will counsel you with My eye upon you."

• He teaches us.

> John 14:26 "But the Helper, the Holy Spirit, whom the Father will send in My name, He will teach you all things, and bring to your remembrance all that I said to you."

• He convicts us of sin and the deeds of the flesh.

> John 16:8 "...He, when He comes, will convict the world concerning sin and righteousness and judgment..."

> Galatians 5:19-21 "Now the deeds of the flesh are evident, which are: immorality, impurity, sensuality, idolatry, sorcery, enmities, strife, jealousy, outbursts of anger, disputes, dissensions, factions, envying, drunkenness, carousing, and things like these, of which I forewarn you, just as I have forewarned you, that those who practice such things will not inherit the kingdom of God."

• He fills us with the fruit of the Spirit-filled life—Christ-like qualities.

> Galatians 5:22-23 "But the fruit of the Spirit is love, joy, peace, patience, kindness, goodness, faithfulness, gentleness, self-control; against such there is no law..."

Who knows? He may even invent a left-handed wrench when needed.

For Personal Reflection:

1. Reflect on the ministry of the Holy Spirit—the Indwelling Helper in your life.

2. Which of His specific ministries, stated above, are you most aware of today?

© Dr. James M. and Karon M. Cecy.

Jim's Veterans' Devotional #13

Where Is Your *Testudo* Today?

> 1 Peter 5:8-9 "Be of sober spirit, be on the alert. Your adversary, the devil, prowls around like a roaring lion, seeking someone to devour. But resist him, firm in your faith, knowing that the same experiences of suffering are being accomplished by your brethren who are in the world."

The ancient Roman army was known for its effective battle tactics. Each soldier was equipped with a curved shield called the *scutum*—roughly the size of a small door. As the *phalanx* (the army formation) marched into the thick of battle, the men in the front placed their shields in front of themselves. The men on the sides placed their shields to the outside, and the men in the middle placed their shields above their heads. In Latin, this was called the *testudo*—the tortoise or the turtle shell. Few enemy weapons could penetrate the solid wall of shields and spears marching toward them.

Modern historians refer to Greek soldiers (called *hoplites*) using this same *testudo*-tactic in the 7th century as "a tank on legs." In the 15th to the 19th centuries, based on the effectiveness of the Roman *testudo*, the Royal Korean Navy used, with great success, the *geobukseon*, an armored ship with iron spikes on its deck and a ring of cannons that fired ship-to-ship darts. It was a formidable offensive and defensive weapon.

As a young sailor in the U.S. Navy, I also benefited from the *testudo*-strategy. Knowing our purpose as an aircraft carrier and our vulnerability to attack, I was very grateful for the other members of our Carrier Group *(Carrier Task Force 77)*, whose job it was to protect us. Our planes in the skies above us, the destroyers and cruisers surrounding us, and the submarines in the sea below us were our *testudo*. I can assure you that I and my fellow carrier sailors are alive today because of that fleet of protectors.

So it is with the Body of Christ. As a soldier in the Army of God, I cannot resist temptation alone. My shield of faith does not protect my flanks against the destructive tactics and the fiery darts of the Enemy (as mentioned in Ephesians 6:11, 16), nor was it designed to do so.

For my protection, I need my fellow Christians with their shields of faith hoisted high. For their protection, they need my shield of faith to do the same. Each of us needs our brothers or sisters in Christ, properly positioned as a spiritual *testudo*—a veritable fortress of faith, our own personal Carrier Group, our private fleet of protectors—surrounding us when we are most vulnerable.

It is in these accountability relationships we have a fighting chance of resisting the devil's attacks, as he seeks someone to devour (cf. 1 Peter 5:8-9). It is then we can succeed in our defense against "the gates of hell," as Jesus promised in Matthew 16:18. Additionally, if we are wounded in battle or let our individual shield of faith down, our fellow soldiers of Christ can move us to the center of the pack, where we can be most protected from further harm.

Where is your *testudo* today?

For Personal Reflection:

List the people in your life who make up your *testudo,* your wall of protection. Take a moment to pray for them. Then write a note to thank them.

(Adapted from *"The Accountable Life: Protecting Myself and Others"* by Dr. James M. Cecy. Available at www.amazon.com and www.jaron.org.)

© Dr. James M. and Karon M. Cecy.

Jim's Veterans' Devotional #14

No Land in Sight

> Psalm 42:3 "My tears have been my food day and night, while they say to me all day long, 'Where is your God?'"

In our nine-month military cruise to the Western Pacific, we spent many days and weeks at sea without seeing land. Oh, how small that giant aircraft carrier feels when bobbing around a vast ocean.

Days without seeing a horizon have a way of getting to your soul. In fact, our ship experienced a great deal of restlessness among the crew. It was not unusual to have a fight break out in the mess hall just for asking someone to pass the salt. I know, I was there! In fact, during our deployment, a riot evolved over a minor altercation.

There are days when we lose sight of the horizon. We get lost in a sea of worry and anxiety. We feel like we are just floating through life without any purpose—with no solid ground in sight.

Rather than share a devotional thought, let me have you sit down quietly and ponder the words of Psalm 42 that is subtitled in some Bibles, *"Thirsting for God in Trouble and Exile."* It is a *maskil*, a teaching psalm presented to teach our hearts a life-lesson that must never be forgotten.

We actually don't know the author, but we have felt his feelings. He used to be right out there in front, leading in spiritual matters. Now he is lost. He used to worship God intimately. Now he is spiritually dry. He used to feel like he was swimming along in life. But now he feels swamped—by God Himself! He used to...he used to...but now...well, we know the feeling!

May I ask you to whisper the words quietly, with three (yes, three) colored pens in hand. In one color, underline this man's deep feelings. In another color, underline the questions this man asks. With another color, underline the answers.

Psalm 42

As the deer pants for the water brooks,
So my soul pants for You, O God.
My soul thirsts for God, for the living God;
When shall I come and appear before God?
My tears have been my food day and night,
While they say to me all day long, "Where is your God?"
These things I remember and I pour out my soul within me.
For I used to go along with the throng and lead them in
procession to the house of God,
With the voice of joy and thanksgiving, a multitude keeping
festival. Why are you in despair, O my soul?
And why have you become disturbed within me?
Hope in God, for I shall again praise Him,
For the help of His presence.
O my God, my soul is in despair within me;
Therefore I remember You from the land of the Jordan
And the peaks of Hermon, from Mount Mizar.
Deep calls to deep at the sound of Your waterfalls;
All Your breakers and Your waves have rolled over me.
The LORD will command His lovingkindness in the daytime;
And His song will be with me in the night,
A prayer to the God of my life.
I will say to God my rock, "Why have You forgotten me?
Why do I go mourning because of the oppression of the
enemy?"
As a shattering of my bones, my adversaries revile me,
While they say to me all day long, "Where is your God?"
Why are you in despair, O my soul?
And why have you become disturbed within me?
Hope in God, for I shall yet praise Him,
The help of my countenance and my God.

For Personal Reflection:

1. Follow this up by reading Psalm 43, a psalm of deliverance written by the same anonymous author.

2. Ask yourself the same question as the Psalmist: "Why are you in despair, O my soul? And why have you become disturbed within me?" (Psalm 42:5).

3. Write out a few thoughts from Psalm 42 and Psalm 43 that serve as a clear answer.

© Dr. James M. and Karon M. Cecy.

Jim's Veterans' Devotional #15

Honor Flight

> Romans 12:10 "Be devoted to one another in brotherly love; give preference to one another in honor…"

> 1 Corinthians 12:26 "And if one member suffers, all the members suffer with it; if one member is honored, all the members rejoice with it."

In 2022, I was blessed to be invited to participate in the Central Valley Honor Flight which provided an opportunity for our local military veterans to visit the various memorials in Washington, D.C. I quite literally wore a number of hats on that life-changing trip.

Hat #1. Chaplain

I was asked to serve as this Honor Flight trip's chaplain, providing emotional and spiritual support for the participants. What a privilege to pray with and for those precious veterans. I was also able to speak to them about "survivor's guilt" and how we honor the dead by living lives that would make them proud. I stood with some who had never quite come to terms with the loss of their fellow soldiers, sailors, airmen, or marines. Some called me "Pastor" while others called me "Chaplain" or "Chappy." I referred to myself as "Brother."

Hat #2. Honor Flight Guardian

I was asked to serve as a chaperone for one of the veteran-participants. My role was simple—to serve this veteran in whatever way that would make his trip an experience of a lifetime. What a joy it was to serve a veteran Air Force officer who was once a Navy officer. We shared some very memorable "sea stories." In fact, during Vietnam, he served on the patrol boats to which I was expected to be assigned. I was well aware of the fellow sailors with whom I was stationed who most likely did not make it home in one piece from one of the most dangerous assignments in the war. It was yet another time I dealt personally with my own "survivor's guilt." Here I was, the Chaplain, being ministered to by the man I was tasked to serve. "Thank you, Lord, for Dennis."

Hat #3. Vietnam Veteran

As a fellow Vietnam veteran, I stood in silence with many at the Vietnam Memorial Wall. We wept. We prayed. We traced names with small pieces of paper. I was not just a chaplain and a chaperone—I was a fellow grieving veteran. That day I was only able to find one name among the others who died on my ship. "May he rest in peace."

On one of the days, while visiting Fort McHenry, I wore my Vietnam Veteran hat. A man passed by and grumbled, "What a waste!" I am not sure what he meant, though it reminded me of the disdain many of my fellow veterans experienced when we arrived back home from Vietnam. Shortly after, another man saw my hat and said, "Welcome home!" It comforted my saddened heart.

Hat #4. Friend

After the trip, I especially connected to a couple of vets, one who has become a dear "brother in arms." As a Vietnam veteran, he admitted he had never really talked about his horrific experiences as a combat Army sergeant. It was not until recently he told the story of his men being pinned down by the enemy. He defied what he believed to be an unlawful order from a ranking officer and hid his men from harm's way. His words to me were deeply felt, "No one died that night!" It was one of his proudest moments in that horrible war. "Atta boy, Greg! Keep on healing!"

As you consider the veterans in your life, what hats are you willing to wear? Prayer-Warrior? Listener? Counselor? Advisor? Friend?

1 Thessalonians 5:14 ...encourage the fainthearted, help the weak..."

Romans 12:15 "...weep with those who weep."

For Personal Reflection:

1. Write a note to a veteran.

2. Look for someone wearing a veteran's hat, shirt, or jacket. Take a moment to thank them for their service. Teach your children to do the same.

3. If you are a veteran, wear your hat or jacket proudly. You are family!

© Dr. James M. and Karon M. Cecy.

Jim's Veteran's Devotional #16

B.R.A.S.S.

1 Corinthians 9:26 "Therefore, I run in such a way, as not without aim..."

1 Corinthians 9:26 "So I run with purpose in every step..." (New Living Translation).

Every "rank and file" military person and veteran knows the term *brass*. When we speak of *The Brass* we are speaking in slang for officers, especially the *Top Brass*—our highest-ranking superiors. The term is also used in business and in law enforcement. In some places, *brass* refers to a police badge—their *shield*. However, the acronym *B.R.A.S.S.* is sometimes used in marksmanship training as a simple reminder:

B.R.A.S.S. — Breath. Relax. Aim. Sight. Squeeze.

I would encourage us to think of this as a spiritual exercise for us as Soldiers of the Cross, as we consider our *top brass*—the Lord Jesus Christ, our Commander in Chief:

• **Breathe** — Pray (P.U.S.H. = Pray Until Something Happens).

Psalm 150:6 "Let everything that has breath praise the LORD. Praise the LORD!"

1 Thessalonians 5:17 "...pray without ceasing..."

• **Relax** — Be less intense and smile more.

Nehemiah 8:10 "Do not be grieved, for the joy of the LORD is your strength."

• **Aim** — Focus on "things above."

Colossians 3:1-2 "Therefore if you have been raised up with Christ, keep seeking the things above, where Christ is, seated at the right hand of God. Set your mind on the things above, not on the things that are on earth."

• **Sight** — Keep your eyes on Jesus.

Hebrews 12:2 "…fixing our eyes on Jesus, the author and perfecter of faith…"

• **Squeeze** — Take action.

Daniel 11:32 "…the people who know their God will display strength and take action."

For Personal Reflection:

Memorize B.R.A.S.S. as a reminder of your daily spiritual routine:

  • Breathe — Pray and praise.
  • Relax — Be less intense and smile more.
  • Aim — Focus on "things above."
  • Sight — Keep your eyes on Jesus.
  • Squeeze — Take action.

Jim's Veteran's Devotional #17

Flashbacks

> Romans 7:24 "Who will set me free from the body of this death?"

Like most in his generation, my father never shared his experiences in World War II. However, every once in a while I caught a glimpse of the painful memories. He was an enlisted soldier in the *Lincoln-Welland Regiment* of the Canadian Army. He never shared the pain of that dreadful war, nor the friends he lost, but I knew it affected him deeply. I would sometimes catch him softly crying when he heard bagpipes.

In those days, we did not use such terms as PTSD (Post-Traumatic Stress Disorder) nor did we really understand it as we do now. As a Vietnam War veteran, I would not describe myself as severely suffering from this deeply painful condition and I do not minimize its effects on my fellow veterans. However, I do have my share of flashbacks—more and more the older I get. They sometimes strike my heart deeply, causing the tears to flow.

Our church is located very close to a civilian and a military airport. As a veteran aircraft carrier sailor, I will sometimes have flashbacks of my time on the ship—often triggered by:

- The distinct smell of jet fuel.

- The dissonant sound of two helicopters flying overhead.

- The deafening roar of fighter jets in full afterburn.

There are other evidences of my time on the ship:

• The hue of red lights in any dark passageway, reminding me of our night operations.

• The worsening claustrophobia from my time spent in my watertight fire control station.

• The recent diagnosis of delayed onset of substantial hearing loss, especially from the whine and deafening roar of jet engines. (I was too cool to wear ear protection.)

• The recurring dreams of being trapped below decks or getting lost as I try to find my General Quarters station.

• The "survivor's guilt" when I see the etched names of shipmates at the Vietnam Memorial or a wounded veteran.

• The pride I feel when I see young men and women in uniform.

• The fear and worry I experience when I read about the new ship-destroying weapons.

• The taste of mixed vegetables (of course, with lima beans) and the lingering memory of powdered eggs and "reconstituted" milk. *Yuck!*

There are, however, more troubling flashbacks that occur in my heart of hearts—the memories of all my youthful and ungodly blunders. On the day I left active naval duty, I gave my life to Jesus Christ, trusting in Him alone to forgive my sins and give me eternal life. By God's grace, I became a new creature. The old things, I was told in Scripture, had passed away:

2 Corinthians 5:17 "Therefore if anyone is in Christ, he is a new creature; the old things passed away; behold, new things have come."

However, I felt like I was still at war—a raging war within—especially with memories of my sinful past. I was not alone. Listen to the testimony of the transformed Apostle Paul who had his own issues with flashbacks of his old life:

Romans 7:24 "Wretched man that I am! Who will set me free from the body of this death?"

He knew the answer:

Romans 8:1 "Therefore there is now no condemnation for those who are in Christ Jesus."

He went on to explain:

1 Timothy 1:15 "...Christ Jesus came into the world to save sinners, among whom I am foremost of all." (The King James Version refers to him as "the chief of sinners.")

Galatians 2:20 "I have been crucified with Christ; and it is no longer I who live, but Christ lives in me; and the life which I now live in the flesh I live by faith in the Son of God, who loved me and gave Himself up for me."

Romans 6:6 "...knowing this, that our old self was crucified with Him, in order that our body of sin might be done away with, so that we would no longer be slaves to sin..."

The Apostle Paul understood what I have now come to realize. The old "me" is crucified and dead. I am no longer that old self—enslaved to sin. My new self, however, will always be at war—a tug-of-war—until I am with the Lord in Heaven.

On the one side, my flesh is prompting me to live in the muck and mire of the deeds of the flesh (Galatians 5:19-21). On the other side, God's Indwelling Holy Spirit is calling me to be filled with the Spirit (Ephesians 5:18) and to manifest the Fruit of the Spirit (Galatians 5:22-23). In other words, it is a winnable war!

And now, when those flashback memories of sin from my old life creep in to try to discourage me, I can recite with the Apostle Paul:

Romans 7:25 "Thanks be to God through Jesus Christ our Lord!"

Of course, the flashbacks still occur. I am still very much a sinner. However, my PTSD might just be my Post-Traumatic Salvation Discovery.

• I do not have to do what I used to do.

• I am no longer in bondage to sin.

• I truly am a new creation.

That freedom is available to you, as well. In the famous words quoted by Dr. Martin Luther King, Jr.:

Free at last! Free at last!
Thank God Almighty.
We are free at last!

For Personal Reflection:

1. When you reflect on your old life before coming to Christ, what images come to mind?

2. When you reflect on your new life in Christ, what comes to mind?

3. In what arena of your life are you still in a tug-of-war?

© Dr. James M. and Karon M. Cecy.

Jim's Veterans' Devotional #18

My Flag-Draped Casket

> Genesis 25:8 "Abraham breathed his last and died in a ripe old age, an old man and satisfied with life; and he was gathered to his people."

Womb to tomb. Cradle to casket. Earth to Heaven. There will come a time when I die, hopefully in a ripe old age—an old man who is quite satisfied with his life and ministry. Born in Canada, I became a naturalized U.S. citizen as a young man. When that time comes, I have asked my family to have a U.S. flag ceremony at my memorial service. There, I have asked that selected military personnel (hopefully Navy) will make the customary thirteen folds of the U.S. flag.

There is no official flag-folding ceremony and no official meaning to each fold. However, there are many interpretations and suggestions regarding the meaning of the folds. I hope to have a flag-folding ceremony presented at my funeral that will represent the same religious principles on which I believe our great country was originally founded. I will have added some personal meanings.

The following was presented by two of my church ministry staff at a Memorial Day gathering. One was a medically-retired Law Enforcement Officer and the other a medically-retired Marine Corps Lance Corporal. It was a very touching ceremony.

In the spirit of the Marine Corps, I have "improvised, adapted, and overcome" the challenges of making that flag ceremony my own. Here is what I am requesting:

• **The first fold of the flag** will be a symbol of life. I pray mine was a life well-lived.

• **The second fold of the flag** will be a reminder of my belief in eternal life made possible by trusting in Jesus Christ alone for my salvation. To God alone be the glory!

• **The third fold of the flag** will be made in honor and remembrance of the veterans departing our ranks, and who gave a portion of their lives for the defense of our country and to attain peace throughout the world. "All gave some; some gave all."

• **The fourth fold of the flag** will represent our weaker nature as American citizens, desperately needing to trust in God for His guidance in times of peace, as well as in times of war. May God bless America. May America bless God!

• **The fifth fold of the flag** will be a tribute to our country. Despite its many challenges, I believe the United States of America is still the best place on the planet to live.

• **The sixth fold of the flag** will represent where a part of my heart lies. It is with my heart I pledged allegiance to the flag of the United States of America, and to the republic for which it stands, one nation under God, indivisible, with liberty and justice for all.

• **The seventh fold of the flag** will be a tribute to the men and women who now serve in our armed forces to protect our country against all enemies, whether they be found within or without the boundaries of our republic.

• **The eighth fold of the flag** will be a tribute to Jesus Christ, the One who entered into the Valley of the Shadow of Death, that we might see the light of day.

• **The ninth fold of the flag** will be a tribute to womanhood. Let this especially be a declaration of my gratefulness for all the women in my life whose faith, love, loyalty, and devotion helped mold my life.

• **The tenth fold of the flag** will be a tribute to the fathers who have given their sons and daughters for the defense of our country. This is also a tribute to all godly fathers who raise their children to be mighty Soldiers of the Cross.

• **The eleventh fold of the flag** will represent the lower portion of the seal of King David and King Solomon and will remind us to give glory to the God of Abraham, Isaac, and Jacob. It is also a reminder to "pray for the peace of Jerusalem"

• **The twelfth fold of the flag** will represent the eternal life I am now enjoying with God, the Father, the Son and the Holy Spirit. It will also be a reminder that I am reunited with my beloved family and friends who have gone before me to Heaven.

• **The thirteenth (and last) fold of the flag**, with the flag completely folded, stars in view, will remind us of our national motto, *"In God We Trust."*

After the flag is completely folded and tucked in, it will have the appearance of a triangular hat to serve as a reminder of the soldiers who served in the Revolutionary War under General George Washington and the sailors and marines who served under Captain John Paul Jones, preserving for us the rights, privileges and freedoms we enjoy today.

Sometimes the Flag Detail will slip three empty shell casings into the folded flag before presenting the flag to the family. Each shell casing represents one of three volleys fired, and the three words: duty, honor, and country. After inspection, the folded flag will be held chest high, then saluted very slowly. The flag will then be presented to my loved ones.

I pray my family will put the flag in a place where my descendants will be reminded how privileged I was to serve in the U.S. Navy. May they appreciate the sentiment expressed by John F. Kennedy:

> "I can imagine no more rewarding a career. And any man who may be asked in this century what he did to make his life worthwhile, I think I can respond with a good deal of pride and satisfaction: 'I served in the United States Navy.'"

I also pray this flag will remind my family that my greatest honor and joy was to serve the Lord Jesus Christ, as my Commander-in-Chief, the One who enlisted me as a Soldier of the Cross (2 Timothy 2:4).

For Personal Reflection:

1. Have you reflected on what you want said and done at your memorial service?

2. More importantly, have you reflected on what kind of life you want to live before that day happens?

© Dr. James M. and Karon M. Cecy.

Jim's Veterans' Devotional #19

Navy Commands

> 2 Timothy 2:4 "No soldier in active service entangles himself in the affairs of everyday life, so that he may please the one who enlisted him as a soldier."

It has been over fifty-five years, but I still remember Navy life. I will never forget the sights, the sounds, and even the smells. On the very day I was released from active duty I gave my life to serve a greater Commanding Officer, the Lord Jesus Christ. I soon took to heart the words of the Apostle Paul, calling me as an active-duty Soldier of the Cross to not get "entangled in the affairs of everyday life" and to have, as my life goal, to please the Lord Jesus Christ, who called me to serve Him.

Over the decades I have often reflected on some of the phrases, announcements, and orders I heard while serving in the military. I have also been able to apply them to my service to the Lord. Here's a few:

- **"Aye, Aye, Sir!"**

Sometimes we would respond, "Roger that," or "10-4," or "WILCO," meaning, "Will comply." So, it is with responding to Jesus Christ, our Commanding Officer: In the words of the simple chorus: *"Yes, Lord, Yes, to Your will and to Your ways."*

- **"Close and report all watertight doors."**

The lesson is simple: The problem is not being in a boat in the middle of the sea (i.e., the world's twisted values). The problem is allowing the sea to get into the middle of the boat.

- **"Fire! Fire! Fire!"** followed by the location (e.g., "Hangar Bay, Port side, Forward, etc.").

On a ship, there is no place to run from the flames. All of us need to hone our fire-fighting skills, personally and corporately. So it is with dealing with sin in our lives.

> Proverbs 6:27-28 "Can a man take fire in his bosom and his clothes not be burned? Or can a man walk on hot coals and his feet not be scorched?"

- **"General Quarters. General Quarters. All hands man your battle stations. This is <u>not</u> a drill."**

Time to act immediately. First, we need to rush to our assigned duty station and do what we were trained to do. When in doubt, ask for help—an essential in the Christian life!

- **"Go get me a left-handed wrench."**

Yes, I fell for this on one of my first days on the ship. Who was I to argue with my superior? Sometimes, it is okay to question authority when the order is not backed by the authoritative Word of God.

- **"Hit the rack."**

Time to get some rest—physically, emotionally and spiritually while holding on to our marching orders: "Rest in the LORD and wait patiently for Him…" (Psalm 37:7).

- **"Liberty Call."**

The actual announcement is: "Liberty Call is sounded; all hands rating liberty may leave the ship" followed by "Away liberty party. Away liberty party."

Sometimes the term is used for sailors heading out for leave or vacation. All of us who serve the Lord know the value of a break from the rigors of ministry. We just don't get to go AWOL (Absent Without Leave—i.e., without permission).

• "Man overboard."

This command was followed by a location (e.g., "Man overboard. Starboard [or port] side. Man overboard"). Sadly, two of my shipmates were lost at sea. Whenever I visit the Vietnam War Memorial in Washington, D.C., I honor their memory. The lesson is clear: We must always keep a sharp lookout for others. "I need you. You need me. We need each other."

• The Navy Motto

There is no official motto for the U.S. Navy. *"Non sibi sed patriae"* (Latin for "Not self but country") is often cited—surprisingly similar to the motto of the *Lincoln-Welland Regiment* of the Canadian Army, with whom my father was assigned. Their motto was *"Non nobis ned patriae."*—"Not for ourselves but for our country."

One of the unofficial Navy mottoes is *"Semper Fortis"*— Latin for "Always Courageous." The Navy's current slogan is "Forged by the Sea." All of these apply to our Christian lives as Soldiers of the Cross: Being selfless. Always bold. Forged by tough times.

• "Sweepers. Sweepers. Man your brooms. Sweep down, fore and aft."

On an aircraft carrier, it is well known that a few grains of sand sucked into a jet engine can take down a multi-million-dollar airplane or helicopter. In the army of God, it is the little things that often pose the most danger. Watch out for the smallest compromises; they can cost us our lives.

• "This is a drill. This is a drill…"

This is an official announcement distinguishing a genuine emergency from a rehearsal. It is a call to practice for the real event. Being equipped with the Sword of the Spirit (i.e., the Word of God) is essential to the effectiveness of Christ's Church.

• "All hands stand by to abandon ship."

The last thing a sailor ever wants to hear. The ship is sinking. Sadly, this is true of too many churches and para-church organizations. The good news is: There are other ships in God's Armada.

• "Permission to board the ship, Sir?" – "Permission granted."

No one had access to the ship without authorization. When it comes to being a part of the Family of God, access is only possible by trusting in Jesus Christ alone for our salvation.

• The Navy Hymn: "Eternal Father, Strong to Save."

The U.S. Navy hymn was written by two Englishmen. Reverend William Whiting wrote the lyrics in 1860. Reverend John B. Dykes wrote the music in 1861. The words are striking:

Eternal Father, strong to save,
Whose arm hath bound the restless wave,
Who bidd'st the mighty ocean deep,
Its own appointed limits keep,
O hear us when we cry to thee,
For those in peril on the sea!

O Christ! Whose voice the waters heard,
And hushed their raging at thy word,
Who walkedst on the foaming deep,
And calm amidst its rage didst sleep,
O hear us when we cry to thee,
For those in peril on the sea!

Most Holy Spirit! Who didst brood,
Upon the chaos dark and rude,
And bid its angry tumult cease,
And give, for wild confusion, peace.
O hear us when we cry to thee,
For those in peril on the sea!

Eternal Father, grant, we pray,
To all Marines, both night and day.
The courage, honor, strength, and skill,
Their land to serve, thy law fulfill.
Be thou the shield forevermore,
From every peril to the Corps.

Lord, guard and guide the ones who fly,
Through the great spaces in the sky.
Be with them always in the air,
In darkening storms or sunlight fair.

For Personal Reflection:

What commands from Jesus Christ, your Commanding Officer, are you having the most difficult time obeying?

© Dr. James M. and Karon M. Cecy.

Jim's Veterans' Devotional #20

Carrier-Talk

> Colossians 4:5 "Conduct yourselves with wisdom toward outsiders, making the most of the opportunity."

As part of the Family of God, we have a vocabulary that is sometimes very strange to unbelievers—the "outsiders." Sometimes I teasingly call our "insider language" *Christianese*. For example, take the word *fellowship*. What does that really mean? Coffee and donuts? Dinner in the Fellowship Hall? Hardly. But that's what many outsiders may think when we who are in the know believe it is much deeper than that. I remember laughing when I first heard the words of a song: *"Fellowship. That's a bunch of fellows in the same ship."* Actually, that's a pretty good definition. Don't get me started on how words like *stewardship, evangelism, Deuteronomy*, and *Zephaniah* cause blank stares among non-believers.

As a pastor, I have a lingo of my own. Sometimes we pastors break out into some of the strangest words in our friendly debates—words like *egalitarianism, complementarianism, predestinarianism, infralapsarianism*, and *sublapsarianism*. And watch out when we start spouting off a host of unfamiliar Hebrew, Aramaic and Greek words. We can definitely make you feel like you don't speak our language. If the truth be told, most of us don't speak the language either.

To give us a feel for how the outsiders might feel when we, as believers, "talk in code," I wrote the following for my veteran shipmates. I have to admit it was quite fun and frankly proves my point. Yes, it is quite wordy. But then again, so are most sailors:

* *

Permit me some time to talk *Navy* and a tiny bit of *Marine* and a modicum of *Military Lingo* from other branches of the service. For those of you who did not serve or who do not *speak the language* or *talk the talk*, this will be *a nautical mouthful*. May those of you who served *onboard ship* enjoy the voyage to *Memory Lane*. We really do speak a different language—not just *Navy-Talk* but *Carrier-Talk*. Feel free to call a *Carrier Veteran* and ask him or her to translate. Then again, give it a try. I think you will do just fine. Every word in *italics* has special meaning to every *carrier sailor*.

It has been fifty-five years, but I still remember life on the *conventionally-powered supercarrier, the U.S.S. Kitty Hawk (CVA-63).* I was a part of the *ship's company*, joined by a *shipboard detachment* of the *MarDet.*" We set sail in November 1971 for a *WestPac Cruise*, on our voyage to *Yankee Station* to primarily provide vital support for our *grunts on the ground in Nam.*

We were also joined *onboard* by an *Air Wing* with their *squadrons* of about sixty-five to eighty airplanes along with their flight and support crew of *Airedales*. We were accompanied by *tin cans* that *covered our six* and *supply ships* that did our *UNREPS*. Then there were those submerged *boats* we never saw, manned by *bubbleheads* (now an acceptable moniker). All of us made up *Task Force 77*—a *Carrier Group* of some 7,500 personnel, all who left their families for nine months. What a toll on marriages and families! I believe ours was one of the last scheduled nine-month cruises. Good decision by the CNO and *CINCPACFLT* (as of 2002, called *COMPACFLT*).

It was hardly a pleasure cruise. Just ask any of the fifty to sixty *bears* on the *flight deck*. You'll recognize them—dressed in the blue, yellow, brown, and white jerseys. They were joined by the *grapes* in purple and the *ordies* in red. They might even direct you *below deck* to the *hangar rats*. Then again, the *plane captains, the*

Shooter, the *LSO,* and the *Air Boss* knew for sure how tough life was on *The Battle Cat.* Just make sure you don't ask the *XO.* The *scuttlebutt* was he was much too busy on the *Bridge,* trying to prove to the *Skipper* he was *worthy of command* someday soon. Then again, that was probably a *sea story* and we all knew what kind of fecal matter they were made of.

To this day I recall the sights, the sounds, and even the smells of *shipboard life* and *ports of call*—places like Hong Kong, Singapore and Subic Bay, Philippines. Who can ever forget *Olongapo,* the smell of the *Po River,* stories of girls with *butterfly knives* or our guys on *sister ships* being *slipped a mickey*? I also remember the sight of the *Russian Bears* playing *cat and mouse* with our *F-4 Phantoms.* One day the *Skipper* called us to *muster on the flight deck* so we could give their bomber crew *a proper U.S. Navy greeting—a finger wave*—as if to say, *"We saw you first!"* One wonders what file in the Kremlin has the photo of what their crew saw that day. *"Greetings from the Hawk!"*

I often reflect on my days on the ship over five decades ago. I can sometimes imagine hearing the ship's *IMC* blasting out orders. Some I loved, like *"Chow Call."* Others made me glad I wasn't a *deckhand* or a *boatswain's mate*: *"Sweepers, sweepers, man your brooms."* Sadly, back then there were others I ignored, like *Church Call*: *"The smoking lamp is out. Knock off all unnecessary work...Keep silence about the deck during divine services."* Oh, how this lonely sailor might have benefited from a word from our *Chaplain*, who I respectfully referred to as *The Sky Pilot.*

In some more detailed times of remembering, I am stuck *below deck* and struggling in my *skivvies* to put on my *dungarees* and find my way *forward* and *starboard*—up, down, over and through *ladders, hatches,* and *knee-knockers*—all the while fighting a *listing* ship and being pushed by my shipmates against the *bulkhead.* I am especially careful to not hit the *overhead.* I end up at my *General Quarters Station—amidships* on the *port side* of the *Hangar Bay*.

There, in my reflections, I *stand my watch* in accordance with my *General Orders* I learned in *Boot Camp*—remembering reciting them as I was blowing snot out my nose in the *Gas Chamber*. I am now locked into a *Watertight Compartment*. I put on my *sound-powered phone* and listen for orders from *CIC*. You might say, *"I was caught between the devil and the deep blue sea,"* and I knew it. However, I am prepared to follow orders. Mine were simple: *"Just push the d - - - - buttons, sailor,"* to which, in an emergency, I would have replied, *"Aye, Aye, Sir!"* No one was going to accuse me of *skating*.

In a real-life scenario we would eventually hear the order, *"Secure from General Quarters."* Even though I was a *pollywog* and not a *shellback,* I was nonetheless no longer a *boot* with *my bluejacket manual* tucked in my *13-buttoned bellbottoms*. After many months on ship, I was now a *deep-water sailor* who was close to becoming a *"salty dog."* I knew my   way around ship— although one day, during *flight ops*, I *scrambled* from my *berthing quarters near the fantail* to the   compartment   near   the *forecastle* to retrieve a telegram in the *Com Center*. Thinking it was an emergency, I *beat feet* in the maze *below decks*. It took twenty minutes! Fortunately, it was just a greeting from my older sister. In those days, any word from home was a blessing. Most of us anxiously waited for   *The COD* to land, carrying any news from *"the world."* *Mail Call* saved our sanity!

At first, I was an ill-equipped *Damage Controlman* doing my duty in a *Hangar Bay Fire Curtain Control Center*. Soon, however, this *red-striped, seaman snipe,* and *bilge rat fireman* would attend Navy school and became *a Personnelman*—eventually a *Petty Officer Third Class* (ultimately a *Second Class P.O.)* while serving in the *U.S.N.R*).

While *onboard*, I worked in the *Reenlistments and Separations Office* alongside the *Legal Office*. The *JAG officers* often asked me to bring messages to the *Marines*, a part of our *MarDet*, guarding my fellow shipmates who were in the *Brig*. I so appreciated the thankless job they did. Thus, I learned some of their *Jarhead* and *Leatherneck* jargon. *Once a Marine; always a Marine—Semper Fi—Oorah*!

After long hours in *General Quarters*, I hoped to earn the right to *turn in*—to *hit the rack*—in my case, located in the *stern* of the ship *aft* near the *fantail*. Then again, having eaten only *sea rations,* I would prefer to *quick step* to the *galley*—the *mess hall.* Some of the names we gave the so-called food are not usually said in polite company. *Mixed vegetables with lima beans, powdered eggs and recombined milk, anyone?*

Once we were *anchors aweigh* at an undisclosed number of *knots,* most of the *Ship's Company, MarDet* and *Air Wing* would eventually be given *permission to go ashore* once we *reached port.* In some cases, my *mates* would join me in searching through our *seabags* or *footlockers* to find our *dress blues* with a pressed *neckerchief* and a clean *dixie cup.* We might even have *spit-shined* our shoes. (No need in the mud-and-manure-soaked streets of *Olongapo).* If it was cold, we would put on a woolen *peacoat.* We knew if we were going to be *let go from duty,* we had to make every attempt to be *squared away* before some *gung-ho shore patrolman* or *MP* flagged and tagged us.

Sometimes we stood on the *flight deck* in our *dress uniforms* as our entire crew would *muster* in order to *dress the ship*—especially in such places as Pearl Harbor, *passing in honor* at the *U.S.S. Arizona Memorial. "May they rest in peace!"*

Before we departed the ship on the *port side,* we would know to *salute the colors* and the *Officer of the Deck.* For some of us, our first *Liberty Call* enticement in the *Port of Call* would be to buy food from the *Geedunk* or *Roach Coach* on the pier. Then again, we might say to a shipmate, *"I'll buy if you fly."*

Thank God nothing happened *underway* that would have sent all of us to *Davy Jones' Locker*. None of us had to *go down with the ship*. Thus, in some way, we said, *"All is well."*

When my memory slips, I have my *Cruise Book* and receive notes from fellow sailors, some who are enjoying their *DD214* and are fellow members of the *U.S.S. Kitty Hawk Association*. In 2009, I was privileged to be invited to join the *Decommissioning Cruise* but was prevented because of a recent illness. I recently flew with fellow veterans on an *Honor Flight* to visit the war memorials in Washington, D.C. There, on the black marble wall of the *Vietnam War Memorial*, we joined each other in saluting the honored dead with whom we served. We wept as young people greeted us with words we rarely heard when we returned from *Yankee Station*: *"Thank you for your service."*

Those of you who are *real Navy*, especially *carrier sailors*, understand most everything I have written. You know this is no *scuttlebutt* or *sea story*. It all makes sense to you, my *shipmates*— whether *swabbies* or those who had *scrambled eggs* on your caps. You *plank owners* get it, too. Even you *shallow water sailors* get it, even though you mostly served on ships less than 1/3 the size of *The Hawk*! So, let me say it with all the affection I can *muster: "Snap to it!"* and *"Full Speed ahead!"* May we all have *fairwinds and calm seas! The Hawk is my ship! Hooyah!*

Gratefully presented to my shipmates and those interested,

> *Petty Officer Third Class James M. Cecy (PN3)*
> *Executive Division, U.S.S. Kitty Hawk (CVA-63). 1969-1971*
>
> *Petty Officer Second Class James M. Cecy (PN2)*
> *Administrative Assistant, U.S. Naval Reserve Center*
> *Santa Cruz, California. 1971-1975*

A Life-Changing Sidenote:

On the afternoon of November 17, 1971, the day I was released to travel home from active duty, I knew I was about to start a new life. Under conviction of the Holy Spirit of God, I prayed to receive Jesus Christ as my Lord and Savior, my new Supreme Commander-in-Chief. Since that day I have endeavored to share my "inside knowledge" with "outsiders" who need to know the language of God's love for them.

In those first years as a new Christian, I also began listening to *The Haven of Rest* radio program as they sang: *"I've anchored my soul to the Haven of Rest."* More Navy talk!

Yes, there is still some Navy in me, and I suppose there will always be. But now, as a Soldier of the Cross, I have a new vocabulary with so many words in my *Christianese* vocabulary that have amazing new meanings—words like *hope*:

Hebrews 6:19 "This hope we have as an anchor of the soul, a hope both sure and steadfast..."

For Personal Reflection:

1. What are some of the words you use as a Christian that may be confusing to non-believers?

2. How might you simplify your vocabulary so that it is understandable?

© Dr. James M. and Karon M. Cecy.

PART FOUR

KARON'S LESSONS FROM A COP'S DAUGHTER

Karon's Cop's Daughter Devotional #1

Cop's Daughter to Pastor's Wife

> Proverbs 19:21 "Many plans are in a man's heart, but the counsel of the LORD will stand."

An Unusual Family History

I came from a long line of first responders:

> • My great, great, great uncle was awarded a Medal of Honor in the Civil War.

> • My grandfather was a fireman in Muncie, Indiana. Some family members say he was a captain or even a Fire Chief in the area.

> • My father was the Chief of Detectives and Lead Investigator in the Santa Cruz County Sheriff's Department, arresting three mass murderers in the 1970s.

> • My father was also a member of the Sheriff's Posse Search and Rescue Team.

> • My uncle, once a Sheriff's deputy with my father, was the Chief of Police in a department he founded in Scotts Valley, California.

On the other hand, my husband came from a long line of…well…the ones that kept first responders busy:

> • His relative was the infamous gangster, Al Capone.

• His uncle was a career criminal who did time at Kingston Penitentiary.

• His first cousin was a diagnosed psychopath, who died in a high-speed police chase.

• He says he would not be surprised to learn he has a few arsonists in the bunch.

When Jim and I met, we were intrigued by the differences in our family histories. When he asked my father for my hand in marriage, Jim was so very afraid. After all, my father knew about some of his more notorious family members. However, knowing Jim's character and love for me, he said, "Yes, of course!"

Here we are, after fifty years of marriage and ministry together—a cop's daughter and Al Capone's relative. Only God makes all things beautiful in His time.

An Unexpected Turn

I did not want my husband to go into law enforcement or become a firefighter. Jim honored my wishes. However, God had a different plan for how He wanted Jim to be involved with both, certainly not in the ways we thought.

• He had tasted the challenges of law enforcement while serving very briefly in the Navy Shore Patrol. His first arrest of a drunken sailor gave him an appreciation for what police officers face.

• He attended Navy Shipboard Fire-fighting School twice and served onboard ship in a fire control station. He became well aware of the threat of uncontrolled fire and explosions.

• He developed a heart for law enforcement officers while doing ride-alongs with my father, even on a horse-back training mission with my father and the other members of the Sheriff's Posse.

• He became the founder and President of JARON Ministries International which contains a special department called CODE 3 Ministries that exists to equip police and first responder chaplains. They also minister globally to law enforcement officers and their families.

• Under his leadership, his CODE 3 Teams minister to the families of fallen police officers and firefighters.

• His CODE 3 Teams have an ongoing confidential counseling ministry for law enforcement personnel.

• He was invited by the South African Police Service to train their officers and minister to their families "from precinct to precinct."

• He was a keynote speaker at the Pan Africa Christian Police Association Conference. He was welcomed into "the family" by hundreds of law enforcement officers from many countries.

• He was the keynote speaker at the Police Officers' Conference at Mount Hermon Christian Conference Center.

• His materials are used internationally to train chaplains, disciple prisoners, and equip ex-cons.

• His office is filled with patches and hats given to him by first responders and military personnel internationally.

• He is, as a pastor, a fellow "minister" with law enforcement officers–the same word (*diakonos*) used in Romans 13:1-7 to speak of government law-keepers. Their worlds are not very different.

• He is, as a counselor, a fellow firefighter, spiritually speaking. Keeping people from experiencing the fires of hell and the flames of interpersonal conflict is his greatest calling.

My Personal Conclusion:

I guess I must admit,

• My husband has the spirit of a pastor, the heart of a cop, and the soul of a firefighter."

• I am not just a cop's daughter. I am a Pastor-Cop-Firefighter's Wife!"

• Better yet, I am a First Responder's backup—his "Second Responder."

That's a job description I would never have planned. However, it is a divine plan for which I will be eternally grateful.

Jeremiah 29:11 "'For I know the plans that I have for you,' declares the LORD, 'plans for welfare and not for calamity to give you a future and a hope.'"

Psalm 32:8 "I will instruct you and teach you in the way which you should go; I will counsel you with My eye upon you."

Proverbs 19:21 "Many plans are in a man's heart, but the counsel of the LORD will stand."

For Personal Reflection:

1. Do you have any famous or infamous ancestors? Any heroes?

2. Reflect on the statement: "I am not responsible for my ancestors, but I can influence my descendants."

3. Do you know any "first responders" personally (e.g., police, fire service, etc.)? In what ways can you encourage them?

4. In what ways has God changed your plans to fit His will for your life?

© Dr. James M. and Karon M. Cecy

Karon's Cop's Daughter Devotional #2

My Police "Family"

> 1 John 4:7-9 "Beloved, let us love one another, for love is from God; and everyone who loves is born of God and knows God. The one who does not love does not know God, for God is love. By this the love of God was manifested in us, that God has sent His only begotten Son into the world so that we might live through Him."

I became a part of the extended police family when I was in elementary school. My father and his brother were both in law enforcement, as were many of their friends. I have fond memories of playing with other police kids. We were truly a band of brothers and sisters.

Every week, we gathered for dinner and games at one of the officers' homes, including ours. Sometimes my sister and I spent the night at our friend's house, and they at ours. There were, of course, all those police department family barbeques! How I remember the fun, laughter, and great food. This brotherhood—this "Thin Blue Line"—of police officers and their families gave me such a feeling of love and acceptance. We really were family!

The yearly Santa Cruz County Fair created special memories for us. My dad and his Sheriff's Posse buddies would ride their horses in the parade and patrol the fairgrounds. We would later meet at the fair with other officers and their families. I now realize they were also "on duty" as they kept their eyes open and their ears tuned to the constant chatter from their walkie-talkies. That was normal for us.

Once in a while, my sister and I got to go to our father's office. I remember distinctly how the other cops treated us. They made us feel very special. They seemed to have understood what it was like to have a Cop-Detective-Dad working different shifts and running out on calls, often in the middle of the night.

It wasn't until I was in junior high school I realized how important this police-family connection was—not until it was taken away. My mother's mental illness had progressed to the point she shut people out, even our uncle's family and the other police families we had grown to love. All dinners, gatherings, and communication abruptly stopped. My sister and I were heartbroken.

Dad's job became all-consuming as he, now the Chief of Detectives, was the Chief Investigator for the mass murders for which Santa Cruz County was famous. Our connection to our police family was broken. My sister and I were left on our own with our mother's irrational and destructive behavior. We missed the gatherings and relationships with other cops and their families.

In 1976, my father died of a sudden heart attack, determined to be a result of his stressful job. Hundreds of officers from all over the nation gathered at his gravesite in tribute. We received many hugs from his fellow officers, especially those we had grown up with. We had missed those fatherly embraces very much!

A few years ago, my husband and I attended his high school class reunion in Santa Cruz. Sitting at a table with old friends, someone I did not know approached me and asked, "Are you Ken Pittenger's daughter?" Puzzled, because my dad had died many years ago, I said "Yes, he was my father. Did you know him?" The man introduced himself and told me he worked in the Sheriff's Department. He began to describe how my father had impacted his life and how much he respected him. I thanked him for his kindness in telling me this.

A few minutes later, a different man approached me and asked the same question. He also introduced himself as a cop and began to describe how honored he was to have met my dad. After this encounter, I left to have a good cry. I was so overwhelmed with gratitude for the kind words about the man I loved and missed.

After getting control of my emotions, I sat down at the table with our friends. We talked about how special it was to hear their words about my father. A short time later, someone else approached our table with the same question and introduction. He continued on with a view of my dad's solid reputation which was such an example to so many in the department and the community. Even though Dad died years earlier, his legacy had continued.

Those three officers gave me three special gifts that day. Not only did their words describing my father's character warm my heart, but they also made me feel like I was still a part of the law enforcement family.

Many years have gone by since I first experienced my youthful connection to other police officers' families. I am certain those feelings instilled in me a lifelong a hunger for "community." My search as a teenager for that belonging contributed to my quest which ultimately led me to trust in Christ and become a part of a new family—the Family of God.

I have since discovered there were definite similarities between our police family and our Christian family. Oh, the love, the fun, and the joy of fellowship! However, unlike our police family that was taken away from us, our Christian family can never be taken away.

I have a special place in my heart for all those in law enforcement. I pray for their protection often. I especially pray every peace officer will come to find personal peace with God through faith in Jesus Christ. I pray they will come to understand that the *"Thin Blue Line"* keeping our society from chaos is found in the *"Shed Red Blood"* of the Crucified and Risen Lord. I especially love welcoming peace officers who respond to Christ into the forever family of God. My family!

The lyrics of an old song by Bill Gaither ring in my heart:

I'm so glad I'm a part of the family of God,
I've been washed in the fountain.
Cleansed by His blood!
Joint heirs with Jesus as we travel this sod,
For I'm part of the family,
The family of God.

For Personal Reflection:

1. Reflect on the gift of those you consider to be "family" even if they are not flesh and blood. Thank them soon.

2. What does it mean to be a part of the forever family of God?

Karon's Cop's Daughter Devotional #3

My Family Heroes

Hebrews 10:10 "By this will we have been sanctified through the offering of the body of Jesus Christ once for all."

Hebrews 10:12 "...but He, having offered one sacrifice for sins for all time, sat down at the right hand of God."

1 John 3:16 "We know love by this, that He laid down His life for us; and we ought to lay down our lives for the brethren."

A hero is defined as a person admired for achievements and noble qualities—one who shows great courage. Who are the heroes in your life? Perhaps it is a favorite Bible character, a person in history, or perhaps you even have a hero in your family.

I am fortunate to have a family of heroes I admire. Although some of these are mentioned in other devotionals, let me review them:

• My great, great, great uncle, Reverend William Pittenger, fought for the Union in the American Civil War and was awarded the Medal of Honor. I am also a direct descendant, on my mother's side, of Confederate General Robert E. Lee.

• My grandfather was in the Army in World War I. He later became a fireman for the city of Muncie, Indiana.

• My father was in the Navy during World War II. In fact, his naval medical ship, *U.S.S. Dorothea Dix*, was a part of the great armada that carried the brave soldiers who stormed the beaches of Normandy. After the war, my father ultimately worked his way up to Lieutenant and Chief of Detectives of the Santa Cruz County Sheriff's Department. In addition, my father was a part of the Sheriff's Posse that searched on horseback for lost people or criminals in hiding.

• My uncle, my father's brother, served as a Navy corpsman with the 1st Marine Division. Later he served as special deputy with the Santa Cruz County Sheriff's Office for eleven years before starting the Scotts Valley Police Dept in November 1966. He retired in 1986 after serving as Police Chief for twenty years.

• My husband was in the Navy, stationed on the attack carrier, *U.S.S. Kitty Hawk*, during the Vietnam War. Two of his older brothers served. One on a Naval missile base, the other at the Navy's *TOPGUN* Training School.

When I think of all the brave men and women who put their lives on the line for others I think of this verse:

1 John 3:16 "We know love by this, that He laid down His life for us; and we ought to lay down our lives for the brethren."

Yes, I am very proud of my family of heroes. I will always admire those who sacrificed greatly to serve others. However, there is another hero in my life—Jesus. His nobility is above all. The courage it took to die on the cross for our sins is unfathomable. What He achieved is the most magnificent work in history: "Jesus, I praise you for your sacrifice on my behalf. You are my hero! Help me to be willing to sacrifice and serve others. Amen."

For Personal Reflection:

1. Inspire your kids by telling them stories of the heroes in your family, community, history, and, of course, the Bible.

2. Talk to your kids about what it means to be a hero.

3. Talk about why Jesus is our Ultimate Hero.

© Dr. James M. and Karon M. Cecy

Karon's Cop's Daughter Devotional #4

Civil War: Up Close and Personal

> Psalm 133:1 "Behold how good and pleasant it is for brothers to dwell together in unity."

> 1 Corinthians 1:10 "Now I exhort you, brethren, by the name of our Lord Jesus Christ, that you all agree, and there be no divisions among you, but you be made complete in the same mind and in the same judgment."

> Colossians 3:14-15 "Beyond all these things put on love, which is the perfect bond of unity. Let the peace of Christ rule in your hearts to which indeed you were called in one body; and be thankful."

Both sides of my family were embroiled on opposite sides in the American Civil War, which was fought April 12, 1861, to May 26, 1865. I am a descendent of the North and the South.

On my father's side (the Union), my great, great, great uncle William Pittenger, a U.S. Army Sergeant, was presented the Medal of Honor on March 25, 1863. He was one of the team of men who, by the direction of General Ormsby M. Mitchell, penetrated nearly 200 miles south into enemy territory. They captured a railroad train at Big Shanty, Georgia and attempted to destroy the bridges and track between Chattanooga, Tennessee and Atlanta, Georgia. This became known as, *The Great Locomotive Chase* and *The Andrews Railroad Raid.*

On my mother's side (the Confederacy), I am a descendent of General Robert E. Lee. He commanded the Army of Northern Virginia, the most successful of the Southern armies during the American Civil War. He ultimately commanded all the Confederate

Armies and surrendered on April 8, 1865, at Appomattox Court House in Virginia.

How do I feel about both of these men in my family tree? I choose to think of their bravery, courage, and determination. I am mostly curious about their faith, hoping to meet them in Heaven someday.

How do I feel about the Civil War itself? It was a horrifying and tragic war for so many reasons. It divided a nation, states, families and friends. Some in the same family fought on the side of the North; some chose to fight on the side of the South. Brother against brother. Blue against gray. Fellow American against fellow American.

My great, great, great uncle William Pittenger and my distant relative, Robert E. Lee would have, if given the chance, killed each other! How might that have affected William's life as a minister and author? How might that have affected their descendants like me?

Many years have passed since the Civil War. However, heartbreaking disunity among family members continues. We are plagued by failed marriages and broken families. Too many friends have become philosophical or political enemies. Too many communities are divided. Sadly, too many local churches are splitting over the silliest of issues.

I am committed to the truth, proclaiming Jesus Christ as the Ultimate Healer of Division. He has provided the Supreme Solution for disunity and civil war on all levels. His work on the cross healed the rift between man and God. His Indwelling Presence is the healing balm for marriages, families, friends, churches, and even nations.

It is often said, "You put two people together you get three opinions." In other words, we love a good fight, even if we don't agree with ourselves! But disunity and division need not be inevitable. We who are "in Christ" should strive with God's help to be at peace with one another. Our churches should display His unity as we live in harmony together. We need to go to war against the civil wars in our homes, churches, and communities:

> Romans 12:18 "If possible, so far as it depends on you, be at peace with all men."

For Personal Reflection:

1. Talk about the American Civil War. Use it as an example of how devastating division can be.

2. Help those close to you by reading and memorizing verses that speak about love and unity.

3. For further study, I encourage you to read *A History of the Andrews Railroad Raid into Georgia in 1862* published in 2001 by Digital Scanning and available at www.amazon.com.

© Dr. James M. and Karon M. Cecy.

Karon's Cop's Daughter Devotional #5

Our Protective Father

> Psalm 91:1-2 "He who dwells in the shelter of the Most High will abide in the shadow of the Almighty. I will say to the LORD, my refuge and my fortress, My God in whom I trust!"

> Psalm 32:7 "You are my hiding place; You preserve me from trouble. You surround me with songs of deliverance."

My dad always wore leather. His policeman's uniform included a leather gun belt, a leather holster, a leather jacket, leather boots, and when riding his horse with the Sheriff's Posse, leather chaps. Of course, his horse was equipped with a saddle, bridle, stirrups, and rifle holster, all made of leather. To complete the look, he often wore a leather cowboy hat.

I remember him frequently cleaning leather. Consequently, my dad always smelled like leather. To this day, when I go into a Western Wear store, the smell of leather sometimes makes me cry.

Every piece of my dad's police uniform was for the purpose of safeguarding himself and others. Being a cop, he was always in "protection mode"—even at home.

My sister and I were often told where we could and could not go. He, of course, had the inside scoop on what was going on in the county and he forbade us to go to certain places. He made a point of explaining that, although he was unable to go into details, we needed to trust him.

Dad's quest to protect the community and his family made the following event especially funny. The following is an excerpt from the Santa Cruz Sentinel, written by reporter, Tom Honig, shortly after my father's death in 1976:

For nearly three years while covering police news for The Sentinel, I came in daily contact with Sheriff's Lt. Ken Pittenger. At the time, he was the head of the department's detective bureau, and it was his job, in addition to running the department, to meet with members of the press to discuss items of interest during the previous 24 hours. Meeting with somebody every morning is an interesting situation. Pitt and I came from different backgrounds; we held totally different jobs, and he was 24 years older than me. But it wasn't long after I first met him that talk became a little less formal and a little more lively. He looked a little bit like George Gobel, and had the kind of innocent expression that made any joke a little more funny. One day, he walked into the detective bureau with a smile on his face and a new gun on his hip. He was showing the other detectives the features of the gun, including a new safety latch which made it impossible to shoot the gun. "Look at this," he said as he pulled the gun and pointed it toward the wall, "it won't even fire when I squeeze the trigger." The next noise was the explosion of the bullet as it fired from the gun and lodged in the wall. Pitt went white in the face, and quietly retired to his desk to write a report on the firing of the gun. The next day, a facsimile of his stamp "K.E. Pittenger --Contents Noted" was drawn over the bullet hole, although nobody ever confessed who drew it. (Tom Honig. Santa Cruz Sentinel)

Since my father was so committed to safety and protection, I know this incident embarrassed him greatly. Much later, he learned to laugh at it. You can be sure his fellow officers did not let him forget it!

I am thankful I had a protective father who watched over me. I never felt his protective nature was restrictive. Instead, my sister and I felt treasured.

I believe our earthly father's protective nature helped us to understand the concept of our Heavenly Father constantly watching over us. Because of Dad, we were able to have a greater grasp of what it means to dwell in the shelter of the Most High, and abide in the shadow of the Almighty—the One who is our refuge, our fortress, our hiding place, and the One who surrounds us with songs of deliverance (cf. Psalm 91:1-2; 32:7).

"Thank you, Dad!"

"Thank You, Heavenly Father!"

For Personal Reflection:

1. In what ways have you experienced someone protecting you?

2. How do those experiences help you to grasp God's hand of protection over you?

© Dr. James M. and Karon M. Cecy.

Karon's Cop's Daughter Devotional #6

Final Justice

> Proverbs 24:20 "For there will be no future for the evil man. The lamp of the wicked will be put out."

My father loved Westerns. As a dutiful daughter, I learned to love them, too. I would sit as close as possible to him and hold his hand while we watched those classic TV shows. The good guys always won!

When he joined the Santa Cruz Sheriff's Department, his life mimicked those Westerns—although, as a murder detective, the good guys did not always win and the bad guys often got away with their heinous crimes. During this time, my father became a member of the Sheriff's Posse. He spent days on horseback, hunting down criminals on the run and searching for lost people in the difficult terrain of the Santa Cruz Mountains.

In the years before his death, he served as the Chief of Detectives and was involved in the hunt for three mass murderers. In 1970, John L. Frazier murdered five people. Herbert Mullin and Edmund Kemper overlapped in their 1972 to 1973 murder sprees, ending with both being arrested within a few weeks of each other, after the deaths of twenty-one people. Relative to its size, our small county became one of the murder capitals of America. The night of our wedding rehearsal, one of these gruesome murderers was finally arrested.

Thankfully, these evil people were caught but at a high price for my father. It was determined my dad's heart attack at the age of fifty-three came as a result of all the pressure, stress, and tragedy he saw first-hand on his job. My grieving family was told this was the first time in the State of California a police officer's heart attack could be attributed to his job. Consequently, my mom received Workman's Compensation—a landmark case in this state.

I wish the world operated like the old TV Westerns where the good guys always won. As a new Christian during that time, I struggled with the age-old questions:

> "Why do people suffer and die at the hands of evil people?"

> "Where is the justice and punishment for the evil they have done?"

My answers were found in the Scriptures. Evil people may be punished here on earth, but the reality is, that justice will not be fully dished out until the Final Day of Judgment before the Throne of God. Our God will execute His justice:

> Psalm 37:1-2 "Do not fret because of evildoers. Be not envious toward wrongdoers. For they will wither quickly like the grass and fade like the green herb."

> Psalm 37:9 "For evildoers will be cut off, but those who wait for the LORD, they will inherit the land."

Quite obviously, Almighty God is the Good Guy who always wins!

For Personal Reflection:

Reflect on all of Psalm 37 regarding good ultimately triumphing over evil.

© Dr. James M. and Karon M. Cecy.

Karon's Cop's Daughter Devotional #7

Another Glimpse of Protection

> Psalm 91:1-4, 11-12 "He who dwells in the shelter of the Most High will abide in the shadow of the Almighty. I will say to the LORD, 'My refuge and my fortress, My God in whom I trust!' For it is He who delivers you from the snare of the trapper and from the deadly pestilence. He will cover you with His pinions, and under His wings you may seek refuge; His faithfulness is a shield and bulwark....For He will give His angels charge concerning you, to guard you in all your ways. They will bear you up in their hands, that you do not strike your foot against a stone."

My father built a reputation of integrity and strong leadership which was balanced quite well with his warm and caring personality. He truly was an example of biblical meekness—strength under control. He was well-liked by his peers and adored by his two daughters. He was also adored by his horse, a beautiful American Saddlebred with dreamy eyes, named Pride. Together they were quite a sight at parades, with her stately walk as he would proudly carry the American flag. Pride was also a "deputized" horse, an official member of the Santa Cruz Sheriff's Department, with a badge on her leather breastplate. Together, Dad and Pride teamed up "To serve and protect" in search and rescue, hunting for criminals, and crowd control.

One day God provided me with a great glimpse of the power of protection from a very unlikely source. I always enjoyed going out each morning to feed my dad's horse. As soon as Pride saw me coming, she galloped across the pasture and stomped into her stable to meet me at the feed trough. She and I did not know our bantam chicken had just hatched her eggs in the stable. A bantam chicken is only 1/5th the size of a normal chicken. Much smaller than a horse, for sure!

As soon as Pride took her first step into the stable, Mama Bantam attacked with such a fury of protection! The next thing I see is the tiny chicken chasing a giant horse around the pasture. I will never forget the sight of Pride kicking and racing around the field with a screeching chicken flying a few feet high in pursuit. In chicken language, I am sure she was screaming, *"Stay away from my babies!"* During all the commotion, I quickly relocated the baby chicks to a safer spot in the yard. I had to hurry so Mama would not come after me. Her tiny body was in "full protection mode" regardless of the threat—equestrian or human.

Psalm 91 declares that Almighty God is the Great Protector of those He loves. He certainly has the power and authority to back it up. No one gets to mess with God's children who, like baby chicks, are truly under His wings of protection. Let's rehearse a quick overview of Psalm 91 in a series of declarations I encourage us to make often:

• "Today, I will dwell in the shelter of the Most High God."

• "Today, I will live in the shadow of the Almighty."

• "Today, I will remind myself the Lord is my refuge and my fortress."

• "Today, I will place my complete trust in the One who is my God."

• "Today, I will remember He will deliver me from entrapment."

• "Today, He will protect me from deadly pestilence (i.e., deadly influences)."

• "Today, He will completely cover me with his pinions (i.e., the edge of His feathers)."

• "Today, I will cuddle under His wings of protection."

• "Today, His faithfulness will be my shield."

• "Today, I will declare He is my bulwark (i.e., my defensive wall)."

• "Today, He will send His angels to guard and protect me."

• "Today, His angels will hold me up and keep me from tripping."

I pray you will write these on the "tablet of your heart" (Proverbs 3:3). In other words, post them as a reminder on the front door of the stable. You never know when you will need protection from even the tiniest of threats!

For Personal Reflection:

1. Reflect on how God has put into nature many examples of His protection.

2. Read Psalm 91 about God's protection over us. Rehearse the declarations.

3. Memorize Psalm 91:4 "…under His wings you may seek refuge…"

© Dr. James M. and Karon M. Cecy.

Karon's Cop's Daughter Devotional #8

My Hero's Funeral

Philippians 4:13 "I can do all things through Him who strengthens me."

I have a gallery of pictures in albums and on the walls of my home. Although décor experts in our present day would consider these as clutter, we treasure these collections. They represent a museum of memories—snapshots of important events, people, and adventures. We had all these precious pictures put on backup hard drives for safekeeping. I have another collection of memories held in safekeeping—i.e., in my heart, my personal backup hard drive.

Throughout my life, God has imprinted Scriptures into my heart during specific events, especially when I am most fearful. For example, passages like:

Philippians 4:13 "I can do all things through Him who strengthens me."

Isaiah 41:10 "Do not fear, for I am with you. Do not anxiously look about you, for I am your God. I will strengthen you. Surely I will help you. Surely I will uphold you with My righteous right hand."

I added these passages to my collection in June 1976, when I got ready to go to my father's funeral. He had died unexpectedly as a result of the stress of his job as the Chief of Detectives. He was only fifty-three years old. His death was a shock to the law enforcement community, and I expected there would be a large crowd. Being shy, terror was added to my grief, and both overwhelmed me!

I took Philippians 4:13 and Isaiah 41:10 with me to the cemetery. As I stepped out of the car, I viewed a vast sea of uniformed officers and officials from all over California and beyond. They stood at attention, some with their eyes dripping with compassion. I will never forget those moments of God's comfort and the comfort of all those people. My husband shared a eulogy, honoring our father who Jim had come to love dearly.

Soon after his death, we received a memorial plaque with my father's picture and his badge embedded. As I gaze at it, I am often taken back to that sad day at the cemetery. In my grief, God was with me. As promised in these verses, He strengthened me, helped me, and upheld me. He has continued to do so throughout these decades. To God alone be the glory.

For Personal Reflection:

1. Bible memory builds the foundation for God to apply Scripture to specific events in your life. Pick a few special verses you make your own—passages you pray God will use throughout your life. Share them with others.

2. Add verses and testimonies of God's faithfulness to your "museum of memories." Store them on the backup hard drive of your heart.

3. Consider writing your faith story for your family and friends. For further help, we refer you to Appendix #1 in Volume One of *"Telling Your Faith Story."* (Available at www.amazon.com or www.jaron.org.)

CONCLUDING THOUGHTS

Our Final Word to Our Fellow Ministers

Our motivations for creating this devotional have been abundantly clear from the beginning.

• We are bound by God's special mandate.

We exist to "serve the servants of God"—especially our fellow Servant-Leaders and Skilled Helpers.

> Colossians 1:29 "For this purpose also I labor, striving according to His power, which mightily works within me."

• We are stimulated by God's special calling.

We exist to encourage one another the closer we draw near to the return of Christ:

> Hebrews 10:24-25 "…let us consider how to stimulate one another to love and good deeds, not forsaking our own assembling together, as is the habit of some, but encouraging one another; and all the more as you see the day drawing near."

• We are motivated to recognize the sacrifices of others.

We exist to pay attention to the struggles our fellow ministers and Skilled Helpers face. We embrace the heartfelt testimony of the Apostle Paul:

2 Corinthians 11:23-31 "Are they servants of Christ?—I speak as if insane—I more so; in far more labors, in far more imprisonments, beaten times without number, often in danger of death. Five times I received from the Jews thirty-nine lashes. Three times I was beaten with rods, once I was stoned, three times I was shipwrecked, a night and a day I have spent in the deep. I have been on frequent journeys, in dangers from rivers, dangers from robbers, dangers from my countrymen, dangers from the Gentiles, dangers in the city, dangers in the wilderness, dangers on the sea, dangers among false brethren; I have been in labor and hardship, through many sleepless nights, in hunger and thirst, often without food, in cold and exposure. Apart from such external things, there is the daily pressure on me of concern for all the churches. Who is weak without my being weak? Who is led into sin without my intense concern? If I have to boast, I will boast of what pertains to my weakness. The God and Father of the Lord Jesus, He who is blessed forever, knows that I am not lying."

• **We are filled with a lifelong passion to encourage fellow ministers to never give up.**

Galatians 6:9 "Let us not lose heart in doing good, for in due time we will reap if we do not grow weary."

2 Thessalonians 3:13 "But as for you, brethren, do not grow weary of doing good."

• **We are excited about the next chapters of our lives and yours.**

Jesus didn't say, "I am finished." He said, "It is finished." His earthly ministry on earth was finished; ours continues on His behalf. Thus, we take His reminder as our daily challenge:

> John 14:12 "Truly, truly, I say to you, he who believes in Me, the works that I do, he will do also; and greater works than these he will do; because I go to the Father."

• **We are not done.**

On to Volume Three of *"Telling Our Faith Story: Earthly Lessons to Our Heavenly Family."* We hope you will join us there.

In the meantime, keep on keeping on, remembering:

> *Coram Deo Laboramus.*
> "We work in the sight of God."

Jim and Karon

APPENDICES

Appendix #1

Taking My Ministry Pulse

A Worksheet for Those Who Serve Others

"Ministry that costs nothing accomplishes nothing. If there is to be any blessing, there must be some bleeding" (J. H. Jowett).

When counseling and encouraging fellow Skilled Helpers and ministers we often ask them to reflect on their ministry. Take some time to seriously think about your ministry condition:

• Some encouraging things that have happened recently in my ministry are:

• Some fresh insights I have recently learned in my ministry are:

• My present concerns regarding my ministry are:

　　1. Regarding my overall ministry I feel:

__abused __angry __appreciated __buried __burdened__burned out __challenged __confident __disappointed __dry__encouraged __excited __falsely accused __fearful__frustrated__fulfilled__hopeful__indifferent __joyful __lonely __misunderstood__optimistic__rejected__stimulated __supported __tired __unappreciated __other: _____

　　Comment:

2. Regarding my relationship to my supervisors, I feel:

__abused __angry __appreciated __buried __burdened__burned out
__challenged __confident __disappointed __dry__encouraged __excited
__falsely accused __fearful__frustrated__fulfilled__hopeful__indifferent
__joyful __lonely __misunderstood__optimistic__rejected__stimulated
__supported __tired __unappreciated __other: _____

     Comment:

3. Regarding my relationship with the community I serve, I feel:

__abused __angry __appreciated __buried __burdened__burned out
__challenged __confident __disappointed __dry__encouraged __excited
__falsely accused __fearful__frustrated__fulfilled__hopeful__indifferent
__joyful __lonely __misunderstood__optimistic__rejected__stimulated
__supported __tired __unappreciated __other: _____

     Comment:

4. Regarding my relationship with my fellow workers, I feel:

__abused __angry __appreciated __buried __burdened__burned out
__challenged __confident __disappointed __dry__encouraged __excited
__falsely accused __fearful__frustrated__fulfilled__hopeful__indifferent
__joyful __lonely __misunderstood__optimistic__rejected__stimulated
__supported __tired __unappreciated __other: _____

     Comment:

5. Regarding how I am presently using my gifts and talents, I feel:

__abused __angry __appreciated __buried __burdened__burned out
__challenged __confident __disappointed __dry__encouraged __excited
__falsely accused __fearful__frustrated__fulfilled__hopeful__indifferent
__joyful __lonely __misunderstood__optimistic__rejected__stimulated
__supported __tired __unappreciated __other: _____

    Comment:

6. Regarding my outlook concerning my ministry future, I feel:

__abused __angry __appreciated __buried __burdened__burned out
__challenged __confident __disappointed __dry__encouraged __excited
__falsely accused __fearful__frustrated__fulfilled__hopeful__indifferent
__joyful __lonely __misunderstood__optimistic__rejected__stimulated
__supported __tired __unappreciated __other: _____

    Comment:

7. Regarding _____, I feel:

__abused __angry __appreciated __buried __burdened__burned out
__challenged __confident __disappointed __dry__encouraged __excited
__falsely accused __fearful__frustrated__fulfilled__hopeful__indifferent
__joyful __lonely __misunderstood__optimistic__rejected__stimulated
__supported __tired __unappreciated __other: _____

    Comment:

(Adapted from *"The Accountable Life: Protecting Myself and Others"* by Dr. James M. Cecy. Available at www.amazon.com and www.jaron.org.)

Appendix #2

Wise Civic Leaders and Their Citizens

Young King Solomon was overwhelmed by the task of leading God's people. He cried out to God for wisdom and God blessed him beyond measure (cf. 1 Kings 3:5-14; 4:20-30). Later, King Solomon authored the Book of Proverbs, where he spends a great deal of time focusing on potential political leaders regarding the wisdom they would need to serve people.

Ultimately, the highest title given to a leader in the Book of Proverbs is "the wise king" (Hebrew: *chakam melek*). Solomon recognizes by experience and by divine revelation that the greatest need of a civic leader is wisdom from God Himself. They are rightly expected to be civil *servants—servant-leaders!*

The following are ancient principles primarily from the Book of Proverbs regarding the rights and duties of civic leaders and the responsibilities of the citizens they are called to serve and protect.

I. The Goals of Human Government

Goal #1: To promote righteousness.

Proverbs 14:34 "Righteousness (i.e., justice/the rule of law) exalts a nation, but sin is a disgrace (i.e., a reproach) to any people" (Christian Standard Bible Version).

Proverbs 21:3 "To do righteousness and justice is desired by the LORD more than sacrifice" (cf. Proverbs 8:18, 20; 10:2; 11:4, 5, 6, 18, 19; 12:28; 13:6; 14:34; 15:9; 16:8, 12, 31; 21:21).

Goal #2: To point the people to God's law as the highest authority.

Proverbs 30:5 "Every word of God is tested; He is a shield to those who take refuge in Him."

Proverbs 29:18 "Where there is no vision (i.e., no hearing from God), the people are unrestrained (i.e., naked and exposed to anarchy), but happy is he who keeps the law."

Proverbs 28:2 "When a country is rebellious, it has many rulers..." (New International Version).

Goal #3: To defend the rights of the people.

Proverbs 31:8-9 "Open your mouth for the mute, for the rights of all the unfortunate. Open your mouth, judge righteously, and defend the rights of the afflicted and needy."

II. The Civic Leader's Responsibilities

Responsibility #1. Civic leaders are to seek godly wisdom in order to judge rightly and make just decisions.

Proverbs 8:15-16 "By me (i.e., wisdom) kings reign, and rulers decree justice. By me (i.e., wisdom) princes rule, and nobles, all who judge rightly."

Proverbs 16:10 "A divine decision is in the lips of the king; his mouth should not err in judgment."

Proverbs 24:5 "...a wise man is strong and a man of knowledge increases power."

Proverbs 14:12 "There is a way that seems right to a person, but its end is the way of death."

Proverbs 28:16 "A leader who is a great oppressor (Hebrew: *ma' ashaqqah*) lacks understanding..."

Proverbs 28:28 "When the wicked rise, men hide themselves; but when they perish, the righteous increase."

Responsibility #2. Civic leaders are to deal with the wicked quickly.

Proverbs 20:8 "A king who sits on the throne of justice disperses all evil with his eyes."

> Note: The throne of justice (Hebrew: *kissa diyn*) is the place where people's rights are considered and where evil is dispersed like a bad seed.

Proverbs 20:26 "A wise king (Hebrew: *chakam melek*) winnows the wicked, and drives the threshing wheel over them."

Proverbs 25:4-5 "Take away the dross from the silver, and there comes out a vessel for the smith. Take away the wicked before the king, and his throne will be established in righteousness."

Ecclesiastes 8:11 "Because the sentence against an evil deed is not executed quickly, therefore the hearts of the sons of men among them are given fully to do evil."

Responsibility #3. Civic leaders are to care for the afflicted and the needy.

Proverbs 28:15 "Like a roaring lion and a rushing bear is a wicked ruler over a poor people."

Proverbs 31:8-9 "Open your mouth for the mute, for the rights of all the unfortunate. Open your mouth, judge righteously, and defend the rights of the afflicted and needy" (cf. James 1:27).

Proverbs 29:14 "If a king judges the poor with truth (i.e., fairness), His throne will be established forever."

III. The Civic Leader's Qualifications

Qualification #1. Civic leaders are to strive to live righteous lives.

Proverbs 14:34s "Righteousness exalts a nation…"

Proverbs 16:12 "It is an abomination (i.e., disgusting) for kings to commit wicked acts, for a throne is established on righteousness (Hebrew: *tsedaqah*)."

Proverbs 29:2 "When the righteous increase, the people rejoice, but when a wicked man rules, people groan (Hebrew: *'anakh* = groan in pain)."

Qualification #2. Civic leaders are to be people of good judgment.

Proverbs 16:10 "A divine decision is in the lips of the king; his mouth should not err in judgment."

(Note: A divine decision [Hebrew: *keh'sem*] is one that considers what Almighty God would do.)

Qualification #3. Civic leaders are to be committed to godly communication.

Proverbs 10:19 "When there are many words, transgression unavoidable."

Proverbs 18:2 "A fool does not delight in understanding but only in revealing his own mind" (cf. Proverbs 17:18, etc.) regarding self-control in speech).

Proverbs 8:6 "Listen, for I will speak noble things; and the opening of my lips will reveal right things."

Proverbs 16:13 "Righteous lips are the delight of kings, and he who speaks right is loved."

Proverbs 11:14 "Where there is no guidance the people fall, but in abundance of counselors there is victory" (cf. Proverbs 1:5; 12:15; etc.).

Qualification #4. Civic leaders are to be committed to loyalty and truth.

Proverbs 20:28 "Loyalty and truth preserve the king, and he upholds his throne by righteousness."

Proverbs 29:12 "If a ruler pays attention to falsehood, all his ministers become wicked."

Proverbs 29:14 "If a king judges the poor with truth, his throne will be established forever."

Qualification #5. Civic leaders are to engage in thorough research of the issues.

Proverbs 25:2 "It is the glory of God to conceal a matter, but the glory of kings is to search out a matter."

Proverbs 29:4 "The king gives stability to the land by justice... (Hebrew: *mishpat*)."

Qualification #6. Civic leaders are to surround themselves with people of character.

Proverbs 25:5 "Take away the wicked before the king, and his throne will be established in righteousness."

Proverbs 29:12 "If a ruler pays attention to falsehood, all his ministers become wicked."

> e.g., 1 Kings 12:1-16 – The story of foolish King Rehoboam, son of King Solomon, who suffered the consequences of listening to the wrong advisors.

Qualification #7. Civic leaders are to refuse bribes or special privileges.

Jeremiah 6:13 "...Everyone is greedy for gain..."

Proverbs 28:16 "A leader who is a great oppressor lacks understanding, but he who hates unjust gain will prolong his days."

Proverbs 29:4 "The king gives stability to the land by justice, but a man who takes bribes overthrows it."

Proverbs 15:27 "He who profits illicitly troubles his own house."

Qualification #8. Civic leaders are to be committed to a life of moral purity.

Proverbs 31:3 "Do not give your strength to women, or your ways to that which destroys kings" (cf. Proverbs 5-9).

Qualification #9. Civic leaders are not to be addicted to any substance.

Proverbs 31:4-5 "It is not for kings, O Lemuel, it is not for kings to drink (i.e., get drunk with) wine, or for rulers to desire strong drink, for they will drink and forget what is decreed, and pervert the rights of all the afflicted."

Qualification #10. Civic leaders are to be decisive.

Proverbs 24:21-22 "My son, fear the LORD and the king; do not associate with those who are given to change. For their calamity will rise suddenly, and who knows the ruin that comes from both of them?"

Proverbs 24:21 "...do not join with rebellious officials" (New International Version).

Qualification #11. Civic leaders are to be subject to the King of kings and Lord of lords.

1 Timothy 6:15-16 "...[Jesus Christ] who is the blessed and only Sovereign, the King of kings and Lord of lords, who alone possesses immortality and dwells in unapproachable light, whom no man has seen or can see. To Him be honor and eternal dominion! Amen" (cf. Revelation 17:14; 19:16).

Ecclesiastes 12:13 "Fear God and keep his commandment, for this is the duty of all mankind."

Proverbs 24:21 "My son, fear the LORD ..."

Proverbs 21:1 "The king's heart is like channels of water in the hand of the LORD; He turns it wherever He wishes."

IV. The Citizens' Responsibilities to Their Civic Leaders

Ecclesiastes 8:2 "Keep the command of the king because of the oath before God."

Ecclesiastes 8:4 "Since the word of the king is authoritative, who will say to him, 'What are you doing?'"

> **Responsibility #1. Wise citizens are to submit to their godly authority.**

Proverbs 24:21 "My son, fear the LORD and the king..." (cf. Ecclesiastes 8:2-5; Romans 13:1-7; 1 Peter 2:13-17).

Acts 5:29 "We must obey God rather than men."

> **Responsibility #2. Wise citizens are to strive to be productive.**

Proverbs 14:35 "The king's favor is toward a servant who acts wisely, but his anger is toward him who acts shamefully."

Proverbs 22:29 "Do you see a man skilled in his work? He will stand before kings; he will not stand before obscure men."

> (Note: The Hebrew word skilled [*mahiyr*] speaks of being quick, prompt—i.e., being ready, willing, and able.)

Responsibility #3. Wise citizens are to be humble and not abuse their personal relationships to civic leaders for their personal benefit.

Proverbs 25:6-7 "Do not claim honor in the presence of the king, and do not stand in the place of great men; for it is better that it be said to you, 'Come up here,' than that you should be put lower in the presence of the prince, whom your eyes have seen."

Proverbs 23:1 "When you sit down to dine with a ruler, consider carefully what is before you..."

Responsibility #4. Wise citizens are not to judge the hearts and motives of their civic leaders.

Proverbs 25:3 "...the heart of kings is unsearchable."

> (Note: We are to judge people's behaviors, but only God can judge their motives [cf. Romans 1:9; Philippians 1:8; 2 Corinthians 1:23; 1 Thessalonians 2:5—e.g., "God is my witness"].)

Responsibility #5. Wise citizens are to be respectful of their civic leaders.

Proverbs 16:14 "The fury of a king I like messengers of death, but a wise man will appease it."

Proverbs 20:2 "The terror of a king is like the growling of a lion; he who provokes him to anger forfeits his own life."

Proverbs 22:11 "He who loves purity of heart and whose speech is gracious, the king is his friend."

Proverbs 25:15 "By forbearance a ruler may be persuaded, and a soft tongue breaks the bone."

Proverbs 29:8 "Scorners set a city aflame, but wise men turn away anger."

The Challenge:

Proverbs 14:34 "Righteousness exalts a nation, but sin is a disgrace to any people" (Christian Standard Bible).

Psalm 33:12 "Blessed is the nation whose God is the LORD."

Praying for Our Civic Leaders

1 Timothy 2:1-4 "First of all, then, I urge that entreaties and prayers, petitions and thanksgivings, be made on behalf of all men, for kings and all who are in authority, so that we may lead a tranquil and quiet life in all godliness and dignity. This is good and acceptable in the sight of God our Savior, who desires all men to be saved and to come to the knowledge of the truth."

Discussion Questions:

1. What do you most expect from your government? Your civic leaders?

2. What does it mean for a civic *leader* to become a civil *servant*?

3. What is the highest duty citizens have to their government and civic leaders?

© Dr. James M. Cecy, Campus Bible Church, Fresno, California

Appendix #3

The Art and Science of Delegation

"When in charge ponder. When in trouble delegate. When in doubt mumble" (Source unknown).

The Art of Delegation is the Science of Management

Delegation is one of the most important management skills that must constantly be improved. It is more than the art of recruiting and wooing willing workers. It is the science of utilizing effective principles that are transferrable, measurable, and repeatable. Delegation is also biblical:

• Moses was rebuked for not delegating (e.g., Story of Jethro in Exodus 18)

> Exodus 18:18 "You will surely wear out, both yourself and these people who are with you, for the task is too heavy for you; you cannot do it alone."

• Jesus delegated, declaring those that followed Him would do "greater works" (cf. John 14:12).

• The Apostle Paul delegated tasks to his less experienced co-workers (e.g., Titus, Timothy, etc.).

• Shepherds are called to equip people for ministry (cf. Ephesians 4:11-12).

> "Delegating means letting others become the experts and hence the best" (Timothy Firnstahl).

Dumping vs. Delegating

• Dumping: Giving responsibility to others without proper training and active oversight.

• Delegating: Giving responsibility to others with proper training and active oversight.

> "Delegating work works, provided the one delegating works, too" (Robert Half).

Effective vs. Ineffective Delegation

• Effective delegation saves time, develops people, grooms successors, motivates and equips others, helps us clarify and refine our own tasks and priorities.

• Ineffective delegation causes frustration, de-motivates, confuses, prevents tasks from being completed, discourages, and causes the organization to be dependent on new people from the outside.

> "No person will make a great business who wants to do it all himself or get all the credit" (Andrew Carnegie).

Delegating S.M.A.R.T.E.R.

No matter how good you are, you can't do everything. The following is borrowed and revised from miscellaneous online sources:

Delegated tasks must be:

> • Specific • Measurable • Agreed Upon
> • Realistic • Time Bound • Ethical • Reportable

The Ten Steps of Successful Delegation

1. Identify the task.

Confirm in your own mind that the task is suitable to be delegated. (Perhaps your supervisor would not approve of you delegating that responsibility.)

"Delegate; don't abrogate."

2. Clarify the task.

Be clear. Be concise. (Who? What? Where? When? How? Why?)

Who else needs to know what's going on? Do not leave the person to inform your supervisor or peers of their new responsibility.

3. Select the individual or team.

What are your reasons for delegating? The benefits? The liabilities?

4. Assess ability and training needs.

Is he/she capable of doing the task? What would they need to have in order to be successful?

5. Explain the reasons for the task being delegated.

• Why is this job being delegated? (i.e., Why aren't you doing it?)
• Why are you delegating to that person or people?
• What is its importance and relevance?
• Where does it fit in the overall scheme of things?
• How does it fit into the big picture?

6. State the expected results.

What must be achieved? How will the task be measured? How will we know that the task is successfully done?

7. Consider the resources required for the task to be completed effectively.

Discuss and agree what is required to get the job done.

Consider people, location, premises, equipment, money, materials, other related activities and services.

8. Agree to specific deadlines, in advance.

When must the job be finished? If an ongoing duty, when are the review dates? When are the reports due? If the task is complex and has parts or stages, what are the priorities?

Methods of checking and controlling must be clearly stated and agreed upon by the other person or this monitoring will seem like interference or lack of trust.

9. Provide regular support and communicate often.

Agree on how and when you will communicate (e.g., phone, email, memo, face-to-face, etc.).

10. Give feedback on the results.

Let the person know how they are doing, and whether they have achieved the expected goals. If not, review with them why things did not go according to plan, and deal with the problems together.

The Levels of Delegation

The more experienced and reliable the other person is, the more freedom you can give. However, the more critical the task, the more cautious you need to be about extending a lot of freedom without the proper training.

Basic Delegation

1. I do it – you watch. (You ask me questions.)

2. We do it together. (I ask you questions.)

3. You do it – I watch. (I inspect what I expect.)

4. You do it alone. (I support and encourage.)

5. You do it – Somebody else watches.

Advanced Delegation

(Note: Level 1 is the lowest level of delegated freedom. Level 8 is the highest.)

Level 1 "Wait to act until I tell you." or "Do exactly what I say." or "Follow these instructions precisely." (Note: There is no delegated freedom in this level.)

Level 2 "Look into this and tell me the situation. I'll decide what to do."

This is asking for investigation and analysis but no recommendation. The person delegating retains responsibility for assessing options before making the decision. This level tests the person's ability to assess a situation and tests your level of confidence.

Level 3 "Look into this and tell me the situation. We'll decide together."

This level of delegation encourages and enables the analysis and decision to be a shared process.

Level 4 "Give me your analysis of the situation (e.g., reasons, options, pros, and cons) and recommendation. We'll discuss it and I'll back your decision."

Level 5 "Decide and let me know your decision, then go ahead unless I say not to."

Now the other person begins to control the action.

Level 6 "Decide and take action. Let me know what you did and what happened."

Level 7 "Decide and take action. You need not check back with me. I trust you."

Level 8 "Decide where action needs to be taken and manage the situation accordingly. It's your area of responsibility now."

The most freedom you can give to the other person, and not generally used without formal change of a person's job role.

What happens if the expected job doesn't get done according to the plan?

The questions to ask:

- Was the agreement and the expectations clear?

• Did something unexpected happen?

• Was this job beyond the person's capability or availability?

• Did I help or hinder the success of this task?

What happens if I get blamed for its failure or lack of completion?

Delegation means allowing people to make mistakes, even if it means we are called to give an account for that mistake.

This requires making a clear distinction between blame and responsibility.

• Blame – "It's my fault."

• Responsibility – "It may be somebody else's fault but it is my oversight. Therefore, I am responsible, regardless of who is to blame."

"You can delegate authority, but you can never delegate responsibility for delegating a task to someone else. If you picked the right person, fine, but if you picked the wrong person, the responsibility is yours–not his. (Adapted from a quote by Richard Kravfe.)

"The best executive is the one who has sense enough to pick good men to do what he wants done, and self-restraint enough to keep from meddling with them while they do it" (Theodore Roosevelt).

(Adapted from instructional aids by Dr. James M. Cecy, Fresno, California.)

ABOUT THE AUTHORS

James Michael Cecy was born in 1950 in Toronto, Canada, and moved to Santa Cruz, California when he was eleven years old. He entered the U.S. Navy in 1969 and served on the aircraft carrier, *U.S.S. Kitty Hawk*, during the Vietnam War. On November 17, 1971, the day he was released from active naval duty, God stirred his heart and Jim trusted in Jesus Christ alone for his salvation. He quickly became an avid student of the Bible.

Jim was called to the ministry in 1974, serving churches in California for fifty years. He has served as the Senior Pastor-Teacher at Campus Bible Church of Fresno (formerly Campus Baptist Church) since 1995. He is known for his commitment to Scripture, his enthusiastic expositional teaching, and his passion to equip God's people locally and globally.

Pastor Jim has a Bachelor of Arts degree in Speech-Communication from San Jose State University (1975). He earned his Master of Divinity degree in Bible Exposition from Talbot Theological Seminary (1978). In 1992, Jim received his Doctor of Ministry degree from Western Seminary (San Jose Campus).

Dr. Cecy is the founder and president of JARON Ministries International. Based in Fresno, California, it is a training ministry committed to equipping pastors, missionaries, chaplains and Christian leaders around the world. Jim has traveled extensively in numerous countries. His training seminars have reached hundreds of thousands of people on five continents. He has produced a number of written, audio, and video materials on a wide variety of subjects, available in several languages through JARON Ministries International (www.jaron.org), Amazon (www.amazon.com), his personal website (www.puritywar.com), and Campus Bible Church (www.campusbiblechurch.com).

Karon Marie Pittenger-Cecy was born in 1950 in Muncie, Indiana and moved to Santa Cruz, California around 1953. She attended elementary, junior high, high school and Cabrillo College in Santa Cruz, California before moving to Dallas, Texas to serve as a Ministry Assistant for a para-church organization. She returned to Santa Cruz County and worked as a receptionist at Twin Lakes Baptist Church. Later, she served as an Executive Assistant for the Executive Director of Mount Hermon Christian Conference Center and later at the Children's Hospital in Los Angeles.

Karon accepted Jesus Christ as her Savior and Lord at the age of eighteen and has served faithfully alongside Jim for over five decades as a pastor's wife. She is presently the Children's Director at Campus Bible Church, a multi-site church in Fresno, California. Karon is also a missionary with JARON Ministries International and, in her Side-By-Side Ministry, serves as a counselor, teacher, and mentor to women, locally and globally. In the words of those who know her, she is "a mother to many."

Jim and Karon were married in 1973 and began a life of ministry together. They raised three daughters and, since 1987, have cared for twenty-three foster children. Two, as adults, remain a part of the family. Karon and Jim are abundantly blessed with fifteen grandchildren and possibly more to come. Jim and Karon enjoy hanging out with family and friends as well as short trips in their recreational vehicle. However, Karon's greatest joy is teaching and discipling her children and grandchildren.

ABOUT JARON MINISTRIES INTERNATIONAL

THE JARON MOVEMENT

So, What's in a Name?

In 1990, Jim and Karon stepped out on an adventure they chose to call Jaron Ministries International, first named by combining the first letter of Jim's name with the last four letters of Karon's (i.e., Jaron = Jim and Karon). As the ministry quickly grew beyond Jim and Karon, they held a re-naming contest in which a young couple from Alaska submitted the winning entry:

> **JARON = Jesus's Ambassadors Reaching Out to Nations**

That new name (note the capital letters) more clearly represented who we wanted to be as a ministry. We are Jesus's Ambassadors, using God's unique giftedness to reach out to people all over the world. Around the same time, one of our first staff members, Dr. Lyndel Moe, designed our JARON seal to help communicate what JARON is:

Around the outside rim are sixty-six stars representing the sixty-six books of the Bible. The cross and wreath represent Jesus's Ambassadors, and the circle reminds us of our mandate to reach out to the world.

Unlike many mission agencies that have a specific calling to a specific people-group using a specific style of ministry, JARON has evolved into a much broader ministry with a very unique purpose.

Our goal is to build a qualified team of Jesus's Ambassadors who will use their gifts and talents wherever and whenever. JARON does not exist to point our missionaries where JARON wants them to go. We exist to equip and empower our missionaries to go wherever God's Holy Spirit has pointed them.

OUR SPECIFIC MISSION:

JARON Ministries International exists to:

• Build a team of Ambassadors of Jesus Christ (pastors, missionaries, chaplains, and Christian leaders) who will teach, disciple, and encourage Christian leaders in the United States and abroad.

• Serve as a ministry of instruction and motivation to local churches and Christian organizations through pulpit supply, classroom instruction, conferences, seminars, retreats, short-term ministries, and special services.

• Produce and provide biblically sound and currently relevant written, audio, and video training materials.

• Provide biblical, Christ-centered counseling to those in need.

JARON is a registered 501(c)3 non-profit organization in the State of California.

ABOUT CODE 3 INTERNATIONAL MINISTRIES

In 1997, yet another ministry was birthed at JARON. Two of JARON's Mission's Department men joined in training and ministry with Pointman Leadership Institute Global, a ministry under the umbrella of Hume Lake Christian Camps, and founded by retired LA Police Chief Robert Vernon. The PLIG program was focused on leadership training for law enforcement leaders. JARON Ministries began leading short-term mission teams, in partnership with international police leaders throughout Africa, as an outreach to indigenous peoples.

JARON's short-term missionary alumni, Josh Carter, was transitioning from youth ministry into law enforcement. He had a burden to continue in ministry, especially to the law enforcement community. However, rather than a "top-down" strategy, Josh and fellow officers wanted to minister to fellow peers—more of a "bottom-up" approach—equipping active and retired officers to serve fellow officers and their families. The name CODE 3 International Ministries was suggested by one of Josh's fellow police officers. CODE 3 is the running code for the emergency use of lights and sirens. The name CODE 3 stands for:

**Christian Officers' Discipleship and Evangelism
Serving God, Serving Police. Serving Community.**

While ministering in Africa, we learned about the movie *Courageous* being filmed by the Kendrick brothers from Sherwood Baptist in Georgia. CODE 3 used the movie as a tool to invite police couples to a red-carpet premiere as part of our Central Valley Police Week. It was a huge success, and the CODE 3 team later took the movie to the Philippines, using it as an outreach tool to over 4,300 police officers. An abundant harvest was a result, and thousands engaged in the Bible study program that accompanied the film.

The CODE 3 team pursues various forms of ministries to local, state, national, and international police agencies and families. Our Chaplaincy Training and equipping ministries are a major part of our strategy. Our chaplains serve in jails and prisons, and provide counseling and discipleship in a number of agencies, locally, nationally, and globally. One beloved outreach is our annual team that travels to Washington D.C. each May for the National Police Week Memorial. There we minister to families of fallen officers who died in the line of duty the year prior.

If you have a desire to help encourage and equip the law enforcement communities, please contact us at:

CODE 3 International Ministries
c/o JARON Ministries International, Inc.
4710 N. Maple Avenue, Fresno, CA 93726
www.jaron.org
559-227-7997

ABOUT SIDE-BY-SIDE MINISTRY

After decades of being a pastor's wife and ministry partner, Karon Cecy started a department of JARON Ministries International called Side-By-Side Ministry. It exists to fortify women in ministry or who serve in a support role, locally and globally. Its goals are:

• To provide an experienced mentor who will befriend and support these women.

• To equip women who need discipleship and specific training as Skilled Helpers.

• To help these women deal with criticism, loneliness, loss of friendship, lack of privacy, and the many challenges in their ministries, marriages, and families.

• To offer individual and confidential counseling to women and their families.

• To connect women with other women who serve in ministry.

If you have a heart to come alongside to disciple, mentor, counsel, and encourage women, please contact us at:

Side-By-Side Ministry
c/o JARON Ministries International, Inc.
4710 N. Maple Avenue, Fresno, CA 93726
www.jaron.org
559-227-7997

THE JARON AMBASSADOR TRAIN

ARE YOU LOOKING FOR A DIFFERENT
KIND OF MISSION AGENCY?

One That Puts <u>You</u> in the Driver's Seat?

Consider Jumping on Board the JARON Ambassador Train

THE TRACK = OUR MISSION

 JARON Ministries International was founded over thirty years ago and has grown to be a special kind of equipping agency that exists to build a qualified team of Jesus's Ambassadors who will use their unique gifts and talents to reach out locally, nationally, and globally. Thus the unique name: JARON = Jesus's Ambassadors Reaching Out to Nations.

THE ENGINES = OUR AMBASSADORS

Simply stated, we put our JARON-approved missionaries, teachers, pastors, chaplains, and workers in front, where they belong. Rather than ask them to fulfill our vision, we exist to help  them fulfill theirs. We go anywhere God leads them. They are the engines—the driving force. We are the caboose. It works so much better this way.

THE CABOOSE = OUR ADMINISTRATION

 JARON's ministry directors and administrative staff are the supply car, providing the resources, communication, training, and support services each of our ambassadors (i.e., our engines) needs.

THE SIGNALS = OUR POLICIES

JARON's policies, procedures, and standards, as well as our doctrinal and ministerial guidelines, are designed to protect and not encumber.

THE CARS = OUR MINISTRIES AND MINISTRY PARTNERS

 Our JARON engines (i.e., our missionaries) often bring along a series of other ministry partners from among the JARON team (i.e., our cars) as well as from outside (i.e., ministry partners). They minister alongside our teaching, pastoral, construction, medical, and chaplaincy teams, as well as other JARON missionaries with a wide variety of skills. We, of course, also encourage them to serve with local churches and world-wide ministry partners.

THE DESTINATION = THE WORLD

"The people who know their God will display strength and take action" (Daniel 11:32).

We exist to empower our ambassadors to make this an even greater reality in their lives and ministries anywhere God leads them.

Who are we inviting to come on board the JARON Ambassador Train?

• Career missionaries who are seeking more freedom to do what they believe they are called by God to do, under the leadership of a ministry committed to empower and not hinder.

• Local church pastors who want to serve in unique ministries beyond the ministry of their local churches.

• Seminary and Bible College teachers who want to be involved in teaching short-term in Bible schools, institutions, and churches, especially in other countries.

• Law Enforcement Officers and Firefighters (active and retired) who desire to be trained to be chaplains, serving locally and, if they so desire, globally.

• Medically-trained doctors, nurses, pharmacists, etc. who desire to use their skills on short-term medical ministry teams.

• Self-motivated servants of God with any kind of skill who desire to do ministry under the protection of a U.S. approved and well-reputed religious, non-profit 501(c)3 organization, along with a committed team of fellow Ambassadors of Jesus Christ.

How does it work?

• Send for an application or go online to www.jaron.org. There you will choose to apply for the kind of missionary position that fits your needs best (e.g., missionary, chaplain, full or part-time, raising full or partial support, etc.). Submit the application with a photo and signed doctrinal statement.

• Our Missionary Application Team will review the application and arrange for an interview in person, by phone, or by internet.

• Once you are approved by the JARON Board of Directors, you will be authorized to raise financial support as well as use our convenient online donation process. If you are new to the fundraising part of missions and ministry, our staff is here to assist you.

• JARON charges an administrative fee from all funds received. These funds primarily provide for the administrative services, legal requirements, and donor receipting by JARON Ministries International, Inc.

• JARON Ministries International, Inc. is a registered 501(c)3 non-profit organization in the State of California.

For further information contact us at:

4710 N. Maple Avenue, Fresno, CA 93726
www. jaron.org
559-227-7997

OTHER BOOKS BY DR. JIM CECY

JARON exists to produce and provide biblically sound and currently relevant written, audio, and video training materials. A catalog is available online at www.jaron.org. Below is the current list of <u>published</u> books by Dr. Jim Cecy:

• *Anger: The Worm in My Apple: Destroying the Rotten Fruit of Anger; Harvesting the Tasty Fruit of the Spirit.* (Also published in Czech and Polish). Available at www.jaron.org and www.amazon.com. An audio version, narrated by Dr. Cecy, is also available at www.amazon.com.

• *Have a G.R.E.A.T. Day: Living Our Lives One Blessed Day at a Time.* Available at www.jaron.org or www.amazon.com.

• *Mastering the Scriptures: A Self-Study Course in Effective Bible Study.* (Also published in Czech). Available at www.jaron.org or www.amazon.com.

• *Men in Action: Equipping Men to Lead in the Home, the Church and the Community.* (Co-authored by Michael L. Wilhelm, J.D.) Available at www.jaron.org or www.amazon.com.

• *Telling Our Faith Story. (A Three - Volume Series)*
    Volume One: Heavenly Lessons to Our Earthly Family (2023)
    Volume Two: Personal Lessons to Our Ministry Family (2024)
    Volume Three: Earthly Lessons to Our Heavenly Family (2024-2025)
Available at www.jaron.org or www.amazon.com.

• *The Accountable Life: Protecting Myself and Others.* (Also published in Romanian.) Available at www.jaron.org or www.amazon.com.

• *The Purity War: A Biblical Guide to Living in an Immoral World.* (Also published in Bulgarian, Czech, French, Hungarian, Polish, Romanian, Serbian, Slovenian, Spanish, and Ukrainian.) Available at www.jaron.org or www.amazon.com or www.puritywar.com. An audio version, narrated by Dr. Cecy, is also available at www.jaron.org or www.amazon.com.

ABOUT THIS THREE-VOLUME SERIES

Telling Our Faith Story

This three-volume series was written to encourage our earthly family, our ministry family, and our fellow Christians—i.e., our heavenly family. The series is presented as follows:

Volume One: Heavenly Lessons to Our Earthly Family

Part One: Jim's Marriage and Family Life Lessons
Part Two: Karon's Marriage and Family Life Lessons

Volume Two: Personal Lessons to Our Ministry Family

Part One: Jim's Ministry and Mission Lessons
Part Two: Karon's Ministry and Mission Lessons
Part Three: Jim's Lessons from a Military Veteran
Part Four: Karon's Lessons from a Cop's Daughter

Volume Three: Earthly Lessons to Our Heavenly Family

Part One: Jim's Life Lessons
Part Two: Karon's Life Lessons

We pray each of these volumes will encourage your hearts so that you may "dwell in the land and cultivate faithfulness" (Psalm 37:3).

SCRIPTURE INDEX

OLD TESTAMENT

NEW TESTAMENT

FOREIGN WORD INDEX

Greek	Meaning
Agapetos tou theou	the beloved of God
diakonos	deacon, hands-on servant
didaskalos	teacher, person of content
dioko	practice
doulos	servant, slave
episcopos	"see from above," oversee
hegoumenos	The careful, thoughtful leader
hoplites	Greek soldiers
huperetes	chained to responsibility
kephale	chief leader, head
nauageo	shipwrecked, stranded
oikonomos	steward, manager
phalanx	a mass infantry formation, a battle array
philoxenos	hospitality, "lover of strangers"
poimen	shepherd who feeds, protects, and warns
presbuteros	elder, mature leader
prohistemi	stand before, upfront leader
tapeinophrosune	humility
zeo	boiling, jealous

Hebrew	Meaning
anakh	groan in pain
aleph	First letter of the Hebrew alphabet
chakam melek	wise king
kanak	train, disciple
keh'sem	divine decision
kissa diyn	throne of justice
ma'ashaqqah	great oppressor
mahiyr	skilled
maskil	teaching psalm
mishpat	justice
ra'a	ruined, broken
tsedaqah	righteousness

Latin	Meaning
Coram Deo Laboramus	"We work in the sight of God."
credo	"I believe." (e.g., creed)
Dei Gratia	"By the grace of God."
Gloria in Excelsis Deo	"Glory to God in the Highest."
magnum opus	the most important work of a person
naufragia	deadly chariot races crashes, shipwrecks
Non nobis ned patriae	"Not for ourselves but for our country."
Non sibi sed patriae	"Not self but country."
res ipsa loquitur	"The thing speaks for itself."
scutum	curved shield the size of a small door
Semper Fidelis (Semper Fi)	"Always Faithful."
Semper Fortis	"Always Courageous."
Semper Paratus	"Always ready"
Soli Deo Gloria	"To God alone be the glory."
testudo	tortoise, turtle shell, a circle of protection
unum diem ad tempus	"One day at a time."
Ut Vuvant Alteri	"So Others Might Live."

Korean	Meaning
geobukseon	armored ship with iron spikes on its deck

Psalm 133:1

הִנֵּה מַה טוֹב וּמַה נָּעִים שֶׁבֶת אָחִים גַּם יַחַד

Hinneh mah tov umah na'im shevet achim gam yachad.

*"Behold, how good and how pleasant it is
for brothers to dwell together in unity!"*

For further information about the ministry, materials, or seminars, please contact:

Jesus's Ambassadors Reaching Out to Nations

Equipping Leaders for Effective Service

". . . the people who know their God
will display strength and take action."
(Daniel 11:32)

4710 N. Maple Avenue, Fresno, CA 93726

559-227-7997

www.jaron.org

Made in the USA
Monee, IL
09 August 2024

62976866R00213